TAX FUNCTION EFFECTIVENESS

The Vision for Tomorrow's Tax Function

TONY ELGOOD

TONY FULTON

MARK SCHUTZMAN

PRICEWATERHOUSECOOPERS

CCH

a Wolters Kluwer business

Printed in the United States of America

CCH
4025 W. Peterson Ave.
Chicago, IL 60646-6085
1 800 248 3248
http://CCHGroup.com

ISBN 978-0-8080-9242-1

ABOUT THE AUTHORS

Tony is a tax partner in PricewaterhouseCoopers LLP (UK) and specialises in tax function effectiveness. Tony is part of the Global Compliance Services (GCS) team, and in particular helps organisations to enunciate and document their tax strategy. He regularly speaks at conferences and has written two leading guides on the subject, namely PwC's 'Best Practice' tax function guide (published 2002, reprinted 2004, 2nd edition 2006) and their Tax Risk Management guide (published 2004, reprinted 2004).

Tony Elgood

Prior to his current role Tony headed up PwC's Bristol tax practice in the UK. He trained in the London office, and after a spell in Amsterdam and as a tax training manager, he moved to Bristol in 1986, becoming a partner in 1988. He is a fellow of the Institute of Chartered Accountants of England and Wales, and has an MA from the University of Cambridge.

PricewaterhouseCoopers LLP (UK)
31 Great George Street
Bristol BS1 5QT
UK
Tel: + 44 (0) 117 9307025
anthony.b.elgood@uk.pwc.com

Tony Fulton is a tax partner with PricewaterhouseCoopers Australia specialising in corporate tax management, compliance and reporting. He advises major corporates in the Asia Pacific region on the effectiveness of the tax function and managing global risk and compliance. Tony leads PwC's Tax Function Effectiveness practice in Australia which has a particular focus on controls, risk management and process improvement in the tax area.

Tony Fulton

Tony has over 16 years experience advising on a broad range of domestic and international tax issues. He is a member of the Institute of Chartered Accountants in Australia and has a Bachelor of Economics from Monash University, Melbourne

PricewaterhouseCoopers Australia
6 Southbank Boulevard
Melbourne
Victoria 3006
Australia
Tel: +61 (3) 8603 6231
anthony.fulton@au.pwc.com

Mark D. Schutzman

Mark is a tax partner with PricewaterhouseCoopers LLP (US). He is a founder and the leader of PwC's US Tax Function Effectiveness practice, regularly consulting with CFO's and Tax VP's to improve the effectiveness of their corporate tax function. He has visited dozens of Fortune 500 companies across the U.S. and leads PwC's efforts to benchmark corporate tax function performance and operational practices.

Mark has consulted with companies on process improvement, technology platforms and tax organization design as each relates to the four primary deliverables required of the corporate tax function. Mark also leads the PwC's tax provision technology implementation services and helps clients to redesign tax accounting processes, leverage emerging tax accounting technology platforms and connect global tax accounting operations via web enabled tools.

Mark received a BS in accounting from the Rochester Institute of Technology. He is a Certified Public Accountant and member of the AICPA.

PricewaterhouseCoopers LLP (US)
300 Madison Avenue
New York, New York 10017
USA
Direct: + 1 646 471 5305
mark.schutzman@us.pwc.com

CONTENTS

ACKNOWLEDGMENTS

In writing this guide we have drawn upon the expertise and experience of many of our colleagues in PricewaterhouseCoopers. We would like especially to thank the two people who produced first drafts of specific chapters. They are Damian De Backer (UK) and Brian Morris (US). We would also like to thank those who reviewed our various drafts and provided their thoughts and comments to us as we wrote this guide. In particular these included John Clymer (US), Angus Johnston (UK), Robert van der Laan (Netherlands), Will More-King (UK), Don Munro (Australia), David Shaw (UK), Chris Tierney (US) and John Whiting (UK).

We would also like to thank Michelle Jones who had the task of bringing this all together into one document and for sorting out all the diagrams. Finally we would like to thank our families for their forbearance on too many Sunday afternoons when we should have been giving them our attention, but instead were writing this guide.

To all the people named above, and all the others who gave us their time and encouragement, thank you.

CHAPTER 1
EXECUTIVE SUMMARY

§1.01 INTRODUCTION

In the last few years the increase in globalisation and the application of new technologies has led to major changes in the way business is done. Over the same period there has been a transformation in the approach by the regulators, with many countries around the world implementing more rigorous corporate governance regimes. This changing business environment has had a dramatic impact on the management of taxation by businesses.

Not only have we seen increasing complexity in managing the cost of taxes, both locally and cross border, we have also seen significant challenges for reporting and compliance. The US Sarbanes-Oxley legislation is aimed at significantly improving the integrity of financial reporting; however this has exposed serious problems with the quality of tax reporting in many companies. Tax continues to be the most frequently cited areas of material weakness under section 404 of the Act and we have no reason to believe that the experience would be any different for tax accounting by non-SEC companies.

The business and regulatory environment of the last few years has thus increased the scrutiny on tax functions and caused a number of behavioural trends within tax functions—some positive, some not so positive. We have particularly witnessed the global pendulum swing towards a focus on risk management and compliance. In many cases this has resulted in companies becoming more conservative and risk averse at the expense of managing the tax costs for their organisation. The increased focus on tax and the tax function is gradually improving the transparency around taxation, the contribution to value and the management of risk.

§1.02 A VISION FOR TOMORROW'S TAX FUNCTION

We are often asked questions such as 'how should I structure my tax function?' or 'how many people should I have in my tax function?' The answers to these questions will depend on both the nature and global footprint of the business and what the business and the tax function is trying to achieve—the objectives for the tax function.

The tax function's objectives should themselves be driven by what is happening in the business and the wider business and regulatory environment. While the objectives of different tax functions will vary in the detail, we believe that the effectiveness of the tax function is fundamentally based on its ability to achieve three core objectives:

—Create, protect and optimise **value** in the context of the organisation's business objectives;
—Manage a wide range of tax related **risks** from carrying on business; and
—Ensure **compliance** with tax laws and reporting requirements.

Tax planning and advisory activities should be focussed on optimising tax outcomes and managing risk, both in respect of strategic transactions and day to day operations. Compliance and reporting activities tend to be process driven activities that are focussed on both risk management and external communication of tax outcomes. It is critical for the effectiveness of the tax function that an appropriate balance is reached between the achievements of the three core objectives set out above.

§ 1.03 A TAX MANAGEMENT FRAMEWORK

We have established a framework for how a tax function should operate. The starting point is the tax strategic plan. For this plan to be implemented there are a number of "enablers" which need to be put in place. The results of the plan, together with the enablers, are the various "deliverables" that are the outputs required for the successful management of the tax affairs of a business. To achieve the right balance, the tax function needs to understand and focus on the enablers as well as the deliverables.

§ 1.04 ENABLERS AND DELIVERABLES

The enablers are the tools, methodologies and skills that are required for the successful implementation of the tax strategy. We have defined eight key enablers which are:

1. Structure of the tax function—how you best organise your people
2. People—establishing effective teams of people who, together with other internal/external resources, have the right mix of skills and experience.
3. Leadership—ensuring tax is aligned with corporate objectives and has an appropriate profile in the organisation.
4. Controls and risk management— integrating risk management processes and controls around the tax function's deliverables.
5. Process—optimising processes to improve efficiency and accuracy.
6. Data management—ensuring both quality data is available and proper data management is in place.
7. Technology—investing in effective systems to enable streamlining and automation of processes
8. Communication–impactful communication to manage relationships with internal and external stakeholders.

The deliverables represent the outputs of the tax function that must be accomplished each year, quarter, month and week in order for the tax function to meet its objectives. There are four key deliverables in respect of managing tax which are:

1. Tax planning
2. Tax accounting and reporting

3. Tax compliance
4. Audit defence

This framework for tax function effectiveness is set out in the 'enablers and deliverables' diagram below.

§ 1.05 PURPOSE OF THE GUIDE

The purpose of the guide is to set out the *Why*, *What*, and *How* of managing an effective tax function based around the above framework. Our starting point is to look at *Why* tax needs managing, putting some additional context around the key external business and regulatory drivers impacting on the management of tax. We then deal with *What* needs to be managed within an organisation in relation to tax, expanding on the concept of the enablers and deliverables and what we mean by tax risk. The *How* section sets out best practice tools, methodologies and approaches for creating a tax strategic plan, developing the enablers and executing the deliverables.

In addition to the enablers and deliverables there are a number of other competencies that are related to managing the effectiveness and sustainability of the tax function. These include performance measurement, benchmarking and managing change. Developing these competencies will enhance the enablers and ultimately the achievement of the tax function objectives. These areas are covered in separate chapters in the *How* section of this guide. The above diagram will act as a roadmap for various chapters in the *How* section, taking you through the enablers first, then the deliverables, followed by the other topics of interest.

In writing this guide we have drawn upon the experiences that we and our colleagues at PwC have had over a number of years in advising tax functions around the world. Our focus has been to help these tax functions be more effective.

§ 1.06 USING THE GUIDE

The guide is aimed at a number of different audiences. Those directly involved in leading a tax function should be interested in all three sections. For executive directors, while the detail in the *How* section may be more than you need, the *Why* and the *What* should be of interest to you. For a non-executive director the *Why* section sets out the context for why tax should be on your boardroom agenda. For other stakeholders in the tax affairs of an organisation, you may want to dip into the various chapters which are directly relevant to your particular interests.

§ 1.07 SUMMARY

Different businesses will do things in different ways, have different corporate practices and indeed different corporate cultures. What we have tried to do in this guide is to set out some food for thought as to the hallmarks of an effective tax function. If we do no more than stimulate the debate around what is best practice in managing a tax function, we will have achieved our objectives.

WHY?

CHAPTER 2

CHANGING BUSINESS ENVIRONMENT

§ 2.01 INTRODUCTION

We will look in later chapters at the increasingly tough regulatory and fiscal environments which obviously impact the tax function. However before turning to these, it is important to look at the bigger picture and consider the changing business environment in which large companies are operating. This chapter is about how these changes will impact the way tax is managed in any organisation.

§ 2.02 A NEW ERA?

The combination of new technologies, together with the post Cold War breakdown of economic and geographic boundaries (bringing billions of individuals into the global economy), has led to major change in the way business is done. Supply chain models are changing fundamentally, business processes are subject to major re-engineering and/or outsourcing, intellectual property is being relocated, finance is being restructured and once stable corporate structures are increasingly subject to corporate acquisition or merger.

This is a challenging environment for those managing companies' tax affairs:

- Many of these changes are areas where any tax specialist will immediately see major tax implications. Cross-border issues, financing issues and changes in structure, contractual frameworks or ownership are all issues where tax functions play an important role in transaction planning, implementation and business support. As there is more and more change in these areas and as the numbers at stake get ever larger, there is increasing need for tax resources to manage the risks and opportunities.
- Secondly, these new shaped global businesses are inherently more difficult for tax functions to oversee. Economic flows cut across borders and entity structures and so tax functions increasingly have to manage across multiple jurisdictions. Communication is compounded by geography, language, cultural differences and time zones. Corporate restructuring and changes in ownership affect established approaches and communications channels. Finance function reengineering/outsourcing presents new challenges in gathering data needed for tax compliance, reporting and forecasting purposes.
- Thirdly, the sheer pace of business change presents a sometimes overwhelming challenge to the tax function. Goals and priorities change. Staff continuity is lost. New technologies appear. Systems and processes change. Time is lost to training and familiarisation with new processes and activities. Resources are diverted to change implementation or to business critical activities. This fast paced change is hard to keep up with and certainly not conducive to careful examination of tax implications and effective operation of controls and processes.

§ 2.03 COMPOUNDING THE CHALLENGE

This new fast paced, changing and uncertain business environment is not just a challenge for the tax function. It is a challenge for governments and tax authorities. As economic activity and resources become increasingly portable, companies are moving their activities to take advantage of favourable regimes (commercial, economic, legal, regulatory and tax considerations all being influencing factors). Governments increasingly recognise that they have to compete for tax revenues, as well as taking steps to defend their own tax bases.

This is leading to:

- Governments considering or offering more favourable regimes in order to attract big business. 'Flat taxes' have moved from being the subject of academic debate to being actual government policy in some jurisdictions.
- Increasingly aggressive anti-avoidance activity in some territories.
- More rapidly changing tax legislation, combined with a break-down in previous precedents and understandings.

§ 2.04 SUMMARY

Business change, and the escalating pace of change, creates increasing uncertainty within which the tax function must do its job. When the 'front end' of a business struggles to cope with the challenges and opportunities the new business environment brings, the tax function may have an even greater challenge managing the tax risks and opportunities that follow.

CHAPTER 3

REGULATORY CONSIDERATIONS

§ 3.01 INTRODUCTION

Undoubtedly the major impact of the financial reporting regulatory bodies is being felt in the US and among US owned groups. While the focus of this chapter is therefore very much on the US regulatory picture, the underlying issues coming out of the US are having a major impact on a much wider global audience outside the US.

There are two broad constituencies that together represent the regulatory agenda:

1. Investor regulatory bodies such as the SEC, ASIC and FSA; and
2. Accounting standard setters such as the FASB and IASB.

In this chapter we examine the role of these regulators together with their impact on how tax is managed.

§ 3.02 THE SEC AND SECTION 404 SARBANES-OXLEY

One of the most significant regulatory impacts on the tax management of a company is section 404 of the Sarbanes-Oxley Act of 2002. This requires a US listed company to include in its annual filing an internal control report which:

- States management's responsibility for establishing and maintaining internal controls for financial reporting;
- Explains management's assessment of the effectiveness of internal controls for financial reporting, as of the end of the fiscal year of the issuer;
- Includes the external auditor's report on the assessment made by management in accordance with standards adopted by the PCAOB.

Where the company has a 'material control weakness' this will be stated in the annual filing.

Looking at the list of material control weaknesses reported over a recent two year period, the first thing to note is that 'tax expense/benefit/deferral/other (FAS 109) issues' is at the top of the list in both years. There are more material control weaknesses in the area of tax than in any other category. While the number of reported tax weaknesses reduced slightly (from 42 to 38), as a percentage of the total number of reported material control weaknesses tax has increased suggesting that other areas are being sorted out rather more quickly than tax.

It is interesting to note that companies who reported material weaknesses in tax accounting lost an average of 6.8% in their share price within 60 days of the announcement (as per a letter to the SEC Advisory Committee on Smaller Public Companies from a US shareholder advisory firm). While this drop is undoubtedly related to many factors beyond tax-related internal controls, the percentage is never the less compelling.

For those of us involved in managing tax and tax functions, to see tax at the top of the list of material control weaknesses is both worrying and disappointing. We believe the key reasons why this is so are:

1. Historically, companies and their internal auditors have not placed that much reliance on internal controls in the tax area. As a result, the design and monitoring of internal controls are not among the skill sets historically emphasised by most tax functions.
2. Without a burning platform, most companies have under invested in technology and process improvement initiatives for the tax function. The cost/benefit analysis simply did not justify meaningful investments in tax until Sarbanes-Oxley.
3. Tax has traditionally brought value to shareholders through tax planning, i.e., expertise in tax technical rules and applying that knowledge to company specific facts and circumstances. The effort necessary to attain and maintain the required level of technical competence is very high and in most cases this effort has been to the exclusion of a focus on tax function operational considerations.

§ 3.03 ACCOUNTING STANDARD SETTERS

Those who set accounting standards are the other key body of regulators who impact on the way tax is managed. The rules have become increasingly complex and difficult for people to understand in their own country. Additionally there is not yet one global accounting standard covering all countries. Tremendous effort and cost is expended by multi-national companies to reconcile US GAAP with IFRS and vice versa in order to comply with both local tax reporting requirements and the financial reporting requirements of those countries in which their shares are listed. A single global standard, if and when it is implemented, promises to alleviate some pressure from the tax function.

One of the major areas for confusion and extra work is the difference between the rules-based approach to financial reporting as compared to the principles based standards. Additionally, for US groups the introduction of FIN 48, which explains how to apply the rules in the US FAS 109 (the accounting standard for tax), has added an extra level of complexity for US groups and in particular for those who are not based in the US. The International Accounting Standards Board is also reviewing the operation of IAS 12 as part of its convergence project with US GAAP and at the time of writing an exposure draft is anticipated to be released shortly. The changes to IAS 12 are expected to lead to more rigorous disclosures in relation to tax accounting and uncertain tax positions.

§3.04 SUMMARY

It is not only the US regulators who are influencing the way tax is managed, though they perhaps have been the main drivers in recent years. The US rules are having an impact on a world wide basis as other regulators are moving in the same direction. In general the regulators are increasing the burden on those who are managing the tax affairs of a business.

CHAPTER 4

INVESTOR EXPECTATIONS

§4.01 INTRODUCTION

Historically many investors have struggled to understand how a company manages its tax affairs. They would review the effective tax rate in the accounts and ask one or two questions around this, but often their knowledge and understanding went little deeper than this high level view. However over the last few years we have seen increasing interest from the investor community in the tax affairs of companies. We believe that this community is therefore becoming increasingly important to those managing the tax affairs of a company.

In this chapter we look at three particular investor reports on tax. We also summarise what we believe the investor community is looking for when they look at the tax position of a company.

§4.02 INVESTOR REPORTS ON TAX

One of the early reports was produced by Henderson Global Investors who, in February 2005, produced a report entitled "Tax, risk and corporate governance". In November 2005 they followed this up with another report entitled "Responsible Tax".

The initial Henderson report was based on the findings of a survey of the UK FTSE 350 companies. They surveyed the chairmen of these companies and had a 48% response rate from those contacted.

In their comments on the background of this survey Henderson states that "A company's management of its tax affairs is directly relevant to shareholders. Tax related figures in the accounts such as the effective tax rate, actual cash tax payments and tax provisions are important factors in analysts' valuations, feeding directly into investment decisions."

Citigroup also produced a report, in September 2005, entitled "An Investor's Guide to Analysing Tax Risk". The Citigroup report starts on a similar theme by stating that "we are concerned that the market generally struggles with or ignores tax risks so we have prepared this comprehensive guide."

It is perhaps no coincidence that these three reports came out at around the same time as a number of groups were starting to report material weaknesses, under section 404 of the Sarbanes-Oxley Act in the US, relating to controls around tax reporting.

§ 4.03 FOCUS ON THE BOARD'S APPROACH TO TAX

In the first Henderson report they state that "in this rapidly changing risk environment it is important that company boards take a strategic review, bringing to bear their full breadth of perspectives and experience, executive and non-executive, financial and non-financial".

They go on to say that in their opinion, the responses to their survey show that many boards are not giving tax sufficient attention. This is based on the fact that fewer than half of the boards of companies responding to the survey have "reviewed tax strategically in the last year or adopted a formal tax policy". Henderson does however welcome a trend they see towards more formalised approaches—and this is a trend which we also recognise.

Henderson commented that they encountered considerable reluctance by some companies to address specific questions on board involvement, policy and individual aspects of tax risk. Despite this they state that they believe it is right and proper for investors to seek assurance that risks in the tax area, just as in any other are being appropriately identified, assessed and managed. In their conclusion they state that "It is important for investors to have adequate information on this [tax] as on other risk issues in order to gain assurance that boards are exercising their governance responsibilities appropriately".

§ 4.04 INVESTOR ANALYSIS OF TAX

The Citigroup report takes a different approach. Citigroup has done a detailed analysis of the tax position of many different companies, from all around the world, over a three year period, pulling the results together by 19 different industry sectors. There are comments on both individual companies and on the different sectors. You might like to look at the report and see if the tax affairs of your company were one of those singled out for detailed analysis.

What Citigroup has set out to provide is a guide to help investors to analyse tax and tax risk. For example they highlight key tax themes including:

1. Unrecognised tax losses which they described as a hidden source of value; and
2. "Use and abuse of tax loss carried forward" which they state allows a company to manage its reported tax rate.

The opening chapter in the Citigroup report states that "despite being one of the most commonplace and material costs any business incurs, taxation is often viewed by the market as beyond meaningful analysis. However, recent changes in both the attitude of government to, and regulation of, tax planning, suggests that significant changes are afoot. Therefore we view tax risk as a key risk facing companies that is worthy of significant analysis."

They go on to say that their report provides "a wealth of information for investors regarding taxation generally, tax terminology, the attitude of specific governments and a comprehensive systemic approach to analysing tax disclosures in companies' financials, often a source of complete bafflement". They add that "we would expect an assessment of expected tax risk to be an important input to investment decisions."

The Citigroup report, in one of its conclusions, also states that "the notes on tax in an annual report are complex, dense and often insufficiently complete to facilitate an outsider to discern how a company is planning and organising its tax affairs. However despite this there is no alternative to undertaking a comprehensive review".

§4.05 SO WHAT ARE INVESTORS LOOKING FOR?

We are hearing three key messages coming through from the investor community on tax matters.

[A] Sustainability

There is a very real concern that groups are pursuing aggressive tax policies which are unsustainable. Investors are looking for a degree of certainty over the tax rate and are less comfortable if they believe that surprises in the tax rate may be on the horizon. They are therefore looking for policies which will deliver this sustainable tax rate.

[B] Reputation

There is a strong belief among investors that companies need to manage their reputation in the area of tax. This is not only their reputation with tax authorities, where a good relationship is seen as beneficial to delivering a sustainable tax rate, but also in the market generally. We will pick up the corporate responsibility theme, which clearly impacts on reputation, in a separate chapter.

[C] Communication

The third key area which investors are looking for in relation to tax is better communication from companies. They are still struggling to understand the tax position of companies. The Citigroup report has gone some way to addressing this but we believe there is still a long way to go.

However where a company is owned either privately or by a private equity house, there is a fourth and possibly overriding requirement we are also seeing—and that is minimising cash taxes payable. There is clearly a potential conflict here with both sustainability and reputation—and the question arises as to how much these latter two really matter for a private company.

§ 4.06 SUMMARY

The investor community has become more interested in the tax affairs of companies and there is no sign of this abating. They are clearly stakeholders who need some attention. They are looking to understand both your tax position and the tax risks in your business. So how often is your head of tax directly involved in investor briefings?

CHAPTER 5

REVENUE AUTHORITIES

"And it came to pass in those days, that there went out a decree from Caesar Augustus that all the world should be taxed." Luke 2:1

§5.01 INTRODUCTION

In Chapter 2, we noted how the changing business environment presented major challenge for the tax function, with this challenge further compounded by the impact of governments' and tax authorities' responses to these changes. In this chapter we focus on the current approach by revenue authorities, how they are working with each other and the trends we are seeing in this area.

§5.02 COMPETITION FOR TAX REVENUES

To quote a recent statement from a revenue official in a major industrialised country:

> *"Enforcement of tax laws has become more difficult as trade and capital liberalisation and advances in communications technologies have opened the global marketplace to a wider spectrum of taxpayers. While this more open economic environment is good for business and global growth, it can lead to structures which challenge tax rules, and schemes and arrangements by both domestic and foreign taxpayers to facilitate non-compliance."*

Revenue authorities clearly recognise that the globalisation of business means potential erosion of the tax base in individual jurisdictions, both by the migration of economic activity/assets to other jurisdictions and by the increased potential for tax planning/avoidance activity that globalisation presents.

Given the threats to their tax bases, tax authorities and governments are acting to protect their revenues in two main ways:

1. They increasingly have to fight to tax 'their share' of global economic activity. Most typically this involves transfer pricing or controlled foreign company intervention as well as challenges to corporate residence/nexus.
2. Greater global mobility means that jurisdictions are increasingly 'in the marketplace' to attract economic activity though offering more favourable business and tax regimes. Major non-U.S. economies are lowering their statutory tax rates and broadening their corporate income tax bases to be more competitive with the developing countries that have captured significant inbound investment. Ireland, for example, has been particularly successful here.

Both these responses have an impact on the way tax is managed, particularly in multi-territorial businesses. An increase in enquiries and disputes on cross-border tax issues potentially demands significant resources to manage, and these will generally be highly skilled, expensive resources given the complexity of the issues and the large amounts at stake.

Similarly, as jurisdictions seek to attract economic activity, tax functions may need to spend greater amounts of time evaluating the impact of varying jurisdictions' regimes and re-examining how the structuring of the corporate value chain impacts on the group's net tax position.

§ 5.03 COLLABORATION AMONG TAX AUTHORITIES

Recognising the implications of globalisation, revenue authorities are increasingly acting in collaboration with each other. Examples of this include:

- The Heads and Deputy Heads of the revenue bodies from 35 countries meeting in Seoul, Korea under the auspices of the OECD's Forum on Tax Administration in September 2006. This meeting concluded with the issuance of the 'Seoul Declaration' which focused particularly on confronting non-compliance with the tax laws in an international context.
- The 2004 formation of the Washington D.C. based 'Joint International Tax Shelter Information Centre' ('JITSIC'), a collaborative approach between the US, UK, Australian and Canadian tax authorities to share information and expertise in respect of tax schemes.
- The 'Leeds Castle Group' which as well as the above mentioned tax authorities, also involves those of China, France, Germany, India, Japan and South Korea.

It is clear that revenue authorities are increasingly sharing information and acting in concert to target some forms of tax management activity. Again, this has risk and resourcing implications for tax functions.

§ 5.04 ANTI-AVOIDANCE ACTIVITY

The revenue authorities' response to globalisation inevitably involves the introduction of anti-avoidance legislation and increased levels of anti-avoidance intervention. A fundamental difficulty here is that such legislation operates on a jurisdictional basis, which does not sit comfortably alongside the trend whereby companies manage their business on a global basis. Such legislation therefore inevitably throws up anomalies, catches 'innocent' business activity and takes time and resource for the tax function to manage.

Defending against such interventions typically requires keeping on top of activities and information across territories, business units, reporting lines, languages, time zones and business practices. Our experience is that revenue authorities sometimes lack understanding of the practical difficulties of managing such issues and obtaining information they require. This therefore leads to a drawn-out enquiry process as well as the prospect that the authorities will exploit such difficulties to generate extra tax.

Given many groups aim to manage their tax rates to what are perceived to be levels acceptable to shareholders or that benchmark with comparable businesses, anti-avoidance activity can result in unforeseen tax charges. Therefore in addition to tax function resources being used to manage tax authority intervention activity, yet more resources are then needed to counteract the impact on the group tax charge of the authorities' interventions and to generate additional tax savings to compensate.

§5.05 COLLABORATIVE RISK ASSESSMENT

A survey of the US, UK and Australian tax authorities' approaches to large businesses shows each authority developing new and more sophisticated approaches to risk assessment. Key features of the respective authorities approaches are described in:

- For the UK, in the 2006 'Review of Links with Large Business' led by Sir David Varney, and expanded on in the 2007 UK Budget.
- For Australia, in the booklet 'Large business and tax compliance 2006'.
- For the US, 'The Joint Audit Planning Process: A cooperative effort of the Large and Mid-Size Business Division of the Internal Revenue Service and the Tax Executives Institute' (2003).

A common theme in each of these proposals is the increasing need for a collaborative approach to risk assessment involving joint working between the taxpayer and the tax authority. Each authority advocates open discussion between taxpayer and tax officials to better understand where risks of non-compliance exist and to take into account companies' own approaches to managing these risks.

Such approaches are not limited to these three jurisdictions. In the Netherlands, collaborative working is being formalised through the signature of 'enforcement covenants' where taxpayer and tax authority agree their relationship will be based on trust, transparency and mutual respect. This approach is also shifting responsibility for control of tax risk from tax authority to taxpayer. In return for the trust of the tax authority and the consequent reduction in audits, the taxpayer is expected to operate a proper tax controls framework and to take responsibility for testing its effectiveness.

There seems to be a general move towards more open dialogue between taxpayer and tax collector. Such approaches seem to be well received and a number of heads of tax have spoken of the benefits that can be realised from more open, trusting and mature relationships between the two parties, provided of course that there is good faith on the part of both parties. Both parties stand to benefit from greater certainty, shorter audit cycles, faster resolution of disputes, reduced information gathering and more appropriately targeted resource. We therefore expect this move towards collaborative risk assessment to continue.

§ 5.06 EMERGING MARKETS

As well as managing the impact of changes in tax authority behaviour in more mature, stable economies, tax functions increasingly have to deal with emerging economy issues. As globalisation increasingly leads to economic activities being sited in emerging markets, these countries' tax systems face the need to evolve rapidly to cope with this change. Indeed this extends well beyond the tax system to wider legal and regulatory regimes, which can also have implications for tax management. Tax functions therefore face having to manage ever larger parts of their global business being sited in countries with rapidly evolving tax systems, and having to establish and oversee local tax functions which will help manage this.

Some of the aspects of taxpayer/tax authority collaboration noted above are also being seen in emerging markets. Approaches do of course differ from territory-to-territory, but some of the more sophisticated emerging jurisdictions do seem to be recognising the benefits of working more closely with the taxpayer. We also note an increased use of on-line technology in some such jurisdictions. As well as streamlining compliance processes, this is believed to be making it tougher for rogue tax officials to abuse the process, as online working makes it increasingly difficult for corrupt or maverick individuals to exercise influence over companies' affairs free of scrutiny.

§ 5.07 LOOKING TO THE FUTURE

There is clearly major change underway in tax authorities' approaches, most notably in their response to the challenges of globalisation. As globalisation continues apace, anomalies will continue to arise given business is increasingly managed globally while tax regimes operate locally. Heads of tax will need to continue to look ahead to predict where this may take us.

This will no doubt include the emergence of new forms of taxation, most predictably in the field of environmental taxation where various governments are starting to float plans for regime change. More fundamentally though, for some years there has been background debate on the need for a global tax authority. The United Nations has supported this concept and the idea of a global 'Tobin Tax' on currency transactions was floated as far back as the 1970s; the European Union continues to work towards a 'Common Consolidated Corporate Tax Base'. Could the pressures of globalisation force governments to put the concept of a global tax authority back on the agenda once again? Heads of tax will need to ensure that their companies' interests are properly represented in any such debate.

§5.08 SUMMARY

Whether or not there are moves towards global convergence, we are currently experiencing unprecedented levels of legislative activity by major jurisdictions, coupled with major changes in approach and working practices. We expect this to continue, and we therefore suggest this is another factor which will require heads of tax to make the appropriate investments in people, processes and technology which will be needed to manage the impact of these changes.

CHAPTER 6

CORPORATE RESPONSIBILITY

"Tax is where the environment was [as a corporate responsibility issue] 10 years ago."
Senior official at an international body.

§6.01 INTRODUCTION

As evidenced by the quote above, tax is now firmly on the corporate responsibility agenda. Some tax planning which only a few years ago was seen in the tax world as legitimate and acceptable is now regarded by many, including tax authorities and regulators, as unacceptable and greedy. Campaigning groups, such as the Tax Justice Network, are calling for companies to make a morally acceptable contribution in taxes in return for the human and physical resources they use.

We would suggest that three emerging trends are likely to develop and persist. In essence these are:

1. A link between tax and corporate responsibility, with the resulting need for companies to integrate their approach to tax with their overall policies on corporate responsibility.
2. A greater interest in tax by a wider group of stakeholders than previously, and hence the need for companies to respond and be more transparent about their tax affairs.
3. The rise of tax up the corporate risk agenda, resulting in tax being seen as a corporate governance issue for the board, rather than solely a financial matter for the CFO and the head of tax.

In this chapter we focus on what the corporate responsibility agenda means for companies and the way they manage their tax affairs. Some of these trends are also picked up in the next chapter where we discuss the other stakeholders, including the board, who have an interest in tax matters.

§6.02 LINK WITH WIDER CORPORATE RESPONSIBILITIES

Most organisations have given a lot of thought to their corporate responsibilities in relation to, for example, labour practices in the supply chain and environmental damage. Where is the case for regarding tax as a corporate responsibility issue and what changes would this mean?

One could argue that by focussing on social and environmental matters the corporate responsibility lobby has spoken up on those issues that would otherwise have no powerful defender, and that this is not the case for tax. As the means of funding government expenditures around the world, tax is already a heavily regulated area and businesses have to deal with tax authorities in all countries in which they operate. However the corporate responsibility lobby (notably the Tax Justice Network and Christian Aid) suggests that in less developed countries the balance of power is with large business—and hence why this is a corporate responsibility agenda item.

> "Corporate responsibility must begin with paying your normal dues to the societies within which you operate"
>
> *Tax lobbying body*
>
> "The payment of tax should be a badge of good citizenship, explicitly linked to public goods."
>
> *Head of the major revenue authority*

We suggest that a call for corporate responsibility on tax is not simply a call for companies to pay more tax. It is about applying the relevant principles of corporate responsibility, which include accountability, transparency and disclosure, engagement with stakeholders, an ethical approach, and commitment to add economic value.

> "The problem of aggressive tax avoidance is a manifestation of systemic failures of global tax policies, leading to market distortions, economic free-riding, slower rates of global growth and widening wealth disparities within and between nation states."
>
> *Tax lobbying body*
>
> "Organised corporate tax avoidance may improve company profits and executive salaries, but it also forces people on the minimum wage, nurses, pensioners and debt-ridden graduates to pay a higher proportion of their income in tax."
>
> *UK national newspaper*
>
> "Every year developing countries lose at least 50 billion US$ in tax revenue as a result of aggressive tax avoidance"
>
> *International non governmental body*

The starting point may therefore be to think about where your organisation sits/should sit on the following scale, where the higher the score the less you are concerned with corporate responsibility in relation to tax.

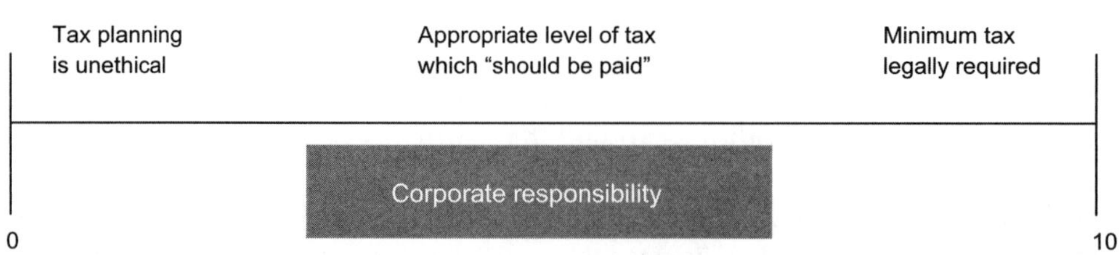

§6.03 TAX PLANNING—ACCEPTABLE OR NOT?

In the past we had a clear distinction between tax evasion and tax avoidance and these terms were generally well understood. Tax evasion is illegal and often relies on non disclosure or concealment. Tax avoidance may be legal in a number of territories but in some circumstances may be against the intention of the legislation and/or rely on exploiting loopholes. The corporate responsibility lobby is urging companies to honour the spirit rather than the letter of the law.

This approach has led to a plethora of terms including unacceptable or immoral tax planning and avoision. The diagram below shows the spectrum between what is clearly illegal and unacceptable and what should just be normal basic tax planning.

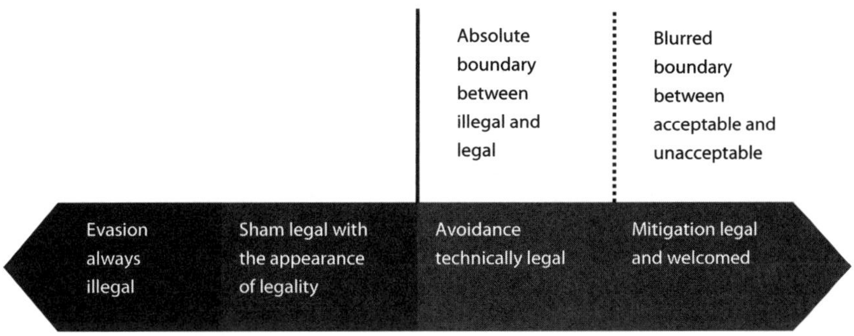

The question again is where a company draws the line on this spectrum. What is acceptable, as opposed to unacceptable, tax planning for your organisation?

> "Arrangements that minimise the amount of tax paid in the short term may be detrimental in the longer term if they prejudice the company's relationship with tax authorities and additional costs are incurred in complex dispute resolution, or if the company's wider reputation is harmed."
>
> *Henderson*

We recognise that it is difficult, in practice, to draw a line on the diagram above. We have divided tax planning into three distinct types.

1. Operational
2. Non-tax driven transactional; and
3. Tax driven transactional

Operational tax planning is that which takes place around the day to day operations within the business. An example of this might be transfer pricing where there is a direct link between any planning and the movement of goods and services between different parts of the business—i.e. the operations of the business.

Non-tax driven transactional planning is where something changes in the business. An example of this might be an acquisition or a disposal, or at a lower level it might be going into a new market and deciding whether to set up a branch or a subsidiary in that new country. Tax driven transactional planning is where a transaction takes place predominately for tax purposes.

However even this distinction can get blurred. Where do financing structures sit? A company needs to be financed and can the financing not be done in the most tax efficient way? When considering what type of planning is acceptable or not, it may be worth considering which of these three headings any particular planning falls into. It could be argued that categories 1 and 2 are more acceptable than category 3.

There is also the question as to where the directors' responsibilities lie. An article in an international newspaper stated that it is not a corporate duty to give shareholders' money to revenue authorities, which is, the article stated, what companies are doing if they are not minimising taxes by all legal means. The article goes on to say that tax should be a matter of law, not morals and that taxation is no more than legalised confiscation of someone else's money. The article concludes that companies are therefore justified in seeking to minimise their tax bills and that as long as the law is observed, paying less tax than the state had expected cannot be prohibited or amoral. The debate clearly continues.

So where on the scale below does your organisation sit?

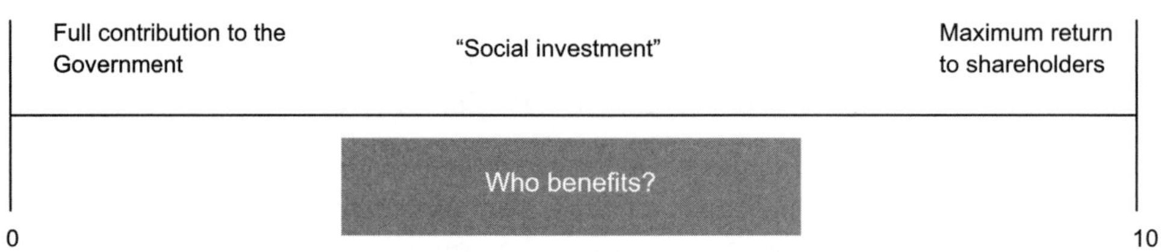

> "Tax avoidance and the industry that drives it are increasingly an international phenomenon and it is vital that we have effective international co-operation to tackle it, as we do for tackling terrorism, organised crime, money laundering and fraud"
>
> *Government official in a major industrialised country*

§ 6.04 THE ECONOMIC CONTEXT

It is of course in the wider interests of society that successful companies make profits and provide appropriate returns to shareholders. If tax regimes do not facilitate this, economies decline and society as a whole suffers. However as noted in an earlier chapter, in a global business world, companies often have a choice where they make investments and they will generally do this on the basis of benefits and costs, including tax. National tax systems raise revenues to fund social expenditure but they also need to be competitive to attract business investment. The economic value added by new investment is of course much wider than additional taxes, notably including new jobs.

Should companies therefore be criticised for paying less tax when they make investment decisions on where to locate or take advantage of government incentives (such as R&D credits)? The different rules in national tax systems provide opportunities for tax planning which companies can not only quite legitimately use to reduce their tax payments, but are actively encouraged to do so by local governments.

§ 6.05 WHAT TAXES?

We come on in later chapters to look at firstly the different taxes that a company pays, and secondly communication around tax. In this chapter we would just highlight that the most 'visible' side of tax is often the corporate tax charge in the accounts. This will usually not include, for example, any employment taxes or indirect/sales taxes. Research indicates that these other taxes can make up, on average, 50% of a company's total tax contribution to governmental authorities—and we are aware of many companies where this percentage is much greater. The natural conclusion from this is that companies not only need to think through where they sit on the corporate responsibility scales above, but also how they communicate the impact of all taxes that they do actually pay.

§ 6.06 SUMMARY

The shorter term financial benefits to shareholders from sustainable tax planning are tangible and measurable, while the longer term benefit of reputation with other groups of key shareholders is less tangible and more difficult to measure. In the past, tax has been seen as a cost, as with any other business cost, to be managed efficiently. In the future it is increasingly likely to be also viewed as a social and reputational issue.

We suggest that companies should spell out the link between their tax strategy and their business ethics and/or policies on corporate responsibility. Many companies have high ethical standards around the way they do business which may not sit comfortably with certain types of tax planning, for example the use of legal loopholes. What ever decisions are made should be agreed and ratified by the board.

CHAPTER 7

OTHER STAKEHOLDERS IN TAX

§7.01 INTRODUCTION

In earlier chapters we have looked at the three key external stakeholders in the tax affairs of a company—namely the regulators, investors and revenue authorities. In this chapter we seek to identify the various other parties, both inside and outside an organisation, who have an interest in that company's tax affairs. We will explore not only who they are but also why they are, or should be, interested in tax.

In our view these other stakeholders can be summarised as:

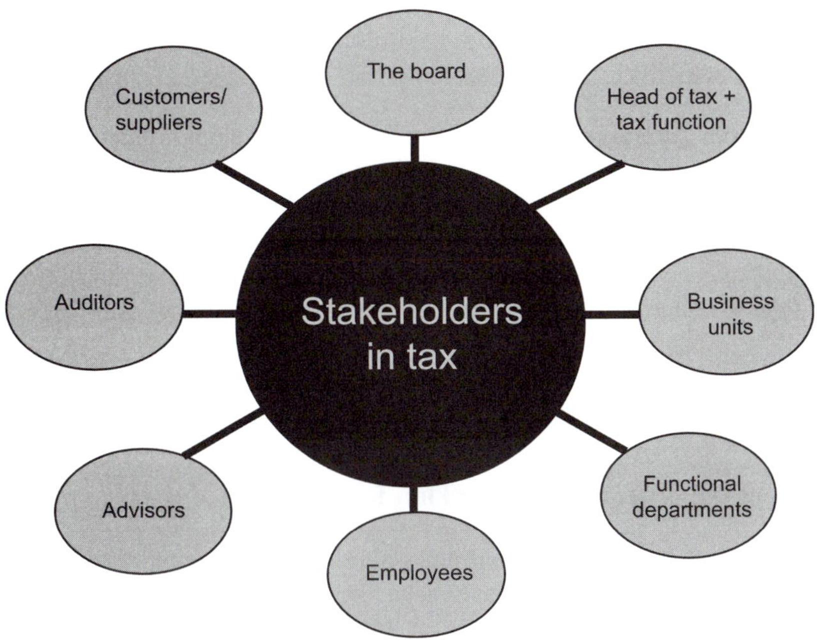

Let us look at each of these in turn.

§7.02 THE BOARD

Historically not all boards have given as much attention to tax as they have to other parts of the business. There has been a tendency for the board to delegate tax matters to the CFO and to rely on the CFO to bring tax matters to the board as and when they deem it necessary. We know of a number of cases where it is intended that tax will be discussed at next month's board meeting—but other items become more immediate/important so tax always stays as next, as opposed to this, month's board agenda item. In practice tax has not, in our opinion, had as much board attention as it warrants.

However we have seen significant changes in this area. We have seen tax rising up the boardroom agenda; this change is being driven, inter alia, firstly by the number of material weaknesses in tax reported by US SEC registrants, secondly by the attitude of tax authorities, thirdly by the increased focus by the investment community and lastly by the increased focus on the corporate responsibility agenda.

There are three key tax concerns which we believe should be on the agenda of all directors. These are the:

- Transparency of information delivered to shareholders;
- Growing pressures on director accountability for certain key processes and decisions; and
- Need to address and satisfy multiple constituents inside and outside the company.

Information transparency and director accountability are obviously closely linked.

What is also clear is that the way tax is run within an organisation is driven by the board's attitude to tax. If the board drives the business on a profit before tax basis, then it will be difficult for those managing the tax affairs of the company to ensure tax, and in particular tax risk, is given the attention it is due. If the board takes little or no interest in tax, then there is a message to the rest of the organisation that tax is less important and is low on the corporate agenda.

In our opinion and in order for the board to give the right overall messages around tax, they should therefore be involved in a number of specific areas.

[A] Setting the Overall Strategic Plan for Tax

While the tax strategic plan will undoubtedly be drafted by the tax function in conjunction with the CFO, we believe the tax strategic plan should be reviewed and discussed by the board at least once a year. In a later chapter we will set out in more detail what might be included in a tax strategic plan but the areas for the board to focus on are:

- The balance between risk and reward;
- The tax corporate responsibility agenda;
- Where the organisation should be focusing its efforts in relation to tax;
- The controls in place around tax risk;
- Communication with external stakeholders; and
- The organisation's reputation in respect of tax.

[B] Reviewing the Tax Risks in the Business

The board should be aware of the major tax risks in the business and what is being done to manage these risks. This is something which should perhaps appear on the board agenda more often than just once a year.

[C] Ensuring the Appropriate Controls Are in Place

While the board will not need the detail, as part of their corporate governance agenda the board should make sure that they are comfortable not only that proper controls are in place for managing tax and tax risk, but that there is a monitoring process in place to ensure that these controls are being implemented.

In some organisations we are aware that tax is delegated to the audit committee as opposed to being reviewed by the board as a whole. Depending on the remit of the audit committee this can give too much focus to tax reporting in the accounts at the expense of the risk versus reward and corporate responsibility agendas.

In our opinion it is vital that the board as a whole does take an active interest in tax. They should not only give support to those managing the tax affairs of the organisation but they also need to approve the agenda for tax.

§7.03 THE CEO AND CFO

As noted above it has usually been the CFO who represents tax at board level and to whom most heads of tax report. However with a number of revenue authorities now making a direct contact at CEO level we are seeing some CEOs becoming more actively engaged in tax matters and this is a trend which we believe is likely to continue. This is why we have combined the CEO and the CFO under one heading.

It is the CEO and CFO, together with the head of tax, who are responsible for the tax strategic plan being executed, on a day to day basis, throughout the organisation. While the board as a whole has responsibility for setting the overall plan for the organisation, it is the CEO and CFO who provide both the support, the structure and the resources to allow the strategy to be implemented.

§7.04 HEAD OF TAX AND THEIR TEAM

It almost goes without saying that the head of tax and their team are key stakeholders in the tax management of any organisation. However in order for them to do their jobs properly they need to understand the wider context within which tax operates in their organisation. They need to understand what their role is, what is expected of them and what the ground rules are for the way they operate. They need to understand the roles of other stakeholders in tax and be party to the overall group tax strategy. Without these basic building blocks, which too often are missing, they are not able to maximise their value to the organisation.

§7.05 BUSINESS UNITS

It could be argued that it is up to the business unit leaders to run their business units and for the tax function to manage tax. However what happens in the business units will undoubtedly have a major impact on the tax position of the organisation, and the business unit leaders and their teams are therefore key stakeholders in tax.

In particular the actions taken by people in business units are one of the main causes of tax risk. To illustrate this point let us give you just one example—transfer pricing. It would be usual for a tax function to be involved with the business units in setting up a transfer pricing system for the movement of goods and services within the organisation. The objective of such an exercise is to arrive at a pricing system which is acceptable to the various revenue authorities around the world. However it is not unusual for people in business units, looking for ways to increase their unit's profitability, to start flexing prices and making adjustments which firstly are not agreed with the tax function and secondly give rise to potential issues with tax authorities at some later date.

There are further issues within business units when organisations are driven on a profit before tax basis. If there is no incentive for a business unit leader to manage the corporate tax line then there is a high risk that tax planning opportunities are missed and less than optimal tax positions are taken.

It is therefore important that people in business units understand their roles in managing both tax and tax risk, and buy in to what they need to do.

§ 7.06 FUNCTIONAL DEPARTMENTS

There are a number of functions within any organisation whose activities have a direct impact on that organisation's tax affairs. Some of the points above on business units are equally applicable to the functional areas in an organisation. However some functions deserve particular mention.

The finance function will be producing figures to go both into the accounts and into tax returns. Their understanding of what is required of them will be crucial to managing compliance risk and also to ensuring that the tax figures in the accounts are correctly stated. Tax is one of the biggest cash costs in an organisation. The treasury and financial planning functions will want to know what tax is payable and when—and also what tax might be payable if various worst case scenarios arose.

The legal department will clearly need to involve the tax function in any transactions in which they are involved. The activities of the HR function will have a direct impact on employee tax matters. Likewise, accounts payable (and receivable) have a major role in how transaction taxes are managed. Additionally, we are seeing an increasing involvement from internal audit in monitoring how tax is managed and controlled.

What these last two sections have shown is that there are a significant number of people in any organisation who can and do have a direct impact on the tax affairs of that organisation. Clearly they need to understand their roles and responsibilities in relation to tax.

§7.07 EMPLOYEES

We have put employees as a separate stakeholder category, notwithstanding they are probably included under the business unit or functional departments headings above. The point we are making here is that many employees are starting to take an interest in the overall tax affairs of the organisation in which they work—either under the corporate responsibility agenda which has been discussed in the previous chapter or as employee representatives on company committees.

§7.08 ADVISORS

We now move on to look at other stakeholders outside the organisation starting with those who advise the business. To be able to advise a company in the management of its tax affairs, an advisor needs to have a good understanding of the taxes payable by that organisation, the overall tax strategy and the key tax objectives. Without this understanding the tax advisor is working in a vacuum, the ideas they bring may well be inappropriate and they will not be best placed to help the internal team meet their objectives. We would encourage both in-house tax teams and CEOs/CFOs to share their tax strategic plan with their external advisors—for the benefit of both parties.

§7.09 AUDITORS

The auditors are a key stakeholder in tax. We have already seen that tax is one of the main material weaknesses being reported under section 404. The auditors need to understand the company's attitude to tax and tax risk, how interested the board are in tax matters, how tax management is being communicated within the organisation—and in particular what controls are in place for managing tax and tax risk.

§7.10 CUSTOMERS/SUPPLIERS

It may seem strange to see customers and suppliers being designated as stakeholders in the tax affairs of an organisation. There are two reasons we have included them. The first is similar to the reason employees are included, i.e. they have an interest in the corporate responsibility agenda. The second is that they are part of the supply chain and hence can be directly impacted by the way an organisation deals with its taxes. What message does it give a customer if the wrong rate of VAT is charged on your invoices? How does it impact your suppliers if you incorrectly calculate withholding taxes on payments to them?

§ 7.11 SUMMARY

The purpose of this chapter has been to show that there are a wide range of different people who either have, or should have, an interest in the tax affairs of an organisation. We have probably omitted a number of people we should have included. However the important point is that you should think through who the key stakeholders are for your organisation and have a methodology for involving them, or at the very least considering them, in the management of your company's tax affairs.

WHAT?

CHAPTER 8

WHAT TAXES?

"The tax function is responsible for all taxes—of whatever form and wherever paid"

§ 8.01 INTRODUCTION

The statement above is a comment we have heard from a number of CFOs—and we can understand where they are coming from. But in considering what this means in practice we run into one or two problems with definitions. In this chapter therefore we look at what is a tax and hence what should be included when we talk about managing taxes.

We also consider the question as to what it is that the tax function should be managing and what more correctly should be managed by other parts of the business. In doing so we consider the difference between taxes borne by an organisation and the taxes they collect on behalf of revenue authorities. Additionally we consider where you draw the line between what a tax function is responsible for on a proactive basis and where tax should support others on a reactive basis.

What is clear to us is that when we talk about managing taxes and in particular the role of the tax function, we need to be sure that everyone is on the same page as to what is included in the term 'tax' and, for these taxes, what we are expecting the tax function to manage—and hence also what is not a tax and additionally which taxes the tax function is not responsible for.

§ 8.02 WHAT IS A TAX?

The answer to the question 'what is a tax?' may seem obvious. There are many payments to governments that a company makes that would fit the general working definition of a tax, which is something that is paid by businesses (and individuals) to government (central or local) to fund government expenditure. However as we look at this in more detail the position is not so clear.

There are some payments where there is little doubt that they fall into the definition of a tax. For a company the most obvious taxes are those taxes which are levied directly on the company's profits. These are the normal corporate income taxes payable under most tax systems. Most countries also have some form of indirect tax, be it a sales tax or a VAT system. There are also withholding taxes on certain payments, such as dividends, interest and royalties. Social security contributions are a feature of all developed countries' tax systems. In countries, such as Germany and France, the social security contribution can be vastly higher than the corporate taxes.

However this is by no means the end of the story. Increasingly we are seeing the introduction of environmental and green taxes, in addition to existing levies such as road fuel duties. There are customs duties on the movement of goods, there are duties on particular transactions (e.g. capital and stamp duties), and there are property taxes to name but a few others. In a recent UK pre-budget report setting out the government's revenues, they list out 25 different taxes and levies, the majority of which apply to businesses.

In some cases you will also have payments to a government which result in a return of value to the company or for a right or asset which is used in the business. This would include for example rents and license fees. In other cases, companies may also receive payments from governments by way of subsidiaries or grants. Should such payments and receipts be included in the definition of tax?

We suggest that where there is doubt you apply three tests in deciding what is and is not a tax:

1. Is it payable to a government authority?
2. Is it mandatory? and
3. Is there no real return of value?

If the answer to all three questions is yes, it is probably a tax. The key here is to reach agreement as to what is to be managed as part of an overall tax strategy. As well as excluding those which are outside this definition, there will also be some where either the amount payable, the opportunity for planning or the risk of getting the compliance wrong are so small that they may be ignored. What should be left are those taxes which do need to be included in the overall tax strategy.

§ 8.03 WHICH TAXES SHOULD THE TAX FUNCTION BE RESPONSIBLE FOR?

Once you have decided what is a tax (for the purpose of 'managing taxes') the next question to ask is which of these taxes should the tax function be responsible for. While there is no right answer here, and each organisation will need to make its own decisions, in answering this question it can be useful to categorise the taxes into five headings that include taxes on:

- Profits and capital (e.g. corporate income taxes);
- People (e.g. payroll/employment taxes);
- Your products (e.g. value added taxes);
- Property (e.g. stamp duties); and
- Others which do not fall into any of the four categories above (e.g. fuel duties).

It is also helpful to look at the difference between taxes borne and taxes collected. We define the two different categories as:

- Tax paid and borne, or tax suffered—the amount of tax that a company pays that becomes a charge to the profit and loss account either directly or indirectly through being capitalised and amortised.
- Tax collected/paid over—the taxes that the company in effect administers on behalf of the revenue authority; in principle there is no tax cost to the business of paying these taxes, only an administrative cost of collection and management.

The purpose of looking at these two different categorisations is to start focusing on the role of the tax function.

Managing tax falls broadly into two main categories: firstly tax planning and advisory and secondly tax compliance and reporting. Tax planning and advisory is the means through which the tax function can contribute value to the organisation as well as managing risk. Tax compliance and reporting is a process activity that is mostly concerned with managing risk. The tax function will not have the resources, or the inclination, to have full ownership of both the planning and the compliance processes for all taxes. Decisions need to be made as to what they are and are not responsible for. For example we might expect the indirect tax compliance processes to be owned by the finance function or business units; whereas the payroll tax processes may be best managed by the payroll function. In general, corporate income tax planning is most effective when managed by the tax function.

§ 8.04 SUMMARY

We do not believe it appropriate for the tax function to be responsible for everything which comes under the wider definition of 'tax'. However there are a number of taxes where it is open to debate as to whether the tax function should or should not have a role. The purpose of this chapter is to highlight that this debate needs to be had in each organisation and for each country in which the group operates. Where the tax function is not involved, it is important to make sure that the accountability for management of these other taxes is clear, so that a situation where there is no ownership can be avoided. The results of this debate need to be clearly spelt out so that there is no misunderstanding as to who is responsible for what.

In making such decisions one of the factors will be the amount of those taxes/levies which the organisation has to pay and also the risks involved in collecting those taxes where the group is acting as a collecting agent for a government authority. We come back to how we calculate the impact of such taxes in chapter 12.

CHAPTER 9

TAX FUNCTION ENABLERS

§9.01 INTRODUCTION

In the last chapter we considered the various different taxes where the tax function might have a role. Having got some clarity on the taxes, we now need to think about what that role might be. As noted in the first chapter of this guide we have established a framework for how a tax function should operate.

The starting point is the tax strategic plan. For the plan to be implemented there are then a number of 'enablers' which need to be put in place. The results of the plan, together with the enablers, are the various 'deliverables' that are the outputs required for the successful management of the tax affairs of a business. In this and the next chapter we introduce the tax function 'enablers' and 'deliverables' in a bit more detail, but we start with the strategic plan.

§9.02 TAX STRATEGIC PLAN

There are limited resources for managing tax and as we saw in the last chapter there are many different taxes. So what are the priorities? Where should these limited resources be focussed? What do you want to achieve this year in respect of tax? How do you monitor progress against the goals you have set for tax?

The starting point for answering these questions is a properly thought through and documented tax strategic plan. In our experience many companies do not have such a document (a number have a list of actions masquerading as a strategic plan). For those who do have a proper plan, it seems to have a very positive behavioural influence.

One of the key benefits of such a plan is that as you pull people together and engage in the dialogue necessary to prepare the plan, you and they will begin to think differently. You will have a better understanding as to the why and what of how you all intend to manage the tax affairs of the business. Having a tax strategic plan therefore greatly increases your chances of attaining your goals.

However not only can a strategic plan help focus your tax personnel, regardless of their geographical location, it can also serve as a primary communication vehicle to your board, CFO and even the regulators. We believe a tax strategic plan is a pre-requisite for a best practice tax function. What such a plan might look like is set out in chapter 13.

§ 9.03 ENABLERS—OVERVIEW

To implement the strategic plan there are various enablers which need to be in place. We have defined the eight key enablers as:

The enablers can be considered the 'operational qualities' of a tax function. The most effective tax functions view the eight enablers as having equal status with the four deliverables (see next chapter) and understand how directly linked the enablers have become to the objective of producing accurate and timely tax deliverables, satisfying the requirements not only of the board and the CFO, but also the numerous other stakeholders in tax. Viewing these enablers as critical to the success of a tax function and not merely as administrative details is an important distinction for heads of tax functions to consider.

In this chapter we put some more definition around these eight enablers, and then in the how section of this guide we discuss how the enablers can best be used.

§ 9.04 STRUCTURE OF THE TAX FUNCTION

There are many different ways in which the tax function can be structured. Historically many tax functions have been structured either by geography or type of tax, or perhaps a combination of the two. The question however which we would ask people to consider is whether they are internally organised with an appropriate focus on things that matter most to enable success and growth? Or, is your internal organisation model an impediment? We will look in chapter 14 at the pros and cons of the different models, and in particular ask what structure is most appropriate to implement your particular tax strategy.

§9.05 PEOPLE

There are also a number of different people issues to be considered when deciding how tax should best be managed in any organisation—and the people are a key enabler in delivering what is required for tax. When we look at the deliverables we will consider who should be responsible for what between the:

- Tax function;
- Shadow tax function; and
- External advisors.

However within the tax function itself, the following people issues will need to be considered:

1. Quantity—do we have the right number of people?
2. Skills—do we have the right mix of competencies that match our business needs? These competencies need to include not only technical, but also all the general business skills such as project management, negotiation, and communication skills.
3. Development—do we have systems and processes in place to ensure our people develop their skills over time?
4. Attracting and retaining talent—are we paying competitive salaries and have we created a great place to work so that we can achieve a competitive advantage in attracting talent?
5. Geography—are we staffed with the appropriate numbers and skills in those jurisdictions outside our home office and country?

We explore each of these areas of people effectiveness in more detail in chapter 15—People development. Historically there has been a predominant emphasis on tax people developing technical skills. This may be one reason many tax functions lack the strong leadership and sensitivity to personnel needs that are necessary to manage a diverse group of people within a flexible organisation. A strong focus on the people element of a tax function is a key differentiator and enabler to becoming highly effective and best in class.

§9.06 LEADERSHIP

What is it about 'leadership' that makes it one of eight key enablers of an effective tax function? In the Why section of this guide we set out why it is so important that the tax affairs of groups of companies are properly managed.

The next step is to have someone in the organisation who makes this happen, someone who will lead the management of tax. Good tax leadership will ensure that tax is taken seriously in an organisation; poor leadership may well result in tax being ignored with potentially significant adverse impact on the business.

Every organisation needs someone to lead the management of tax—and where there is an in-house tax function this will be the head of tax. In the chapter on the role of the head of tax (chapter 16 in the How section) we have set out some examples of where strong leadership is required in order to manage the tax affairs of a business effectively. In our experience a number of these examples are relatively new in the tax world—and it is these changes which have brought leadership to the fore.

§ 9.07 CONTROLS AND RISK MANAGEMENT

The next key enabler, and one which needs to permeate all parts of how tax is managed within an organisation, is 'controls and risk management'. Risk management has become increasingly important over the past few years, driven by both the corporate governance agenda and some high profile risk issues (including material weaknesses in tax accounting). Many organisations are still trying to come to grips with what risk management means for tax and what controls need to be in place to manage these risks. In view of its importance we have devoted a whole chapter in the What section to tax risk (chapter 11). In this next chapter we will spell out how we define tax risk, and then in chapter 17 set out what controls are needed and how tax risk can best be managed.

§ 9.08 PROCESS

The tax function is being asked to do much more with the same or even fewer resources (both people and financial) than it was in the past. The tolerance for risk of error in tax reporting, in particular, is substantially lower than it was previously. At the same time, tax is being asked to contribute value to the organisation through positively contributing to the business strategy. These all lead to the need for a tax function to be more efficient than it has been—and to embrace process improvement.

In our experience many tax professionals do not have a process orientation and do not have an innate appreciation for the value that process improvement projects can deliver. Process improvement represents an opportunity to redeploy resources to pursue risk management, put in controls, communicate with stakeholders and with the business units, undertake tax strategic planning, ensure transparent disclosure and appropriate tax planning efforts—tasks that yield greater value and employee satisfaction than some others. Consequently, tax functions increasingly need to look to process improvement to extract additional efficiencies across a range of processes, especially tax reporting and compliance related activities.

In addition to the technology enhancements described below, process improvement is one of the best ways we know substantially to increase the chances that a tax function will consistently deliver on its commitments in the future. How this can be achieved is set out in more detail in chapter 18.

> **Process improvement value proposition**
>
> *Successful PI projects result in fewer hours necessary to complete a process than originally required. This represents an opportunity to redeploy the newly created capacity to pursue higher value—add activities. Secondarily, this often leads to improved job satisfaction and better staff retention.*
>
> *In other words, PI enables the opportunity to accomplish more without an increase in headcount (i.e. cost).*

§9.09 DATA

"I spend more time collecting the data I need for the tax provision and tax returns than I spend doing analytics, the real tax work I should be doing."

Domestic Tax Manager
Fortune 500, US based MNC

This is the sort of comment we come across on a regular basis. Many tax functions are mired in, for example, extracting data for tax accounting and compliance purposes, reconciling information from overseas subsidiaries and chasing data to compute book/tax differences. The implications are obvious and not good.

With data as the starting point for the entire annual tax reporting lifecycle it is clear that starting with poor quality data will almost always result in inaccuracies and presents risks nearly impossible to manage, control or share. Quality, tax sensitised data is therefore one of the foundations of leading tax organisations.

For too long, tax professionals have been content to simply accept any data they can get to meet the analysis and reporting requirements of the tax function. This approach has resulted in an inordinate amount of effort spent on manipulating rather than analysing data. For the tax function to add value to the organisation they must be able to spend time examining data and relationships of different data sets (year-over-year) to identify these value added opportunities.

In a 2004 PricewaterhouseCoopers survey of CIOs and IT directors, respondents estimated that the value of their company's data represented 37% of the worth of their organisation. This clearly illustrates the value that data can have to the organisation. The challenge for tax is assuring that the data needs of the tax function are clearly communicated and incorporated into the data management processes of the organisation.

For these reasons we have chosen to distinguish data as an enabler that is separate and distinct from technology. Technology is the engine that when running efficiently produces the output needed to drive the machine forward. Yet that engine can not even begin to run without quality fuel. Data is the fuel that drives not only tax but the entire business.

§ 9.10 TECHNOLOGY

Do your people have to place an order for information with IT or the financial controllers group and wait for the report to show up in lieu of getting it themselves? Do your people take printed reports from IT systems and re-key the reporting into a spreadsheet to be able to report the data in another way than presented on the report? These are but a few symptoms experienced by the tax function that is not realising the full benefits of available technology solutions.

You might like to consider where you are on the continuum below:

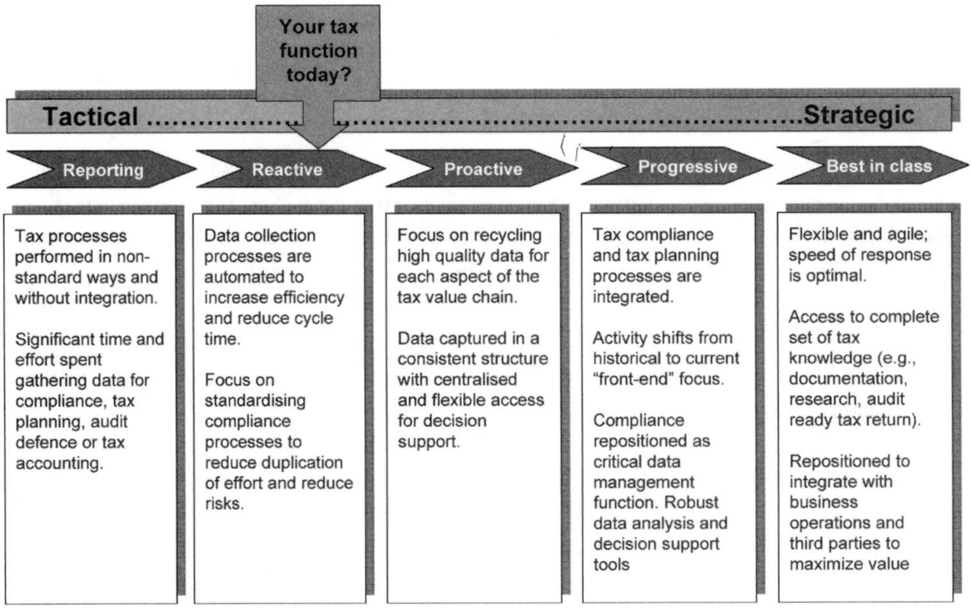

We believe that technology can be a major enabler of overall tax function effectiveness. In a majority of cases we have observed, it serves as the foundation for those companies who have moved along the best in class continuum shown above. While all the enablers we are discussing have considerable impact, technology does stand out as a critical success factor in the movement from left to right along the continuum . . . from a Tactical—Reporting centered tax function to a Best in class—Strategic tax function.

While there are certainly limitations as to what tax can accomplish on the technology front without the buy-in and close collaboration of both finance and IT leaders, and in some cases the board and CEO, there are sufficient opportunities that are tax specific and wholly within the control of tax that can be addressed. As with process improvement efforts, technology investments are first all about managing risk, streamlining and automating repetitive processes, and improving quality of output from the tax function. An example of a best in class approach to technology is set out in chapter 20.

Technology investment value proposition

Successful technology investments result in faster and easier access to higher quality data and thereby can reduce or eliminate the need for time consuming data collection, validation and manipulation tasks within the tax function. This represents an opportunity to redeploy newly created capacity to pursue higher value-added activities, which often leads to improved job satisfaction and better staff retention.

In other words, technology investments enable the opportunity to accomplish more with the same staff complement while reducing risk in tax reporting.

§9.11 COMMUNICATION

There are many facets of communication that make it often misunderstood and misapplied in practice. Communication is complicated by the existence of multiple stakeholder groups each having different interests and agendas. In terms of communication as an enabler our message is simple. Those tax functions placing a high priority on effective communication by anticipating the needs of each stakeholder group and appreciating the nuances that make some forms of communication superior to others will enjoy more success, acceptance, latitude and potentially more rewards.

The most effective tax functions are very skilled in two key aspects of effective communication:

1. Identifying the varying stakeholders and their specific interests.

In the Why section of this guide we dealt with the various stakeholders in tax and what they are/should be interested in. A few examples of these stakeholders and their different agendas are set out in the table below. This table is not intended to be all-inclusive but rather to challenge the readers thinking about stakeholder management and why communication is so important.

Stakeholder Group	*Primary Interest*
Audit committee	Tax strategy, risk management, accuracy and quality of tax related financial disclosures, reputation.
CFO	Tax strategy, risk management, accuracy and quality of tax related financial disclosures, cost of the tax function, tax personnel competencies, IT requirements, adequacy of tax reserves, accuracy of current and deferred tax provisions in all jurisdictions.
Financial controllers	Coordination during the closing process. Ensuring accuracy in the tax accounts and no delays caused by tax during the close cycle.
Business unit leaders	Impact of tax accounts on their BU books, addressing tax related issues emanating from their business, equitable sharing of tax burden across all business units. Higher sensitivity to above the line transaction taxes (Sales tax, VAT)
IT leaders	Understanding and anticipating the technology needs and requirements of the tax function.
Financial planning/treasury	Cash taxes, cash tax forecasting, refund claims, cash requirements/benefits emanating from tax audits. Minimizing taxes on financial transactions. Timely collaboration of cash requirements, no surprises.
Tax employees	Career opportunities, continual learning and skill development.

2. Designing the appropriate method of delivery for each stakeholder group.

Have you ever sent a well crafted email to a large group and wonder why nothing came of your message? Have you ever organised a meeting for senior executives only to have previously confirmed attendees drop out minutes before the scheduled session? Highly effective communicators understand that varying types of stakeholders and different types of messages require thinking about the means of communication delivery.

It is important for tax executives to use similar strategies deployed by their successful peers in the finance organisation to disseminate information about important tax matters. We advocate effective communication designed to bring about change, inform, educate, persuade and collaborate. In many cases this is not a well developed skill set for tax professionals but, in our experience, it is clearly a differentiator for those considered best in class. Chapter 21 provides some thoughts as to how this can be achieved.

§9.12 SUMMARY

To implement the tax strategic plan efficiently the best in class tax function will need to have the right structure, the right people, good leadership, proper controls and risk management, together with the right processes, good data and the right technology, as well as excellent communication with the other stakeholders in tax. These eight enablers are crucial to the delivery of the four deliverables discussed in the next chapter.

CHAPTER 10

TAX FUNCTION DELIVERABLES

§10.01 INTRODUCTION

In the last chapter we considered both the overall tax strategy for a business and the key enablers which are needed for the strategy to be implemented. In this chapter we focus on the outputs of that strategy—the tax function's deliverables. The deliverables represent the work that must be accomplished each year, quarter, month and week.

The deliverables apply to all taxes and not only those where the tax function has a role. We have also considered in this chapter who should have ownership of the deliverables for different taxes; it is not only the tax function who manages taxes.

§10.02 WHAT ARE THE DELIVERABLES?

Following on from the tax strategic plan, we see the four key deliverables for tax as being:

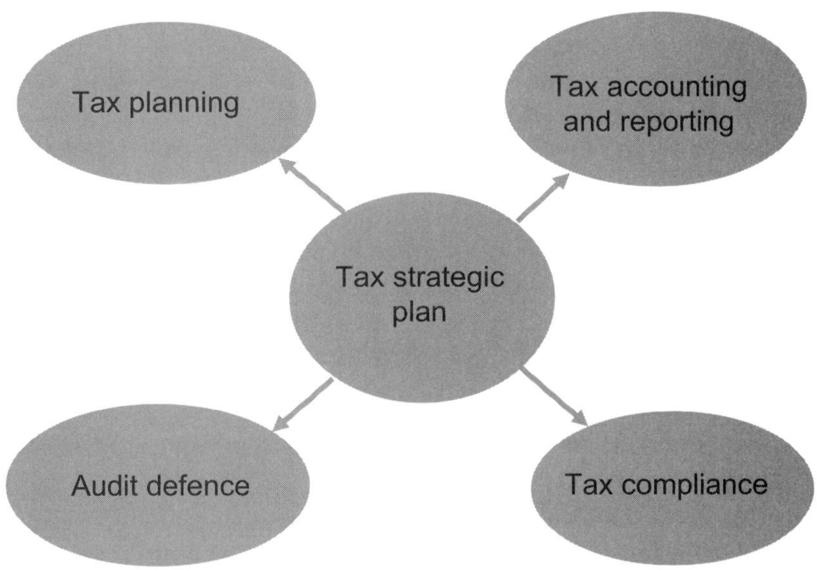

Let us look at each of these in turn.

§10.03 TAX PLANNING

A key role of tax functions is to contribute value for the organisation, not just to act as a risk and compliance manager. Accordingly a major component of managing tax is ensuring that the business plans its affairs in a way which ensures it does not pay more tax (globally) than it needs to. The first core deliverable for tax is therefore tax planning, ensuring that opportunities are considered and, where appropriate, implemented. A key to success in this area is a tight alignment with business units and their decision making processes.

The business' strategic plan and agreed risk profile will drive the approach taken to the tax planning. The tax planning deliverable also requires broad interaction within the organisation including senior management, other corporate functions and the business units. Accordingly, a key measure of success for the head of tax is the degree of involvement (and the timing of that involvement) in key business decision making. Secondly, it is crucial that the tax function fosters a collaborative approach in tax planning with the business, and is viewed as a proactive driver of solutions rather than just providing a reactive 'yes/no' sign-off.

§ 10.04 TAX ACCOUNTING AND REPORTING

Tax accounting and reporting has also become a core tax deliverable over the last few years. Increased demands in this area have put a real strain on resources which has highlighted many of the challenges that have largely been tolerated in the past. Perhaps the main driver for this has been the number of material weaknesses reported in tax accounting under section 404 Sarbanes-Oxley. The main focus has been on the reporting for corporate income taxes—but we should not lose sight of the other taxes a business has to pay.

We will look later at who delivers the deliverables, but it is worth making some particular points about tax accounting and reporting. We are aware that in many organisations, but not in all, the tax function has a major part to play in producing and reviewing the corporate income tax figures for the accounts. However the skills and knowledge required for tax accounting are not necessarily the core skills for many tax function people, in particular those who have come up through a legally based training. Equally those in finance functions, who hopefully do understand accounting standards, often do not have a good enough grasp of the tax issues underlying the figures.

§ 10.05 TAX COMPLIANCE

The next core deliverable is the completion of tax and other regulatory returns. We suspect that over the years the completion of corporate income tax returns has been the key deliverable for a number of tax functions. Indeed our surveys of time spent by tax functions show that of the four deliverables this is the one where tax functions have spent most time—perhaps to the detriment of the other three. One of the challenges for tax functions is to get the balance right between all four deliverables.

However it is not only corporate income tax returns which come under this heading. The vast majority of the taxes that a company has both to pay and collect will be submitted to a revenue authority with some type of formal return. A significant number of these returns will be dealt with outside the tax function—but they are all part of the tax compliance deliverable.

§10.06 AUDIT DEFENCE

The final core deliverable is audit defence, dealing with revenue authorities once a tax return has been submitted to them. Whether this is as a result of a formal tax audit or not will depend on how the local tax system works for that particular tax.

There is an interesting debate to be had in many organisations as to who should be responsible for revenue audits, in particular for those returns which have been submitted by someone other than the tax function. During an audit there may be requests for more detailed analysis of particular figures, requests for further factual information (such as details of a transaction) and discussions around the interpretation of tax law and practice. Non-tax specialists can get out of their depth very quickly when dealing with tax audits and a great deal of care is needed to ensure they are properly managed.

§10.07 OTHER TAX FUNCTION DELIVERABLES

We would suggest that the four deliverables set out above are the key deliverables in respect of tax and they are expanded on in more detail in chapters 22 to 24. However we are aware of tax functions whose scope extends rather wider than just these four deliverables. For example we are aware of tax functions that have taken on the role of preparing local statutory accounts due to the fact that the tax authorities are the only people who need these accounts; if the tax function did not take ownership then the accounts would not be prepared and consequently the tax returns could not be submitted. There are undoubtedly other examples.

Our view is that activities/deliverables over and above the four we have discussed in this chapter are usually not activities which should come under the heading of 'tax'. If there are management decisions that the tax function's role should be extended beyond that of tax, so be it. However it should be recognised that such activities are not normal tax function activities and are carried out by the tax function for purely pragmatic reasons. Whether the use of skilled tax people to carry out non-tax activities is a sensible use of scarce tax resources is a question that requires serious consideration from those who provide the financial resources for the tax function.

§10.08 WHO DELIVERS THE DELIVERABLES?

The tax function will not be responsible for delivering all the deliverables for all taxes. For example it would be unusual for the tax function to be responsible for the accounting of withholding taxes. As noted in an earlier chapter this raises the question as to what deliverables the tax function should be responsible for, and where they are not responsible, who else should be.

As already noted there are basically three categories of people who are involved in running the tax affairs of any organisation. These three are:

- The in-house tax function;
- The shadow tax function, and
- External advisors.

We would define the in-house tax function as those who are designated within an organisation as tax specialists, irrespective of who they are reporting to (and we often see local tax people, whether they be local to a business unit or local to a country, reporting to local CFOs). Where people have part time tax roles (and, for example, part-time finance roles) the picture can become a bit confused and it may be better to designate these people as being part of the shadow tax function.

The term 'shadow tax function' probably needs a bit more explanation. The term includes anyone in the business who is not formally in the tax function, but has a role in managing the tax affairs of that business. In addition to the above example there will be people in the finance function who provide critical information for both tax accounting and compliance: there may also be people in the finance function who have responsibility for completing indirect tax returns; there may be people in the HR function who deal with benefit packages and the tax impact of these packages; there will be people in operations who are effectively managing tax risk. They are all part of the shadow tax function.

The term external advisor is fairly self-explanatory. What is perhaps more difficult is for the tax function to be clear as to where external advisors should be used, and indeed to be aware of when they are being used. For example local CFOs may have the authority to take advice without the tax function even being aware that advice is being taken.

If we now go back to the tax strategic plan and the four deliverables, you need to be clear within your own organisation which of the three categories of people is responsible for the strategy and each deliverable for each tax. Different businesses use different models and we do not believe there is any one right answer. However we would recommend that a table along the lines of the one below is completed for your organisation and it may be that a number of tables need to be completed for different parts of the business.

In each box one of the three categories of people who manage tax need to be inserted. Probably when this exercise is first attempted, there will be some gaps and possibly also some duplications—and these in themselves will show where further discussion is needed.

The completion of this table is the starting point for discussions as to how the tax function should be structured and the budget for the tax function. We will come back to these points in later chapters, as well as looking at how the most effective tax functions might approach production of their deliverables to the highest quality standards, and do so consistently and in a cost effective way.

Deliverables / Types of tax	Ownership of tax deliverables				
	Strategic plan	Planning	Accounting and reporting	Compliance	Audit defence
Corporate income taxes					
Indirect/sales taxes					
Employment taxes					
Customs duties					
Environmental taxes					
Withholding taxes					
Property taxes					

You might also like to complete this table in respect of the tax function's involvement. We suggest you either put high, medium or low in each box, or alternatively put proactive, reactive or no involvement, to show what the tax function's responsibilities are for each tax. Particularly where there is a low, reactive or no responsibility score, this prima facie means that someone other than the tax function has responsibility for this area—and they need to be fully aware of this.

There is clearly no one right way of completing this grid and each organisation will ultimately need to take a view on what elements of its own total tax affairs it wishes to be managed by the tax function, and this may even vary between different parts of the business and indeed different countries in which the business operates.

§10.09 SUMMARY

The four deliverables for tax include both added value activities (tax planning) as well as more regulatory matters (tax accounting, tax compliance and audit defence). In preparing the tax strategic plan thought needs to be given as the role of the tax function and where it wants to position itself. This then naturally leads on to the role of the shadow tax function and external advisors in managing the tax affairs of the business.

Audit defence
Planning
Communication
Structure of
tax function
Technology
People
Tax strategic
plan
Data
Leadership
Process
Controls/
risk management
Compliance
Accounting and reporting

CHAPTER 11
TAX RISK

§11.01 INTRODUCTION

As noted in chapter 9, one of the key enablers for the tax function is controls and tax risk management. In order to manage tax risks it is important to understand firstly what the tax risks are in your business. The purpose of this chapter is to provide an explanation of what we see as the main areas of tax risk and why they arise, so that we can start with a common understanding of what it is we are talking about when we move on to what controls are needed and how tax risk can best be managed.

§11.02 WHAT IS TAX RISK?

The decisions, activities and operations undertaken by an organisation give rise to various business risks. Some of these risks will be in respect of tax. These risks may be in relation to uncertainty regarding the application of tax law and practice to particular facts (including future changes to the law). It may be uncertainty over the facts themselves or the standard of documentary evidence to support the position taken. It may be uncertainty as to how well systems operate to arrive at the tax results of the business activities and operations. These uncertainties give rise to tax risk.

Tax risk can be defined as the risk of not meeting organisational or tax group objectives in relation to tax strategy. In its broadest sense, tax risk includes any consequence relating to the application of tax strategy and planning, day-to-day operations, compliance or external reporting that adversely impacts a business in the form of cash tax liability, financial statement errors or misstatement or reputational damage. Acknowledging that tax risk can relate to the risk of not meeting tax strategy objectives underlines the fact that risk can relate to failing to realise particular planned results or outcomes, sometimes referred to as "upside risk".

§11.03 OBJECTIVES OF TAX RISK MANAGEMENT

A key element of a company's tax policy is articulating how much risk the organisation is prepared to accept. We are often told that a particular business' tax risk management objectives are to minimise risk. Our core proposition is that managing risk is not about minimising risk, but is about optimising risk and value by determining what level of risk is acceptable to that business relative to value and then managing and monitoring the risk. It is about managing tax risk, not minimising it. Indeed in our dealings with some clients we have challenged them as to whether they are taking enough risk. Businesses make profits by taking risks and a no-risk strategy is probably neither cost effective nor right for any business.

Like other business risks, there is a clear trade off between tax risk and value created (or defended) by the tax function. In managing tax risk, an organisation therefore needs to find the appropriate balance between the risk taken and value (or return) achieved based on the agreed risk profile of the group—and we will consider this in more detail in chapter 13.

We should make it clear that we believe each business has a responsibility and duty to pay the appropriate taxes in respect of its business operations. We also consider it critical that organisations manage and plan their tax affairs to optimise after tax outcomes within the parameters provided by the laws in the countries that they do business. However, we work on the assumption of full and proper disclosure and accordingly, none of the following has regard to what some might term detection risk.

§ 11.04 TYPES OF TAX RISK

In our view there are four specific categories of risk associated with taxes. These are:

1. Strategic and transactional risk;
2. Operational risk;
3. Compliance risk; and
4. Financial accounting risk.

However there is further category of risk that could arise in conjunction with any of the specific categories above. This is reputational risk which is a potential impact or consequence that is initially non-financial, but which can have a major impact on the tax affairs of an organisation. Given its importance to tax management, we will treat it as a separate category. The specific areas of tax risk are explained in more detail below.

§ 11.05 SPECIFIC RISK AREAS

[A] Strategic and Transactional Risk

This type of risk concerns the exposures associated with strategic planning and major or non-routine transactions undertaken by a company. In any strategic transaction there may be uncertainty as to how the relevant tax law will apply to the factual circumstances and positions will need to be taken that require judgement. For complex transactions, there may be a number of interrelated tax uncertainties potentially across different jurisdictions and taxes.

The more unusual and less routine a particular transaction is, then generally the greater the likely tax risks. One-off, non-routine transactions, such as acquisitions/disposals of businesses or parts of a business, or significant restructuring projects and reorganisations will generally bear greater tax risks than the routine every day business such as selling products and services. In addition there are likely to be well-designed procedures and systems in place for the processing of routine transactions, which would usually not apply to non-routine, one-off transactions.

In terms of strategic and transactional tax risks, more important than minimising the risk is ensuring that the risk assumed is commensurate with the value of the business outcome for the organisation. We have seen many cases where the incremental benefit of pursuing a particular strategy is debatable when compared to the incremental tax risk.

Additionally tax risks can arise from failures, such as:

- The tax department is not involved in the transaction or is brought in only at the last minute;
- There is no organisational agreed framework against which to judge acceptable risk; and/or
- There is a failure to properly document, implement or maintain a transaction.

In our view this last point often carries the greatest risk for strategic transactions. Failure to implement, properly document or maintain what has been planned and agreed upon is, in our experience, the cause of a significant amount of tax risk for companies. The tax treatment may depend on a particular sequence of events, board meeting or wording in documentation and there is often a significant risk that the standard of documentary evidence will not adequately support the tax positions being taken in the event of being challenged.

The question then arises as to how much tax risk are you prepared to take in particular transactions and how much risk are you actually taking over the correct implementation of the transactions? What is your profile in relation to transactional risk?

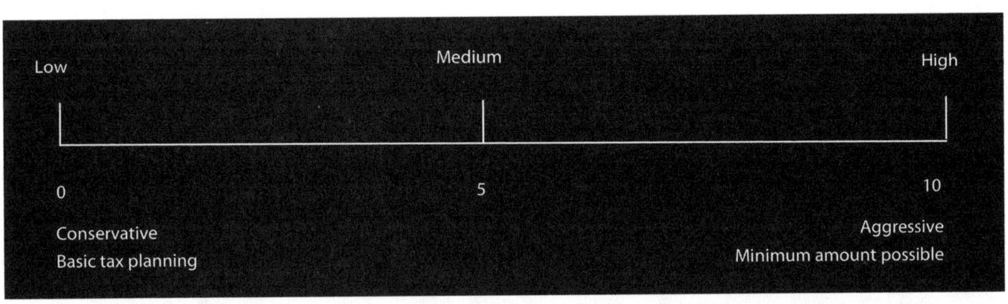

It is important in considering this scale to indicate where you want to end up as distinct from the inherent risk in the transaction or tax planning strategy. Risks identified can in many cases be managed, such that a risk initially identified as being at an unacceptable level may be capable of being brought down by a tax ruling or some other approach. This recognises that risks can be managed so that the potential upside benefit is not lost.

[B] Operational Risk

Operational risk concerns the underlying risks of applying the tax laws, regulations and decisions to the routine every day business operations of a company.

Different types of operation will have different levels of tax risk associated with them. For example, compare normal third party product sales with intra-group cross-border products sales; there are greater tax risks associated with connected party cross-border transactions (primarily transfer pricing issues). This is one example of tax risks that can occur from the normal ongoing business of a company.

Another example that can arise is associated with the increasing globalisation of trade. This can result in an ever increasing risk of operational people inadvertently creating a taxable presence or permanent establishment (PE) in another country. An inadvertent PE can arise from an array of situations such as:

- Companies who contract employees to work on overseas assignments;
- Agents of companies working in other jurisdictions who enter into agreements on behalf of the local company;
- Setting up a representative office in a foreign country;
- Companies looking to expand services overseas; and
- Companies who work on a project basis where employees can be relocated for an extended period of time.

The tax consequences of having a PE can extend to a number of different taxes and obligations including direct tax, VAT, employment taxes and transaction taxes such as stamp duty and can represent an absolute cost to the business.

In our experience the closer the tax function is to the business operations the better these types of risks are managed. Communication between the various parties is key.

Where are you today on the operational risk scale—and where would you like to be?

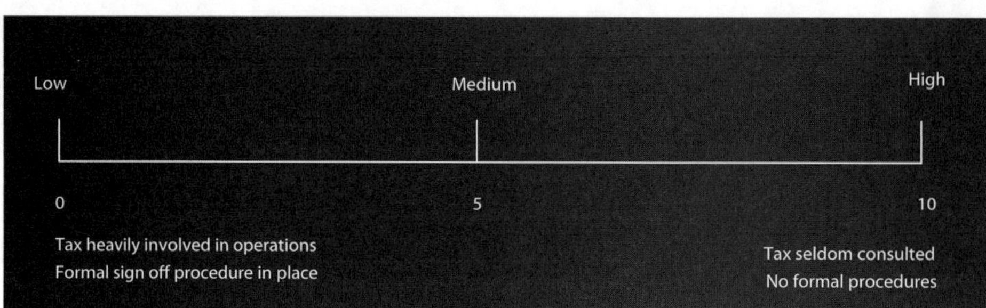

[C] Compliance Risk

Compliance risk concerns the risks associated with meeting an organisation's tax compliance obligations. As we noted earlier, we do not believe risk of discovery by tax authorities is a factor. One must assume full disclosure and that the authorities are aware of and will review your activities. From a tax perspective compliance risk would primarily relate to the preparation, completion and review of an organisation's tax returns (of both corporate tax and other types of tax returns) and the risks within those processes.

Compliance risk addresses the risks implicit in the systems, processes and procedures adopted by a company to prepare and submit its tax returns and in responding to any enquiries/issues raised in the process of reaching an agreed position with the authorities.

What we are talking about here is:

- The integrity of the underlying accounting systems and information;
- The effectiveness of processes to extract tax sensitive information from the accounting system;
- Ensuring the tax compliance analysis processes are based on up to date knowledge of the latest tax law and practice; and
- The proper and efficient use of technology in the processes.

There are clearly cost implications in where you position yourself on the scale below and there will be a trade off between costs spent and risks taken. To achieve no errors in any tax return will undoubtedly be cost prohibitive. Alternatively, are you over engineering the process and could you reduce the cost with little or no impact on your risk position? What is your attitude to tax penalties? Where do you want to be on the scale below—and what changes need to happen in the way you operate to get you there?

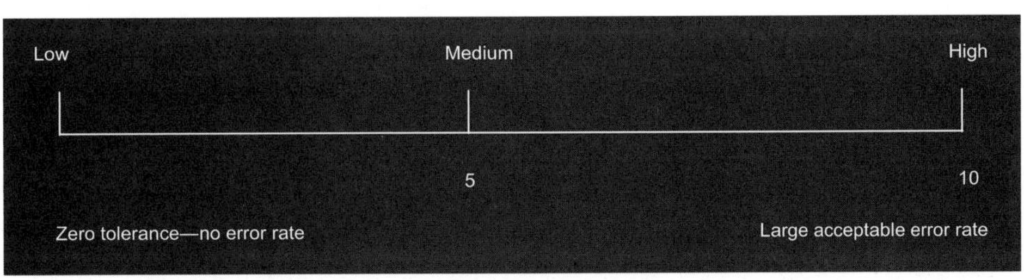

Tax compliance risk also includes the risks arising from agreement of tax returns and from enquiries on, or the audit of, submitted tax returns by fiscal authorities. In a number of countries the final agreement of a tax return often ends in a 'horse trade' between the taxpayer and the relevant revenue authority; one might even argue that it may make sense to have a number of aggressive positions in the return so that there is something to give as part of any negotiations.

Additionally, with how many of the group's tax returns is the tax function actively involved? What about payroll tax returns, indirect tax returns, and customs and duty returns? If it is not the tax function, who is managing the risks associated with these returns?

> We have come across a situation where a CEO of a multi-national group had been informed by a tax authority in one of the territories that the group does business, that a subsidiary had not filed tax returns for 3 years and the local tax authority would be making arrangements for the deregistration of the business at the end of the week unless the tax returns were brought up to date. In this real life example, the global tax director was not even aware of the problem.

There is also an interaction between compliance risk and reputational risk (see below). How do the revenue authorities rate you on a risk scale? Do they see you as an aggressive tax planning group and have 'marked your card' as one where they have to do a lot of work—or are you seen as a more conservative group where they have little to go for?

[D] Financial Accounting Risk

The Sarbanes-Oxley Act of 2002 brought the risks in the financial accounting area into sharper focus. A particular challenge for many tax departments is the requirement in section 404 requiring documented and tested internal controls over financial reporting.

In most jurisdictions, the figures included in the tax accounts, at the time the financial statements are issued, will be estimates as the income tax return will not have been completed and time does not allow for any detailed work to be undertaken. Deferred tax accounting generally calls for the estimation of future taxes to be paid under tax regimes on transactions that are recorded in the accounts in the current year. However, with the introduction of new corporate governance initiatives, there is much less tolerance for errors in the tax accounts and the CFO and the board are generally expecting 'no surprises' when it comes to movements in the tax accounts.

The release of interpretation FIN 48 for the application of US GAAP tax effect accounting under FAS109 is causing serious tightening of tax provisioning practices for SEC registered companies and their subsidiaries. FIN 48 requires a more rigorous approach to the recognition and disclosure of the accounting for uncertain tax positions for US GAAP purposes. At the time of writing, the International Standards Board was also considering more rigorous standards for recognition and disclosure under the international standard for tax effect accounting, IAS 12.

As well as looking at the processes in arriving at the accounts figures, and the internal controls around these processes, the following questions need to be asked:

- How much uncertainty is there in the interpretation or application of the tax law(s) used to compute the tax figures?
- What is the quality of the data received from or used in the transactional, operational and compliance areas?
- Are there issues or questions as to the application of the tax law to the data?
- What provisions are needed to cover these uncertainties? and
- What level of materiality is acceptable?

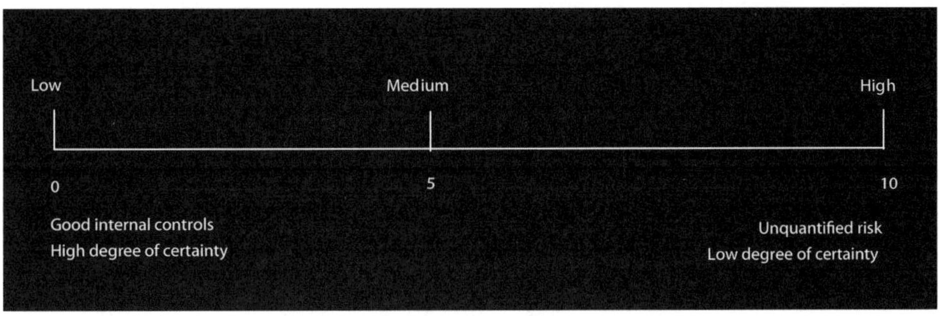

The experience with applying section 404 has shown that many companies have struggled to demonstrate robust tax controls, with the area of tax accounting continuing to produce a significant number of material weaknesses. There is no reason to believe this is an issue peculiar to US multi-nationals.

Clearly it is not only the statutory financial accounts where financial accounting risk arises. Tax figures appear in cash flow planning, forecasting, and in managing investor expectations of the future.

[E] Reputational Risk

We have collected a file of press cuttings relating to the tax affairs of companies—and this file is becoming increasingly bulky. How will your CEO or the board react to seeing your tax affairs splashed all over the front page of a national newspaper?

Reputational risk concerns the wider impact on the organisation that might arise from an organisation's actions or errors if they become a matter of public knowledge. By their very nature such risks will impact wider business interests. For example, consider the impact on a company if, as a result of pursuing a tax issue through a public arena such as the courts, information about the company's activities or practices result in changes to the perception of the company by its customers, suppliers, or employees. Consider also the impact of being seen to pursue considerably more aggressive tax planning—does this matter to you?

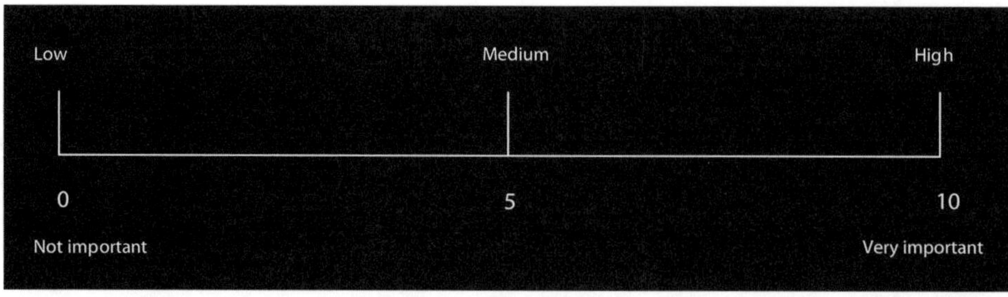

For multi-national groups this issue may also go to the heart of good corporate citizenship, particularly in foreign jurisdictions where reputational impacts may be more important in some countries than at home. It is also where cultural differences and policy clashes can occur. Identifying and managing issues such as the impact of aggressive tax planning, reputational issues just from major tax authority challenges, and policy and practices around corruption, are all elements of reputational tax risk management.

Reputational risk is also relevant to a company's relationship with tax authorities in its head office jurisdiction as well as in foreign jurisdictions. Consequences that impact the company's reputation in the eyes of a tax authority tend to negatively impact relationships with those authorities and increase the perception of the risk profile of the company. Some common results of being perceived to have a higher risk profile could be more frequent and more focussed attention in terms of the reviews and audits, more difficulty getting revenue authority clearance or rulings on proposed transactions and less discretion likely to be applied in terms of interest and penalties for late/underpaid tax liabilities.

[F] External Risks

The comments so far have focussed on the risks that are manageable inside an organisation. There will also be risks that are external and by their very nature are unmanageable—but are very real and equally important nevertheless. Examples under this heading are unexpected change of legislation or court decision on a particular point, or even a change of government. In designing tax risk management procedures these external risks should not be overlooked. Some, but not all of them, can be anticipated.

§ 11.06 DRIVERS OF TAX RISK

In order to manage tax risk to the level expected by your organisation, you need to understand not only what the risks are, but also how they arise. That means considering both the drivers of risk and the business activities and characteristics that create them. We set out below a summary of some of the key drivers of risk based on our experience.

[A] Errors of Judgement

Risk driver	*When it arises*	*Typical risk areas*
Tax positions adopted	Judgement regarding tax positions adopted that are rejected or challenged by tax authorities	Strategic and transactional risk Operational risk Reputational risk
Tax provisioning/ reserving	Judgement in relation to expected outcome of a tax position or dispute	Financial accounting risk Reputational risk

[B] Errors in Implementation

Risk driver	*When it arises*	*Typical risk areas*
Technical errors	Errors in the understanding and application of tax laws	Strategic and transactional risk Operational risk
Process errors	Errors in underlying source data or calculations of tax liabilities	Operational risk Compliance risk Financial accounting risk
Oversights or omissions	Where actions required by law are not taken due to oversight	Operational risk Compliance risk

[C] Failure to Monitor

Risk driver	*When it arises*	*Typical risk areas*
Changes in tax law or application	Where changes in the application of tax law or how particular transactions are treated leading to unsustainable tax positions	Strategic and transactional risk Operational risk Reputational risk
Control weaknesses	Errors resulting from failed or non-effective tax controls such as adequate sign-offs	Operational risk Compliance risk Financial Accounting risk Reputational risk

Managing the risks requires you to do more than just recognise the drivers of risk; you need to understand the business activities and characteristics that create the risks. For example, an organisation that has high volumes of transactions involving multiple products sold by different business units has a higher inherent risk of operational tax issues across the whole range of transaction based taxes. An organisation that has a significant and diverse workforce inherently has higher inherent risk in relation to employment related taxes including taxes borne and collected on behalf of employees.

For global organisations, the drivers of tax risk are multiplied across the number of territories where the group carries on business and magnified in territories where there is limited finance and tax presence. We are regularly told by tax functions that ensuring robust implementation of transactions and monitoring changes in the tax laws across multiple territories are key challenges. Accordingly, the response needs to focus on addressing these global drivers of risk.

§ 11.07 SUMMARY

An understanding of the different types of tax risk and the key drivers is an important starting point for managing these risks. In chapter 17 we will set out a framework as to what controls are needed and how these risks can best be managed.

HOW?

CHAPTER 12

CALCULATING THE TAXES

§ 12.01 INTRODUCTION

In chapter 8 we considered what is a tax and what should a tax function be responsible for. Looking at the amount of specific taxes paid or collected by a business, together with the risks associated with those taxes, will give you a good steer as to where you best focus both the tax function and other tax management resources. In chapter 13 we will use the amounts paid (or charged) and collected as the starting point for setting the overall tax strategic plan.

It may be that you can work out the amount of taxes paid, charged and collected on a rough and ready basis, and that is all that is required for the purposes of setting your strategic plan. However you may decide you need more accurate figures both on which to base your overall strategy and planning, and also for wider communication. In this chapter we therefore look at some of the issues in arriving on a consistent basis, year on year, at figures for taxes paid, charged and collected and we consider how these figures might be calculated.

§ 12.02 OBJECTIVES OF THIS EXERCISE

We suggest that the main reason for collecting information of taxes paid, charged and collected is to understand better where the scarce resources of the tax function should be focussed. However this may not be the only reason, and therefore before looking at any methodologies it is worth considering some of the other uses to which such information can be put.

We have talked in earlier chapters about the different stakeholders in tax. Many of these stakeholders will better understand the tax position of the group if there are proper figures attached to any communication with them. For example when dealing with the corporate responsibility agenda and the fact that headline corporate tax figures do not give a full picture of a company's total tax contribution to government authorities, it is extremely helpful to have details of all the other taxes paid by a business. Similarly when lobbying government bodies, having figures to back up your argument is vital.

There may also be a need to ensure a clear understanding of trends in the data. For example, where there is an upward trend in irrecoverable VAT is this due to increased business volume, change in cost base or changes in legislation? We do not therefore believe that collecting the information is a one off exercise. It should become something which takes place every year so that trends can be recognised.

Internally, it is extremely helpful for those managing risk (and particularly those in the business who are involved with managing tax risk) to understand the quantum of what is at issue. Finally it may be useful to benchmark the data against other organisational results (turnover, profit, employment costs) or against some other external metric (comparable organisations, contribution as measured against GDP). If a number of organisations are using comparable methodologies and publishing the results (for example in their accounts) then there starts to be good comparable data for benchmarking purposes.

§ 12.03 SOME ISSUES TO BE ADDRESSED

Assuming that you want a methodology which can both be used on an ongoing basis and give sensible comparisons year on year, consider the following questions:

- Do you use a cash or accruals basis?
- How should items disputed with government authorities be reflected?
- How should adjustments from prior years be dealt with?
- How should provisions for possible adjustments be dealt with?
- Do you include penalties and interest in your calculations?
- How should deferred tax be dealt with?

§ 12.04 OVERALL APPROACH

Collecting information for cash taxes paid in a fiscal year will require a different approach to collecting data regarding tax obligations (potentially) falling due within a reporting period, i.e. an accrual basis. Which approach is most appropriate may depend, for example, on whether profitability/the effective tax rate is more important than cash management, or vice versa.

The approach will also depend on how the information is to be used. If it is purely for the purpose of setting the tax strategic plan and communicating with the board then perhaps an accruals breakdown for the company's financial year is appropriate. However if the information is also to be used to lobby and deliver messages to governments, then a cash basis might be more appropriate. It may even be necessary to prepare different sets of information for different purposes—but such an approach can get complicated, and probably the best approach is to decide on one method and stick to it.

As already explained, in order to arrive at meaningful results, measurements should be taken on a consistent basis across a number of reporting periods. Using the example of corporate income tax on an accruals basis, the figures produced will be potentially vulnerable to distorting effects, which may make it difficult to interpret a single year's data in isolation. These distorting effects may be due to the availability of losses brought forward, material timing differences or other exceptional events. These measurement issues and potential distortions are likely to be more relevant to corporation tax than other 'above the line' business taxes. However they need to be considered for all taxes in the calculations.

§ 12.05 THE STARTING POINT

At the heart of any approach must be the ability to substantiate the results produced. When communicating the output of this exercise, it is essential that the data is robust, defensible and presented in a way that makes sense to the potential readers. As far as possible, the ability for the reader to develop alternative hypotheses in respect of the data should be minimised. This suggests that the financial accounts of a company must be the primary data source and that any results should, in some way, relate back to and be validated against the audited financial statements.

§12.06 WHAT ARE THE MEASUREMENT STANDARDS?

As noted above, the approach to data collection depends on the planned deliverables and objectives. There is also a need to keep the collection exercise manageable. So are the 'raw' financial accounts tax figures to be used or should the impact of prior year adjustments and true ups be considered? If a sensible trend analysis is to be performed, then almost inevitably adjusting items would have to be understood, but too many adjusting items can devalue the overall picture.

Using the corporation income tax figures in the accounts as an example, the main reconciling items between the tax payable in the returns and its actual rate in the accounts could be:

Tax item	*$'m*	*$'m*
Cash tax (per returns)		X
Adjusted by:		
Provisions for uncertain positions	X	
Prior year adjustments	X	
Interest and penalties	X	
		X
Current tax charge (per P&L)		X
Deferred tax charge (per P&L)		X
Total tax charge in P&L account		X

Which of the figures in the right hand column will you use for your year on year comparable and which of the three adjustments would you adjust for? Indeed there may be a need to go back and revise prior year figures for adjustments made in later years. While there is no one right answer, the key to this question is to arrive at a basis which can be applied consistently and can show trends from one year to the next without obviously being distorted by adjusting items.

§12.07 WHAT TAXES SHOULD BE INCLUDED?

The example above is purely a corporate income tax example. However for this exercise to achieve its objectives all material taxes need to be included. Additional similar reconciliations may need to be performed for these other taxes and a decision taken as to which corresponding figure from the right hand column is used. As deferred tax is basically a corporate income tax related item, the position on other taxes may be a bit simpler, but you still need to consider how you want to deal with the three different types of adjustment.

In deciding which taxes to do the calculations for there is both a practical and a 'technical' issue. From a practical perspective, there is certainly merit in taking an 80:20 approach based on the (perceived) organisational importance of the tax and the difficulties of obtaining the data. This may require a preliminary assessment of previously un-quantified taxes by developing proxy measures of the potential cost of those taxes. The technical issue is one of determining which taxes should be included in the data collection exercise—and, from a strategic viewpoint, this was discussed in an earlier chapter.

§ 12.08 WHAT ARE THE DATA SOURCES?

As suggested above the preferred starting point is the statutory accounts, with adjustments being made to those figures. This is a sensible approach where the tax is a P&L item in its own right or is an aggregated number embedded in another P&L figure. Taking this approach means that the derived figures can be easily reconciled back to the accounts.

However, if the data is not an aggregated figure in the P&L (e.g. VAT not recovered on employee expenses) or is an item where the company acts as a tax collection agency and the figures do not hit the P&L account, then this approach is unlikely to be the most effective way to collate the data. In situations where the P&L is not the starting point alternatives need to be considered.

It may be possible to create the required reports directly from the company's accounting systems. If the decision is to create a free standing process, then the following issues may be worth considering:

- Is there any possibility of including the exercise as part of the year-end process?
- Are there extraction protocols and programs that could reduce the amount of manual work required?
- Are there any changes to internal procedures that could help better track costs (which may additionally have cost management benefits)?
- Is it possible to create a reporting platform in one country that, if desired, could be rolled out to other territories?

Finally, you may want to consider the administrative costs of tax compliance. This is not dealt with in the data collection exercise because its computation is highly subjective and organisation specific. However, this does not invalidate the idea that there is a cost and that cost should not be lost sight of in the way tax is being managed in your organisation.

§ 12.09 CHECKING THE COLLECTION EXERCISE

Apart from the reconciliations and reasonableness checks of the data, an overall sense check would also be appropriate. This overall sense check requires knowledge of the drivers of the business. For example in a substantially people based business, does it make sense that irrecoverable VAT exceeds employer's social security payments? The sense checks will clearly be a more subjective assessment of the data but may help create a better explanation of the data.

§12.10 WHAT IS THE COLLECTION PERIOD?

Clearly the more extended the measurement period is the more informed any trend analysis will be, and the less likely that decisions are made just based on a snapshot of one year alone. However, recognising the practicalities of analysing historic data an initial two year comparison period may be appropriate as a starting point.

§12.11 SUMMARY

Some form of calculation of taxes paid and collected is important in deciding where scarce tax management resources should be deployed. However there are a number of other good reasons why having good comparable information is important. Collecting such information is not straightforward and a number of decisions have to be made as to what basis to use. Ensuring that you can substantiate the information produced is the key to the credibility of such information.

CHAPTER 13
DOCUMENTING THE STRATEGIC PLAN

"Strategy is choosing what not to do"

§13.01 INTRODUCTION

We have seen many 'tax strategic plans' which are no more than a list of action points. They often start with the things which are easy to measure (e.g. we will get all our tax returns in on time). We have to question whether such documents really warrant the term strategy.

In this chapter we discuss what a best practice tax strategic plan might look like, how the document might be produced and how the plan might be implemented. At the end of this chapter we put forward a structure which could act as a template for producing a tax strategic plan. How you produce such a plan and arrive at this document will vary from company to company, but there are certain underlying steps which need to be taken whichever route you choose. Once written there remains the question as to how it is communicated and rolled out to the relevant parties.

§13.02 THE EXTERNAL ENVIRONMENT

The starting point for any strategic plan is the external environment. This includes an understanding of where regulators are coming from, the attitude of revenue authorities, and the agendas of the other stakeholders in the tax affairs of your organisation. The Why section of this guide covered this external environment in generic terms; in arriving at your plan which of these issues/pressures is relevant and how important are they to you?

§13.03 ALIGNING WITH THE BUSINESS

For a plan to be effective it should be aligned with the overall business. The days of the tax tail wagging the commercial dog (if they ever existed) are long past. Therefore in producing a tax strategic plan it is necessary to understand what we call the 'fixed parameters', i.e. those things which are predetermined and within which the tax plan has to be developed. These might include the group's overall commercial strategy, the group's corporate responsibility position, the group's approach to corporate governance, the group's attitude to risk and even the group's business model. These are the things which the tax function, much as it may want to, can not readily change.

§13.04 TAXES PAID, CHARGED AND COLLECTED

In chapter 8 we looked at how we define the term tax and hence which taxes should be included in the tax strategic plan. They included not only the taxes which the business bears, but also the taxes which it is responsible for collecting on behalf of government authorities. We also reflected on which of these many taxes should be managed by the tax function and which are best managed elsewhere in the business. The point to make here is that it does not matter who is managing the particular taxes; if they fall under the definition of tax they should be part of the overall tax plan for an organisation.

However the amount of effort to be put into managing each tax will be driven by the impact of that tax. This will include not only the overall cost to the business of that tax, but also the risks involved in dealing with it. To put the different taxes in context we therefore suggest that the strategic plan should include a brief summary of all the major taxes paid by an organisation, as well as details of the major taxes collected on behalf of government authorities.

A number of businesses are more interested in the tax charge in the accounts, as opposed to cash taxes, and so you may want to include deferred taxes under this heading. It is also worth reflecting on what tax holidays or special treatments the business is getting; these 'tax assets' also need to be considered under the 'taxes [not] paid' heading. How you calculate the taxes paid has been discussed in the previous chapter; what is important is that this exercise is done even if only on a rough and ready basis before the strategic plan is developed.

§ 13.05 RESEARCH

In arriving at the tax plan, the fixed parameters need to be researched and understood, and their impact on the plan needs to be thought through. A similar point applies to the external tax environment and its impact, as well as the taxes paid. We would normally start a discussion/workshop on a tax strategic plan by asking the head of tax (or someone they have appointed) to provide feedback on the three points discussed above, having researched them prior to the meeting. This is the key background information that is needed before you can have meaningful discussion on the plan itself.

§ 13.06 OVERVIEW

Staying with the big picture, and before diving down into the detail of what needs managing, the strategic plan needs to set out the overall approach to managing taxes. From our work in helping many businesses produce a tax strategic plan we have developed two 'tax strategy templates' one of which deals with tax planning and the other with tax compliance and accounting. They are both overview tools to promote discussion and help clarify the group's overall approach to managing its tax affairs. We would stress that they are not meant to be scientifically perfect models; however what they do very effectively is get people thinking and stimulate debate, particularly at board level.

The tax planning template:

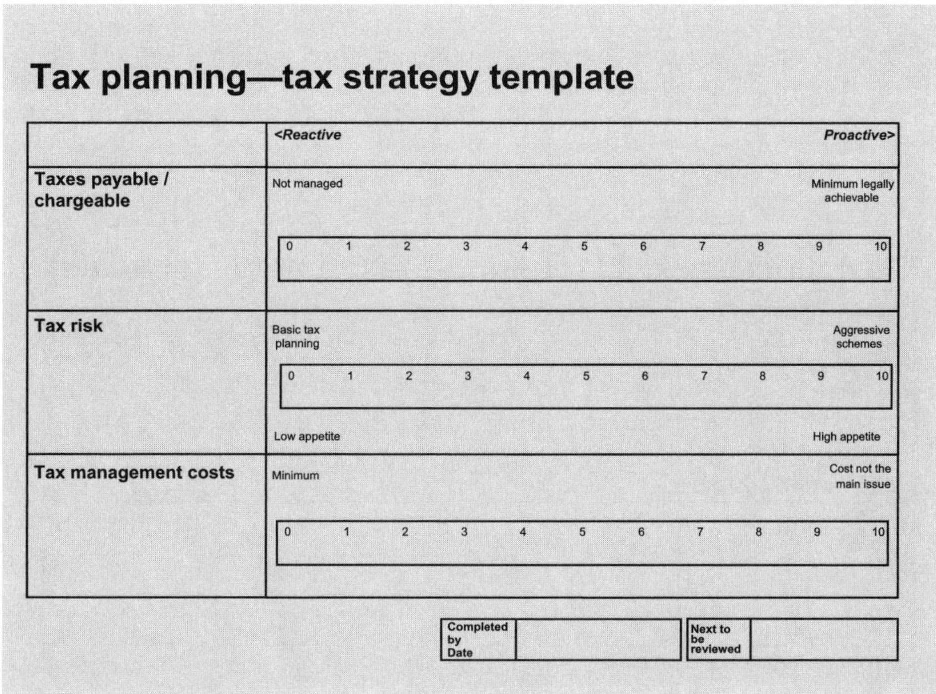

For the tax planning template above there are three scales:

- Taxes payable or chargeable;
- Tax risk; and
- The costs of managing the planning side of tax.

The scales run from zero to ten. Zero represents a very reactive approach to tax planning. Ten represents a very proactive approach, where the head of tax would be prepared to spend time fighting a case in the senior law courts. We believe that, broadly, the three scales are correlated. One cannot have a very aggressive approach to managing the tax charge without incurring some (legitimate) tax risk and without incurring some extra costs.

To get an overall view of someone's approach to their tax planning, and because of the correlation noted above, we ask people to draw a vertical line down the template giving a single overall 'score' between zero and ten. The more conservative and reactive groups would have a lower score than those who manage their tax more aggressively and proactively. In deciding where to draw the line down the template, you might also like to refer back to the scales used in chapter 6, the chapter on corporate responsibility.

Similarly for the compliance and tax accounting template below there are three scales, this time being:

- The effectiveness of the processes around tax compliance and accounting;
- Tax risk—or tolerance of error; and
- The costs of managing the compliance/accounting side of tax.

Compliance and accounting—tax strategy template

	<Reactive										*Proactive>*
Tax compliance / accounting	Haphazard processes										Effective processes
	0	1	2	3	4	5	6	7	8	9	10
Tax risk	High tolerance of error										Low tolerance of error
	0	1	2	3	4	5	6	7	8	9	10
Tax management costs	Minimum										Cost not the main issue
	0	1	2	3	4	5	6	7	8	9	10

Completed by Date		Next to be reviewed	

Again we believe there is a trade off between the three items, and again we ask people to draw a vertical line down the template giving a single overall 'score' between zero and ten for compliance/accounting. Those groups who are fairly relaxed about their compliance and tax accounting will have a lower score than those who are more concerned about errors and want to get their compliance and accounting 'right'.

It does not follow that the scores on the two templates have to be the same. A group which is more focussed on planning than compliance will have a higher score on the planning template (see below), and vice versa. What we believe does follow is that there is a correlation between the scores on each template and the way resources and budget are allocated. If one score is significantly higher than the

Tax planning—tax strategy template

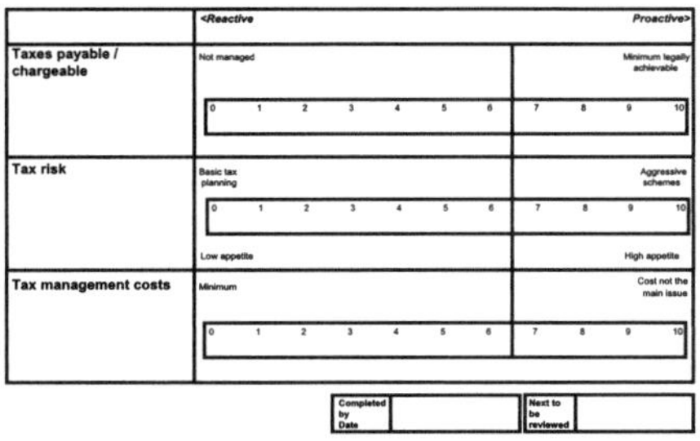

Compliance and accounting – tax strategy template

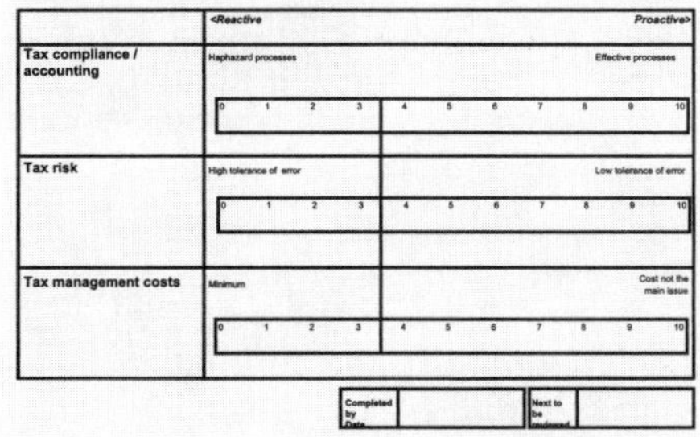

other then that is where we would expect to see more resources; if the two scores are similar then there will be a more even allocation of resources.

Some real life examples we have seen when using the template include:

- A tax function which told us they had a good shared understanding of their tax planning strategy, but then when each member of the team individually completed the template, their 'scores' ranged from two to nine.
- A company who completed the templates while recruiting a new head of tax, and then tore up their draft recruitment advertisement as they realised that their desired strategy suggested they needed a very different individual from that which the draft advertisement suggested.
- A group where the board identified that the tax function's 'robust' approach was fine in current circumstances, but going forward would need to become less aggressive as the group needed 'steady' results due to a forthcoming flotation.

In helping clients formulate a tax strategic plan, we often start by getting them to identify where on the scales they are at present and then where they would like to be in two/three/five years time. That exercise gives an idea of the amount of change that the strategic plan needs to bring about.

§ 13.07 AREAS OF FOCUS

Strategy is about choice—and hence focus. Having got clarity as to where your business might sit on the two tax strategy templates above, you need to decide what are the important things which need managing (your 'areas of focus'). The answer to this question will obviously vary from group to group. The diagram below sets out some examples of typical areas of focus for a business.

We do not pretend that these are the only possible areas of focus—and indeed in your organisation you may want to be a lot more granular than the high level items in the diagram below. However what we are attempting to do here is to

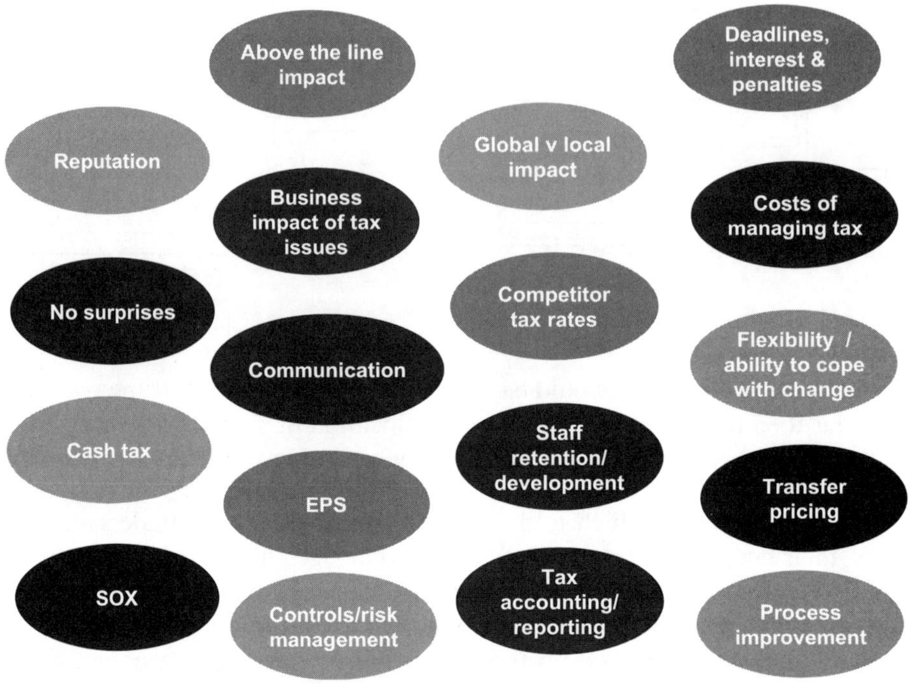

encourage those running the tax affairs of a business to think through what is important, and come up with a maximum of 5 headings which are the most important areas for their group—and the answer to the question from the board as to 'what really matters for the group in relation to tax?' Undoubtedly there will be other things which need to be dealt with but, as noted earlier, a strategy is about making choices and putting some focus around limited resources.

We have worked with many groups in helping them decide where they should be focussing their resources. What is very clear is that individual people will each have their own thoughts as where the group should be focussing. For example the indirect tax manager's views may well be different from the head of tax, and their views may be different from the CFO.

In order to get both a consensus and to get buy in from the various different stakeholders, we have found that brainstorming sessions work well here—where everyone is encouraged to have their say and initially, at least, nothing is ruled out as being inappropriate. Those we have worked with will recall walls covered in different coloured 'post-its' on which all those present have set out their own thoughts. The next part of the brainstorming exercise involves moving the post-its around the walls to see what are the common themes.

We have often broken this exercise down into two halves with the first half focussing on managing the tax planning and second the compliance and reporting (with tax risk being a common thread through both). Where we have run this as a two part exercise, common themes come through from the two parts and bringing the 'long list' down to no more than five key areas of focus is not often an issue.

§13.08 SCENARIO PLANNING

A more sophisticated approach to choosing your areas of focus, and one used by a small number of groups, is the use of scenario planning. This is not the place to go into a detailed analysis of scenario planning, but it is a technique that has been widely used in politics and certain sectors, like the defence industry, for some time. Rather than making certain fixed assumptions about the future, scenario planning advocates the consideration of different decisions against a range of different values and outcomes. These scenarios can then be weighted against the likelihood of them happening—and a decision made which is right in the overall scheme of things and not just against the most predictable scenario.

In a tax context, you would need to determine the main influences on your group's tax position or the tax function. You would then need to consider what might happen in different scenarios. In turn, what would be the position if each of those influences became extremely significant or insignificant? Further, if you can judge the strength of the forces pulling you in the directions of those influences and the risks involved, you will be better placed to decide future requirements for both resources and skills, and where you need to focus going forward.

§13.09 SMART OBJECTIVES

We believe that a tax strategic plan should set out clear objectives as to what is to be achieved. Having decided upon the most important issues to be managed (the key areas of focus), the strategic plan should then spell out how these issues are to be addressed and what success looks like.

We encourage people to use the SMART approach to objective setting (objectives should be Specific, Measurable, Acceptable, Realistic and Timely). To ensure objectives are realistic we also encourage people to think through the barriers to achieving the objectives—and these are often barriers where support and assistance is needed from those outside the tax function.

In practice, often the most difficult part of setting the strategic plan is in agreeing SMART objectives around the areas of focus. However without such objectives, implementation becomes problematic (see below) and the time spent in setting the strategic plan can be partially (or even wholly) wasted.

In our experience it is therefore vitally important to allow enough time for the objectives around each area of focus to be fully debated, and challenges to be made as to whether they are SMART enough. This does become a bit of a wordsmithing exercise—but time invested here is usually time well spent.

§ 13.10 OTHER POSSIBLE ITEMS FOR INCLUSION

There will always be a debate as to how much detail needs to be included in a tax strategic plan. The discussion so far has been at a reasonably high level and you could argue that you need go no further and that everything else is about how you implement the plan.

However there will undoubtedly be a number of different stakeholders who are interested in the tax strategic plan and it may therefore follow that more than one document is required. For example what we have already discussed may be enough for the board, but for the members of the tax function you also need to include comments around some of the headings below.

1. Roles and responsibilities;
2. Reporting lines;
3. People development;
4. Stakeholder communication;
5. Use of external advisors;
6. Controls;
7. Process improvement;
8. Data management;
9. Use of technology;
10. Budgets; and
11. Detailed performance measurements.

In future chapters we discuss each of these items in a bit more detail and hence do not do so here. However what is important it that whatever document you come up with is right for your organisation and is also right for those stakeholders you are looking to communicate with—and with the multiple different stakeholders, even if that means having more than one document.

§ 13.11 THE STRATEGIC PLAN

Based on the above analysis we have set out below what a tax strategic plan might look like. We have included some, but not all of the items listed in the section above.

I. High level overview
   1. The external environment
   2. Taxes paid, charged and collected
   3. Attitude to tax planning and risk
   4. Tax strategy templates

II. Key areas of focus (no more than 5)
   1. [Area of focus 1]
      - What is the issue
      - Objective(s) for addressing the issue
      - Barriers to achieving the objectives—and how to overcome them
      - Action plan
   2. [Area of focus 2]
      - What is the issue
      - Objective(s) for addressing the issue
      - Barriers to achieving the objectives—and how to overcome them
      - Action plan
   3. [Area of focus 3]
      - What is the issue
      - Objective(s) for addressing the issue
      - Barriers to achieving the objectives—and how to overcome them
      - Action plan
   4. [Area of focus 4]
      - What is the issue
      - Objective(s) for addressing the issue
      - Barriers to achieving the objective—and how to overcome them
      - Action plan

III. Role of the tax function
   1. Structure of the tax function
   2. Role of 'shadow tax function'
   3. Reporting lines
   4. Using external advisors
   5. Developing the team

IV. Stakeholder engagement and communication
   1. Who are the stakeholders in tax?
   2. The communication plan

V. Performance metrics—the balanced scorecard

VI. Summary

Clearly each group will have their own style and way of working. If the strategic plan is being presented to the board for approval, we might add a section into the Introduction entitled 'What the board are being asked to comment on' and in the Summary a section entitled 'Matters for board approval'. We might also remove all/parts of section III and IV if it is felt that this is too much detail for a board paper—but we would probably leave these sections in when communicating with the tax function.

§ 13.12 IMPLEMENTATION

We have seen many excellent strategic plans which have fallen down in their execution. 'We had an excellent away day where we agreed upon our overall strategy; unfortunately we have been too busy to implement it'.

As we discussed in early chapters, the eight key enablers (structure, people, leadership, controls and risk management, process, data management, technology and communication) are the tools, methodologies and skills that are required for the successful implementation of the tax strategy. As a result, the implementation plan for all the key areas of focus should include a discussion of the changes necessary in each of these key enablers in order to achieve the desired results.

Having considered the enablers and set SMART objectives for the key areas of focus for the group as a whole, the next stage is to give individual people ownership of these objectives. By defining the implementation in terms of the enablers, it will be easier to assign individual accountability for each action that is required so that individual plans and performance measures can be integrated into the overall tax strategy. When the group objectives start appearing in people's personal objectives—and you start measuring people on how they deliver against them—you have then started to make the link between the overall strategy and what happens day to day on the ground.

This leads onto a debate around resources and who does what. In a later chapter we will explore this in more detail—and in particular the role of the shadow tax function and of external advisors. Suffice it to say at this stage if there are a number of key areas of focus which are top of the tax agenda, you need to have the right resources to deliver against the objectives set and, as noted above, the people tasked to do so need to have these objectives at the top of their own personal agendas.

§ 13.13 APPROVAL

It is our view that the board should consider and sign off the tax strategic plan at least once a year. We believe that a board paper needs to be produced, and it made very clear to the board what they are being asked to opine on. We also believe that it is very important that the head of tax is actually present when the board discusses tax. In some cases we are aware that the person representing tax at board level is the CFO. If the head of tax is not allowed to present to the board, it firstly gives a message as to where tax is on the board agenda and secondly makes it very difficult for the head of tax to understand fully where the board are coming from on tax matters.

§13.14 COMMUNICATION

Once a tax strategic plan has been agreed it needs to be communicated to the relevant stakeholders. In a later chapter we look at communication in more detail. We do recommend a proper tax communication plan. In relation to the tax strategic plan, the questions which need to be asked are:

- Who are the stakeholders in the tax plan?
- What do they need to understand?
- What behaviours are you looking for from them?
- What is the best form of communication with them—and it will undoubtedly vary from stakeholder to stakeholder?

§13.15 REVIEW

If it is right that the board should review and sign off the tax strategic plan at least once a year, it logically follows that the head of tax should also instigate a review of the plan at least once a year. We can debate as to whether you need to go back to a blank sheet of paper every year, or whether this is done every second or third year. However as we all know the external environment for tax is changing very fast and this suggests you should err on the side of more frequent reviews as opposed to less. Having said that, we would suggest that strategic reviews happening more than once a year could be counter productive unless something significant has happened (such as a merger or a major acquisition).

§13.16 SUMMARY

Best practice demands that a proper documented tax strategic plan is produced. For the document to be a true strategy (rather than just a list of high level objectives), it should:

- Set out the overall high level attitude to tax management;
- Be clear as to the key areas of tax which need managing;
- Set out clear objectives as to what is to be achieved; and
- Be aligned with and embedded in the business.

The overall approach can best be summarised in the attached diagram—where we link up the overall strategic plan with peoples' day to day activities.

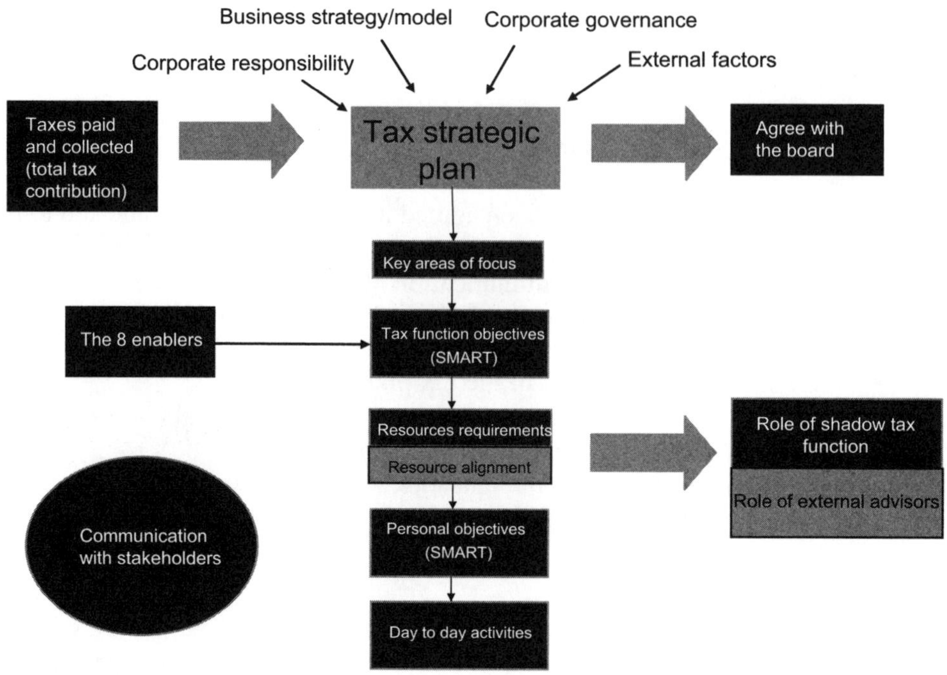

Business strategy/model
Corporate governance
Corporate responsibility
External factors
Taxes paid and collected (total tax contribution)
Tax strategic plan
Agree with the board
Key areas of focus
The 8 enablers
Tax function objectives (SMART)
Resources requirements
Resource alignment
Role of shadow tax function
Role of external advisors
Communication with stakeholders
Personal objectives (SMART)
Day to day activities

CHAPTER 14

STRUCTURING THE TAX FUNCTION

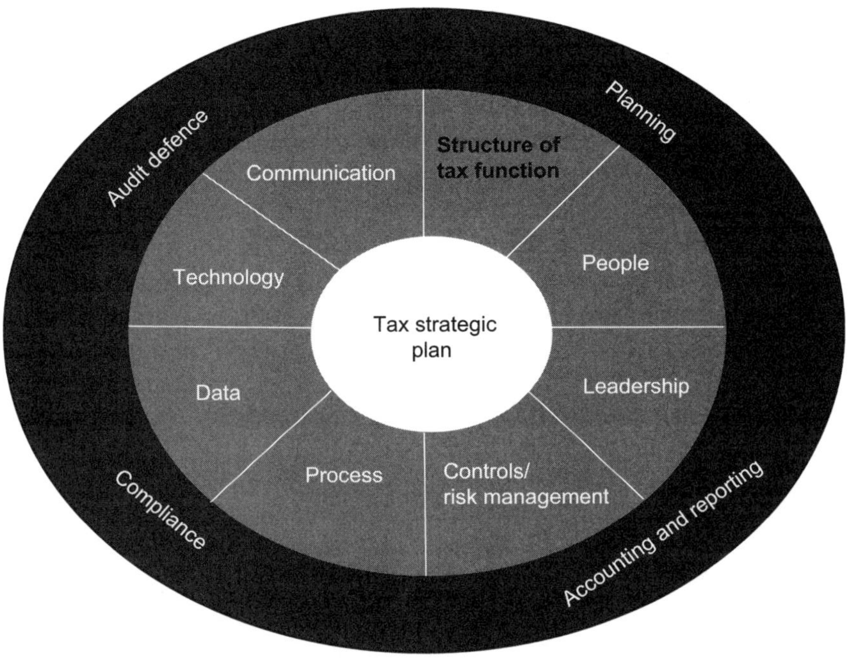

§14.01 INTRODUCTION

In our work with many tax functions around the world we have seen a number of different ways in which the tax function is structured and organised. There are clearly a number of different options and we do not believe that there is only one right answer which will suit all businesses.

The purpose of this chapter is to set out some of the options, with comments on the pros and cons of each. Indeed the correct answer for your business will probably be a matrix system which combines two or more of these different options.

§14.02 ROLE OF THE TAX FUNCTION

In chapter 10 we set out the three different types of people who are involved in the running of the tax affairs of any business, namely:

- In-house tax function;
- Shadow tax function; and
- External advisors.

It is beyond the scope of this guide to consider, for example, how the finance function or the HR department organises their part of the shadow tax function. Nor would we attempt to comment on how the external advisors might be organised. In this chapter we will be focusing purely on the first of these three, the in-house tax function, the people who are dedicated tax specialists and probably have tax somewhere in their job titles.

The starting point for organising the structure of the in-house tax function is a decision as to which activities are carried out by the in-house team and which are dealt with by these other parties, the shadow tax function or the external advisors. In chapter 10 we included a table entitled ownership of tax deliverables which looked at who was responsible for each deliverable for the various different taxes which need managing. It is those activities which fall within the tax function's ambit that this chapter is about.

§14.03 KEY QUESTIONS

Whatever the size of your tax function, in designing the structure of the function you should be looking to answer two key questions:

- How should the tax function be grouped into distinct organisational units and teams, to enable the people to:

  —Focus sufficient attention and resources on the priority requirements that the tax function must meet (the key areas of focus and the four deliverables), and

—Obtain the best value from the company's overall tax resources?

- How should the relationships between those teams be managed?

There are a number of different ways that you could structure your in-house tax function. You might like to consider the alternatives set out below.

§ 14.04 HEAD OFFICE v BUSINESS UNIT MODEL

Particularly for larger businesses, the first question to consider is whether you wish to operate the head office model or the local business unit model. In the head office model the tax function is highly centralised; in the business unit model, local businesses take more responsibility of their tax affairs and have in-house tax resource within that business.

In answering this question you should consider the company's overall organisational strategy with respect to the roles and functions of the corporate centre and its relationships with individual business units. Additionally you will need to consider the environment in which the tax function must operate. For companies that have numerous disparate businesses, a more decentralised model may be more appealing so that resources can be aligned more closely with where and how key business decisions are made.

Some companies give prime importance to the benefits of scale and greater specialisation that are achievable within a centralised structure, while others place greater emphasis on the benefits of delegating accountability and control to the management team of individual business units. Should the tax function not be consistent with the rest of the business in this respect?

It has been interesting to note over the past few years that even where businesses operate the local business model, there has been an increasing tendency for these local tax people to have their main reporting line into the global head of tax, with perhaps a dotted reporting line to the local business. This structure may be of value in embedding a consistent approach to tax while keeping the tax function close to its internal business stakeholders.

A comparison of the advantages and disadvantages of the two models is set out in the table below.

	Advantages	Disadvantages
Head office model	• Strong focus on group tax charge • Easier to align with group strategy • Good co-ordination • Easier to restrict headcount • Provide a pool of expertise	• Can be seen as remote from businesses • Will not have detailed territory specific skills for overseas entities • Can be perceived as a 'head office overhead'
Business unit model	• Close to business • Likely to have local-territory specific tax skills • Can reduce reliance on local advisers	• Less focused on group co-ordination or strategy • Can lead to inconsistent positions with different tax authorities • Transfer pricing can be difficult to co-ordinate • Harder to supervise activity and control group tax costs • Reporting and/or loyalties will often be to local management • Harder to ensure optimum resource levels • Tax staff in smaller locations can feel isolated

§14.05 THE ORGANISATIONAL OPTIONS

The options for both head office tax functions and local business unit teams include organising the people by:

- The main deliverables, namely tax planning, tax accounting, tax compliance and audit defence.
- Different types of tax specialism, such as corporate income taxes, indirect taxes and employment taxes.
- Geography e.g. by county or region maybe headed up by an international tax manager.
- Business unit—in line with the rest of the business.
- A project-based organisational structure, whereby people in the tax function are organised in team-based structures of limited duration—typically 12 to 18 months—with specific responsibilities for the current key areas of focus (i.e. the near-term priorities for tax).

- The enablers (e.g. people development, controls and risk management, process improvement, data management, technology and communication), though this is not something we have seen implemented in practice.

These basic options are often combined into matrix structures, so as to obtain the benefits of focus in two (or possibly even more?) distinct areas. For example, a matrix structure might be created whereby the line management structure was defined according to the main deliverables, but functional reporting lines were established to run across the geographies. Matrix structures typically however have one management dimension that predominates, which in practice can limit the scope for achieving a really sharp focus on more than one of the alternative options summarised above.

For those groups aligned with the deliverables, it is worth noting that we are increasingly seeing a tax controller role within tax functions, someone one who is responsible for the tax figures within the financial statements and related reporting. The skills of this role are more around accounting than tax. Additionally we are also seeing people with ownership of people development, controls and risk management, process improvement, data management, technology and communication (i.e. the enablers) but it would be unusual for the enablers to be the predominant arm within a matrix structure. Our experience has shown that some level of alignment around deliverables is desired but unless the right matrix is also implemented, these deliverables based structures tend to result in silos that can result in dysfunctional organisational models.

Where the geography structure is combined with a tax specialisms structure there is a tendency for the corporate tax people to be in the more senior roles with sometimes undue emphasis on these taxes at the expense of the others. The technical competency is but one part of the overall skills of tax professionals, and to have this as one of the key drivers of the tax function's structure is perhaps an historical position which needs challenging.

One of the key drivers in selecting the best organisational structure is to carefully consider how the rest of the organisation (outside of tax) is structured and where and when key strategic decisions are made. Our experience has been that if the company as a whole is structured tightly around global business units, key strategic decisions tend to be made at that level. If tax is then structured by functional specialty and geography, it may be some time before tax is engaged in the process (usually after decisions are made and corporate geographies are asked to implement changes). If tax is to be a relevant business partner to other business units, it must structure itself to facilitate collaboration with key stakeholders. One highly diversified company assigned its senior tax planning resources to business units but retained a deliverable/geography matrix for the rest of its organisation. The tax function's ability to interact with key stakeholders has since improved dramatically. In the right circumstances, this approach is clearly a best practice.

A comparison of the typical advantages and disadvantages of these different organisational structures is set out in the table below.

Organisational structure	*Advantages*	*Disadvantages*
By the deliverables	• Facilitates development of particular expertise • Facilitates efficient and consistent delivery	• Could limit the scope for focus of attention on key priorities/ areas of focus
By different types of tax specialism	• Facilitates development of deep expertise in particular types of tax specialism	• Could lead to business processes that are inconsistent across the organisation and costly to operate
By geography	• Provides for focus on country-specific/regional issues • Often aligns with the business	• Could involve focus at the country/regional/ BU level at the expense of corporate issues
By business unit	• Clearer alignment with overall corporate strategy • Alignment with senior business unit leadership	• Possibly more resources needed to collaborate with business units and other tax professionals
Adopt a project-based organisational form	• Provides a sharp focus on key priorities • Provides for flexible deployment of resources according to business requirements	• Could limit the scope for providing robust structures within which to develop deep expertise and structured career development of staff

We do recognise that in the smaller tax functions there will undoubtedly be significant 'multi-hatting' with the same people responsible for a number of different areas. However in our opinion this does not do away with the underlying principle that the organisation of the tax function needs to thought through and be appropriate to that business.

Finally you need to consider how the tax function will be managed as a whole in order to obtain the best value from the company's overall tax resources and the benefits from collaborative working among people in the different teams. This might include a 'staff pool' concept at the lower levels, which overcomes the potential for narrow technical focus too early on in a tax career. This can give you the deep expertise at the higher levels, and a situation where much of the routine work is attractive to younger staff since its new and offers exposure to things they have not experienced before.

§ 14.06 REPORTING LINES

Within the overall organisation design consideration needs to be given to:

- The breadth of the spans of control of individual people and in consequence the number of management levels in the organisation.

  Within a large tax function a balance is needed between providing an economical structure with no more levels of management than are really needed and one in which the number of people whom each person has to supervise is few enough to enable that person to give sufficient attention to each. It is particularly important for the head of tax not to have too many direct reports, so they have time to deal with some of the bigger issues which should fall within their role.
- Clarity as to the areas of accountability of each position.

  The design of each individual job needs to set out a clear area of performance for which the jobholder is accountable. The job and organisation design should also, so far as possible, facilitate the jobholder's direct report in assessing whether or not the jobholder is performing the role to a sufficiently high standard.
- Mechanisms for facilitating collaborative working between different parts of the tax function where these are important for performance.

  A major source of failure in organisation design is the establishment of structures in which it is assumed that particular organisational units and teams will work together collaboratively but in practice do not do so. Mechanisms for managing these interrelationships should be developed in sufficient detail to ensure that they will work effectively in actual practice. This will be particularly important for those tax functions designed around the tax specialisms or geographies.
- Adaptability to change.

  The organisation design should take into account potential requirements for the tax function to adapt to organisational changes, such as changes in the company's tax strategy, mergers between business units within the company's portfolio or acquisitions.

It is perhaps worth at this point picking up a practical issue in relation to the de-centralised model for a tax function. Where a member of the tax function is physically situated in a business line, and even more so where they are situated in a country other than the head office country, then there will be a tendency for them to look to the local CFO as their direct report even if this officially is not the case. The question often comes down to who is responsible for their pay and benefits; if the local CFO is the person most closely involved then human nature dictates that the tax person will see this CFO as more important to them individually than the head of tax.

There is then also the question as to whom the head of tax should report. In our opinion, and as set out in the Why section of this guide, the head of tax should have a direct report into the CFO (and should also have access to the board on a regular basis). We have seen a concerning trend in one or two places for the CFO to delegate tax down to financial controllers and we do question whether this is appropriate. It is no surprise that while this approach remains in the minority, these companies seem to have a disproportionately high amount of problems, especially controls weaknesses and resource issues, as compared to their peers. We are also aware of a number of cases where an organisation has a 'head of tax and treasury' and in many cases this person's background experience is in treasury rather than tax. Again there can be a question as to whether tax is properly and fully represented at the senior levels in the organisation.

§ 14.07 FLEXIBILITY

We started this guide highlighting the major changes which have taken place in both the business and the tax world over the last few years. The tax function and the organisation of the tax function needs to be flexible enough to cope with this change. We would therefore recommend, along with the overall tax strategy, that the organisation of the tax function is reviewed on a regular basis. Our recommendation was that the tax strategic plan should be reviewed and presented to the board at least once a year. We would suggest that the organisation of the tax function follows the same route to ensure it is still appropriate.

§ 14.08 SUMMARY

There are a number of different roles within a tax function and due to resource and budgetary constraints, there are usually rather less people within the tax function than there are specific roles to be carried out. This normally drives organisations to some sort of matrix structure whereby individual people have a number of different responsibilities.

We would suggest that the matrix will be based on one or more of the options we set out above. One of the challenges for heads of tax is to consider whether the traditional structures which were based around the different taxes and different geographies are appropriate to today's best in class tax function.

CHAPTER 15

PEOPLE DEVELOPMENT

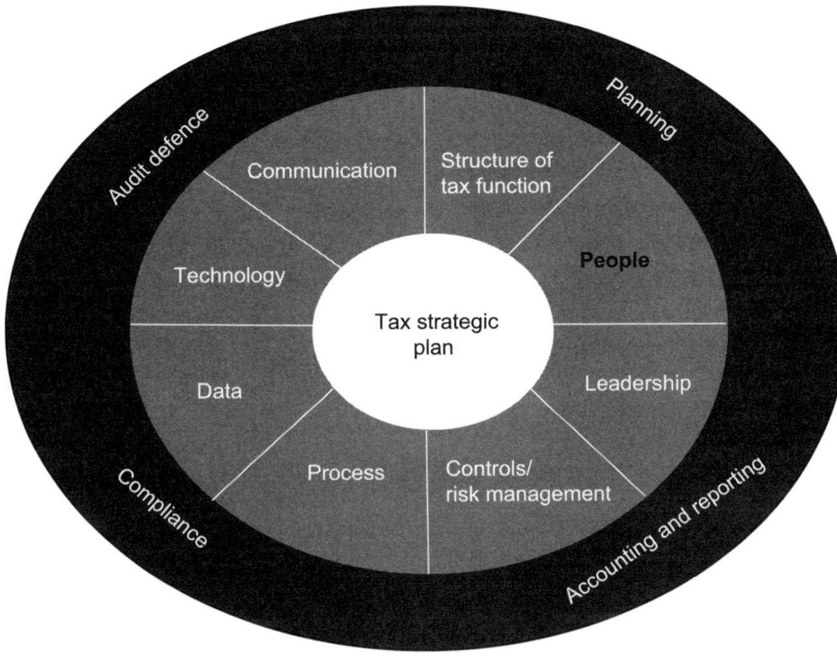

§15.01 INTRODUCTION

In chapter 14 we explained how the head of tax might organise and structure their people most effectively in order to implement the tax strategy. The purpose of this chapter is to focus more on the people agenda and less on the organisational structure. We set out firstly some comments about the skills required for those in a tax function. We then discuss a number of the common people issues which we see when working with tax functions and finally set out a suggested methodology for addressing these issues.

§15.02 SKILLS REQUIRED

Tax functions have come a long way from the days when tax technical skills were all that was seen as being important. While for most tax functions, strong technical skills will constitute a basic requirement, other 'softer' business skills will prove crucial if the tax function is to be effective. Even when dealing with tax authorities, tax technical skills are probably less important than negotiating ability.

The skills required today clearly need to link in with what the tax function is being asked to manage. Taking this to its logical conclusion you could argue that technical skills are less important and the key skills required are:

Perhaps this is taking things too far and there should be a box for technical skills as well—but it is worth considering whether that statement is correct for your organisation.

One particular comment we have heard from a number of CFOs is that tax people sometimes seem to need too much base information before a decision can be made; another typical comment is that tax people seem to over-engineer even the simplest requests. Tax is of course an area where one cannot divorce planning from the underlying base data, but given that decisions increasingly have to be made quickly on the basis of imperfect/incomplete data the tax function needs to be flexible in the way it provides advice when commercial circumstances are changing, for example providing advice in relation to a proposed transaction such as an acquisition or disposal.

The key point here is to think through what skills are required to deliver what the tax function is expected to deliver. The methodology set out below takes us through identifying the gaps between what is needed and what exists, and how these gaps might best be filled. Firstly though let us look at some of the other people issues we see in our work with tax functions.

§ 15.03 PEOPLE ISSUES

[A] Shortages of Staff

There seems to be a common theme wherever we go around the world, in that there is a shortage of good, quality and well trained tax staff. This is as much to do with increasing demand for tax staff, as it is to do with supply. The changing business environment has resulted in greater needs for good tax people, and there is undoubtedly a time lag between the demand being recognised and the appropriate numbers of people being properly trained. This imbalance between supply and demand is therefore putting pressure both on recruitment and retention of good tax people.

The internal organisation also needs to be flexible enough to accommodate sharing work during peak periods. Tax functions that are too siloed and rigid tend to use resources ineffectively and have a tendency to feel perpetually undermanned.

[B] Keeping Staff Motivated

Most heads of tax are keen to ensure they retain the staff they have so that experience and continuity is preserved. However this can present particular problems:

- Career development—unless you have a particularly large tax function, providing good career development for tax staff is an increasing issue. Good people will be looking to further their careers and, with demand out-stripping supply, they will be looking for, and are often able to get, a role change on a reasonably regular basis. This is probably even more so in the early stages of their careers as they work their way up the corporate ladder.
- Specialisation—if this happens too early on a person's career this can lead to high staff turnover; younger people want to experience variety. If they

can not get it at company A they are very comfortable moving on to company B.

- Overqualified for role—if there is a lack of opportunity for people to change roles and develop their careers, staff can become overqualified for the roles they hold. Most staff will also look for regular salary increases. Thus not only can they become overqualified for the role they are carrying out, they can also become an expensive resource for the role they are doing.
- Keeping fresh—staff can start to go stale if the work they do is repetitive or lacks development opportunity. Particularly in the reporting and compliance area it is sometimes difficult to ensure fresh thinking from those who have been doing this work for a number of years.
- Resistance to change—if staff do not have the chance to change their roles and develop it is very easy for inertia to set in and for work to continue much in the way it always has. This can of course sometimes be an advantage, but given the rate of change that most businesses (and indeed their tax functions) are currently experiencing, we believe that flexibility and ability to change are important advantages for tax teams.

[C] Learning and Education

While there is a whole plethora of people who run external tax related courses, it is often either very difficult or very expensive to find training which is specifically tailored to the needs of the individuals in a particular business. As a result of this, what we see in practice is either people not getting sufficient training or alternatively going on external courses which have some benefit in imparting knowledge but are often poor in developing people's skills and behaviours.

[D] Succession Planning

Succession planning is an issue, particularly for smaller tax functions. In such tax functions senior roles are often filled by external recruitment. In the larger tax functions, internal succession planning is possible and links in with career development point note above. However there will still be issues matching up the timing of vacancies arising with the career aspirations of those coming up the development ladder.

[E] The One-Person Tax Function

For those medium sized businesses where a decision is made to have a tax department, but the in-house tax department is to consist of just a single individual, a key issue is whether the individual should have high level 'Head of Tax' skills or should be more suited to detailed compliance and tax accounting work. It is rare that a single individual will be suited to both. This will obviously impact on the allocation of work between the in-house tax individual and external advisors/service providers. In our experience the more successful model for one person in-house tax functions is where the person has the higher-level skill base and uses outside consultants for compliance services.

[F] Compliance v Planning

There has been a danger, and even with the increasing focus on compliance and reporting matters there will continue to be a danger, that the more skilled people will want to focus their time and efforts on what are seen as the more exciting areas of tax management such as tax planning and dealing with transactions such as acquisitions and disposals. As a result we do see the compliance activities being carried out in a number of tax functions either by people who are not looking to stay in such activities or people who have been there for some years and are perhaps not as quick as they might be in embracing first the changing approach from revenue authorities and secondly developing processes and technologies for dealing with compliance matters.

Additionally one typical scenario is that staff shortages combined with increased demands have caused tax managers to prepare more and review less. In addition to the increased overtime and low morale, the head of tax is forced to spend more time reviewing the work performed by their managers leaving less time for the higher value planning and analytics.

[G] Work-Life Balance and Fun

The late 1990s and early 21st Century have seen an increasing focus on quality of life issues and on the business benefits of improving people's working lives. We believe that a team will perform more effectively if it is happy and the team members are content with their working life and therefore 'keeping it fun' is important. Many leading companies are starting to pay serious attention to such issues and tax functions need to ensure that they reflect this.

At the time of writing however, many tax functions are burdened with increasingly tough tax reporting demands, and this is typically 'high pain, low reward' work, often carried out under considerable pressure. Overtime has also been on the rise as a result of these increased demands and a tight labour market. Companies may need to consider how to counterbalance this effect if they are to continue to recruit and retain quality staff.

§ 15.04 PEOPLE STRATEGY

The answers to some of the issues set out above may be resolved by having a clear people strategy and the methodology below discusses what might be included in such a strategy. The diagram below summarises what this might look like.

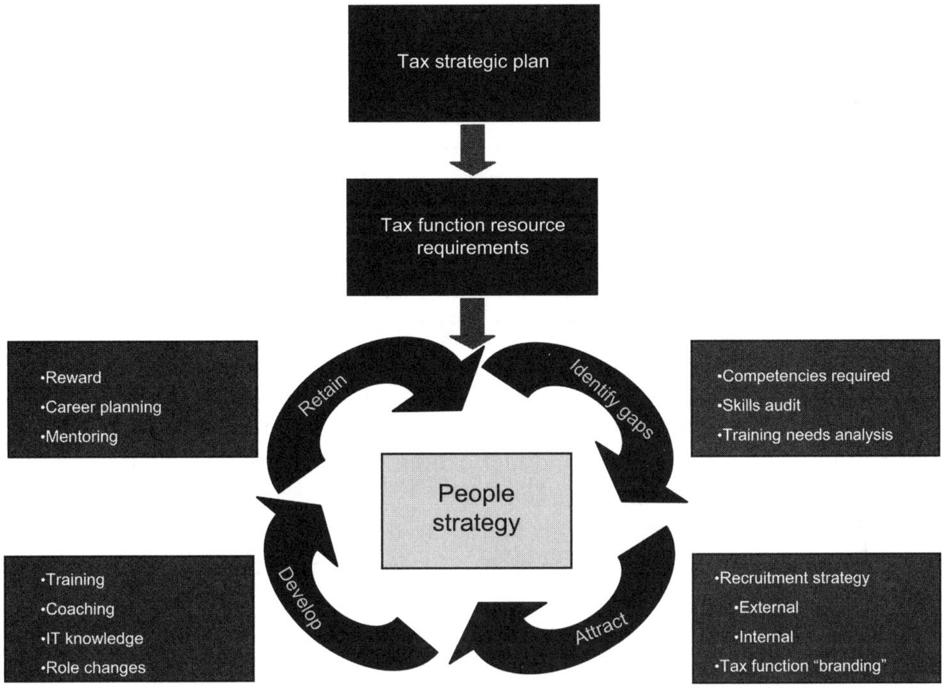

The resource requirements for the tax function will be driven from the overall tax strategy, and, as noted in an earlier chapter, will take into account the role of the shadow tax function and external advisors. Having decided what activities will be carried out by the tax function you are then well placed to carry out the four step methodology below.

[A] Identify Gaps

Assuming that both the numbers and the skills and competences of those in the tax function are not a perfect fit for what is needed, then the first stage is to analyse where the gaps are. This gap analysis will allow you to start thinking about whether you need to recruit new people, change the roles of existing people or perhaps just to give existing people some training in either technical competences or different skills.

In our view this gap analysis should be carried out on a regular basis, say annually. It actually fits well into an annual review of the tax strategy and could easily become part of that overall process.

[B] Attracting the Right People

Assuming that the gap analysis shows either that new people need to be recruited or alternatively new roles need to be developed in the tax function, then the next step is to find the right people to fill these roles. Whether these roles are best filled by moving someone within the tax function, recruiting someone from within the business as a whole or external recruitment will be a matter of debate (and possibly headcount issues). We mention tax function 'branding' at this point as the overall reputation and the perceived attractiveness of the tax function will have a direct impact on the ease of recruiting people.

[C] Developing the People

One of the real challenges for a tax function is how it develops its existing people. Under the issue section earlier in this chapter we talked about the problems of finding training which was sufficiently focussed on people's individual needs. Best practice would dictate that formal training plans are developed annually for each member of the tax department in order to address both the skills gaps in the tax function and the needs of the individual people, both from a technical viewpoint but also to address their behavioural needs.

Training of softer skills for in-house tax departments is, in our experience, seldom given the importance we believe it deserves. Indeed our experience is that training in this area is often fairly ad hoc. The softer skills the tax function needs is often linked in to whatever training is being provided within the rest of the organisation and, while this may be appropriate, the design of such training is usually not tailored to the specific needs of the tax function.

However one of the best forms of training is that which takes place on the job and we would encourage more senior people in tax functions to involve the more junior people in what they are doing and at the same time to provide on the job coaching. Doing something for real, and ensuring that you get proper feedback on it, is usually considerably more effective than any classroom training. While this may not be that efficient in the short run, it is usually well worth the investment. Another alternative is to align staff with technical projects performed by outside consultants. This is a great way to develop staff and to transfer knowledge to your tax function.

An effective training plan is also part of a robust evaluation and coaching process. It is critical to maintain these processes even in today's tough marketplace. Allowing development to be abandoned in times of resources shortages and overtime will lead to a future loss of talent which will only serve to exacerbate the problem.

Another good way to develop people is to give them new roles within either the tax function or the organisation as a whole. These might be full time moves or just secondments. We do recognise however that there are considerable practical difficulties in doing this, particularly within a smaller tax function. However the longer term benefits can often heavily outweigh the short term disruptions.

In the larger tax departments, where providing career progression is rather easier, it is beneficial that those staff who are the 'stars' are identified and a career path is discussed with them. These are often the staff who the business can least afford to lose and not providing them with a chance to progress is the surest way to lose them. Rotating these staff to, for example, the finance function or internal audit (may be on an exchange basis) can build a broader base of skills that can be utilized by the tax department and position the most talented performers for promotion both within and outside of tax.

If career progression is not possible inside the tax function, then there are often other opportunities elsewhere in an organisation—and having ex tax people in other parts of the business is very beneficial in ensuring the importance of tax is recognised outside the tax function.

[D] Retaining Good Staff

While proper reward for the job is one way of retaining people it is clearly not the only factor which encourages people to stay with an organisation. The opportunity to develop, opportunities to progress and a culture whereby people are encouraged to grow their skills and competences are often better ways of retaining staff than any financial reward. We would therefore encourage heads of tax to have meaningful conversations with their team members on a regular basis so that people are aware of the opportunities opening up for them in the future.

Some heads of tax we know actively encourage a reasonable degree of staff churn in order to keep the tax function fresh. This is often particularly the case for more junior tax staff, typically those who have joined the company shortly after obtaining the appropriate qualifications. Such staff, in conjunction with their heads of tax, are often quite open that they only intend to stay with the company for a couple of years in order to build up their experience and then move up the career ladder elsewhere. We see this as a healthy and open approach; the more these things are discussed the more staff feel that someone is taking an interest in them as individuals.

§15.05 SUMMARY

The key asset of a tax function is its people. Having the right people, with the right competences, in the right numbers, doing the right things will be crucial to the success of the tax function. Keeping them focussed and motivated is hence a key part of the role of the head of tax.

CHAPTER 16

LEADERSHIP—THE ROLE OF THE HEAD OF TAX

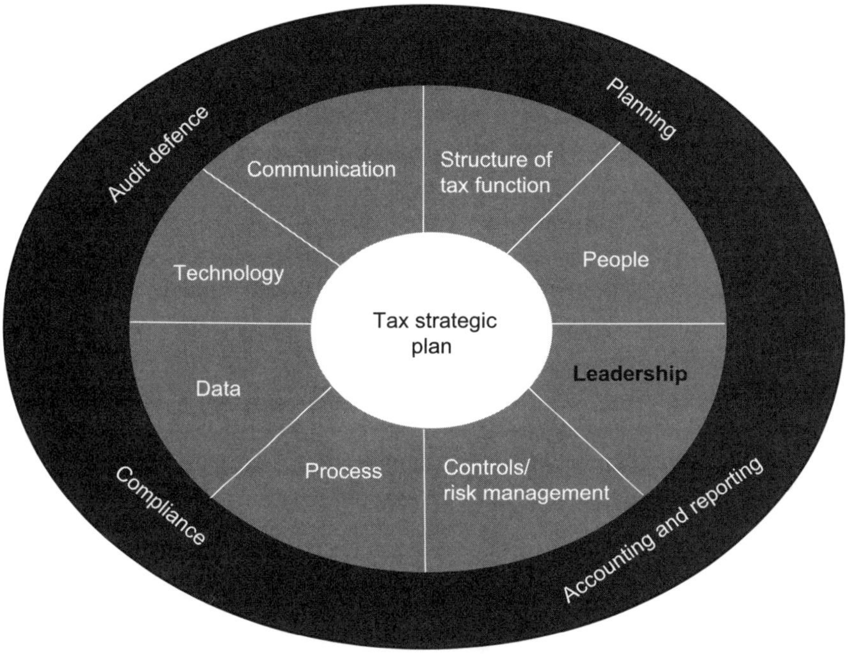

§16.01 INTRODUCTION

One of the enablers for the tax function which we set out in chapter 9 was leadership. While various members of the tax function will have leadership roles in their own particular areas, the main leadership role will clearly be carried out by the head of tax. This chapter examines this particular role.

§16.02 WHERE IS LEADERSHIP REQUIRED?

In the table below we have set out some examples of where effective leadership is required in order to manage the tax affairs of a business effectively. In our experience a number of these examples are relatively new in the tax world—and it is this change which has brought leadership to the fore.

Driver	*Leadership*
Tax executives are spending more time interacting with the audit committee or full board.	It is increasingly important for senior tax executives to communicate with the board and/or the audit committee about the tax strategy, the key tax risks, status of tax accounts, contingencies, and tax audits. The ability to speak at the highest level in an organisation on behalf of the tax function and represent how tax is and can impact shareholder value is a key leadership quality.
The setting of strategy	We have talked about the development of a strategic plan being one of the key deliverables for the tax function. In many instances it is head of tax who must demonstrate leadership around the need for the tax strategy and actively seek input and support from senior management for that strategy.
Increasing importance of interaction with the business	Getting engagement from the leaders of the business is key for both managing tax risk and for ensuring that tax planning is both properly conceived and implemented.
Shorter financial close cycles	One of the best ways to address the tighter and tighter financial close deadlines is to increase collaboration with those in accounting/finance. Tax can no longer operate effectively as a silo but must be fully integrated with finance, IT functions and the business units. Strong tax function leadership will be necessary to bring tax further into the business, bring a higher level of collaboration with finance, and to drive through process improvement.

Driver	*Leadership*
Speed of change	Not only is the tax world changing very fast, but so is the whole business world. The ability to cope with change, keep the big picture in mind and ensure that the tax affairs of a business are not swamped by these changes are key leadership qualities. Additionally these changes will often result in an increased workload for the tax function. The head of tax will be responsible for negotiating for increased budgets/ headcount as required—often well in advance of these resources actually being needed.
Making change happen	External forces will drive changes within the tax function—and adapting to these changes will require leadership. Those tax functions which do not adapt will experience a higher risk profile, whether they like it or not.
Recruiting, developing and retaining quality staff	There is a general shortage of qualified tax talent in the market. Leadership skills can help increase staff recruitment and retention leading to a long term favourable impact on the quality of the deliverables and on staff morale. The tax leader and his directors and managers should excel at coaching and mentoring less experienced staff. A collaborative approach to management will increasingly lead to an environment where people can learn, grow and develop into future leaders.
Managing within resource constraints	Almost every head of tax will be managing the tax function with limited resources. This means that the head of tax needs to be able to focus their time and their key people on the most important issues for the company and avoid getting drawn into every discussion that has something to do with tax. We have observed that successful heads of tax are equally adept at choosing what not to do as what to get involved in.
Managing revenue authorities	It is becoming increasingly important to build excellent working and collaborative relationships with local revenue authorities in order to manage risk appropriately.

§16.03 SKILLS REQUIRED

We set out in the previous chapter a list of the key skills required for people in a tax function. This list applies even more so to a head of tax as it does to other members of the tax function, and other than include the list again we would refer you to the previous chapter for further comments.

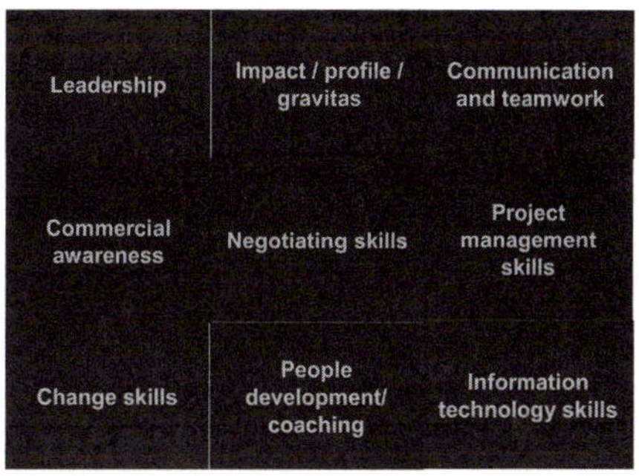

One Finance Director told us he was seeking a Head of Tax who "didn't know too much about tax"—admittedly a slightly 'tongue-in-cheek' comment, but he did want a tax manager who would focus on managing the impact of tax on the business, rather than become drawn in to technical research and computational work.

§16.04 THE ROLE

The head of tax needs to decide what role they personally wish to carry out. At a high level we suggest that in a best practice tax function the head of tax's role should encompass:

- Developing and implementing the tax strategic plan;
- Being a business advisor to senior management;
- Having an international focus;
- Being an ambassador who champions tax within the business;
- Managing relationships with key internal stakeholders including the business units;
- Lobbying and external relations;
- Advocating the risk management agenda; and
- Managing the tax function (although we have seen this being delegated at least partially to a number two).

However bringing this down to a lower level, the head of tax will need to decide how much time to allocate to operational and functional activities such as:

- Transactions;
- Discussions with revenue authorities—both in their home territory and overseas;
- Tax accounting;
- Review of tax returns;

- Risk management controls;
- Process improvement;
- Communication with the different parts of the business;
- Recruitment;
- Managing the people in the tax function; and
- Technology enhancements.

The head of tax will also need to choose carefully which non-tax specific projects they (and their team) will get involved in. Organisation wide projects and initiatives, such as a new IT system implementation, may present an important opportunity for the head of tax to integrate tax with the broader finance and operational areas as well as demonstrating their broader commercial skills. As noted above, equally important for the head of tax will be choosing what projects not to be get involved in. These might be projects where the connection with the tax function's overall strategic objectives and the value the head of tax can add through their involvement is less clear.

One of the challenges for the head of tax is to keep above the detail and ensure that they focus on the bigger picture. The danger is that they will become too focused on one particular area at the expense of the wider agenda.

§ 16.05 SUMMARY

As in a number of areas in this guide, there is no one right answer as to how a head of tax should operate. However the head of tax should work out what their role is and if it does not include the majority of the high level points in the section above then they should challenge themselves as to whether they are doing their role properly.

CHAPTER 17

CONTROLS AND RISK MANAGEMENT

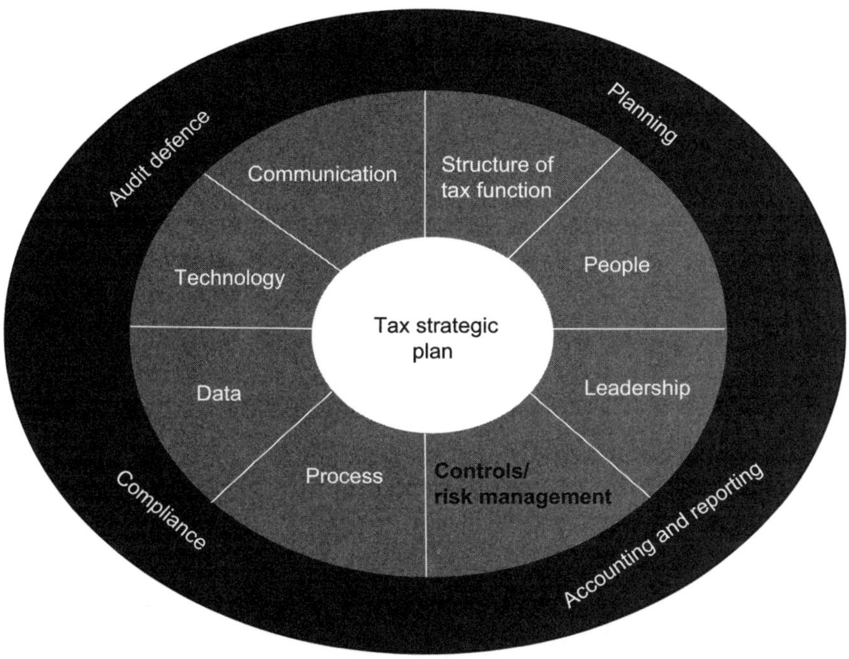

§17.01 INTRODUCTION

Tax risk management has been a hot topic for some years now. For tax practitioners however, it remains a challenge, blending as it does issues of technical assurance, data management, processes, governance and stakeholder management. Having set out in chapter 11 what we mean by tax risk and what causes tax risk to happen, this chapter sets out how to ensure that, within an overall risk management framework, appropriate controls around tax are in place.

The introduction of the US Sarbanes-Oxley rules and the outcomes in the years since its inception have brought controls in the tax area into much sharper focus. Prior to this, the effectiveness of controls and the control environment were relatively foreign concepts in relation to tax. We therefore start this chapter with a discussion on designing effective controls and then set out a practical tax risk management framework, dealing with a number of different components of control from establishing the tax risk policy through to reporting on tax risk.

§17.02 DESIGNING EFFECTIVE CONTROLS

As already discussed, US public registrants have collectively reported more material internal control deficiencies in tax than in any other area. This is due in part to the lack of historical reliance on internal controls in the tax area, but there is more to the story. It is no secret that tax professionals generally do not possess the level of expertise related to internal controls as compared to their counterparts in finance and internal audit. Additionally when compared to highly automated and process oriented areas, tax is much more difficult to control. Rather than a series of repetitive transactions, one tax account can often be the product of dozens, if not hundreds, of complex and often manual calculations.

One could argue that when section 404 of the Sarbanes-Oxley Act was introduced, the initial approach to tax internal controls taken by many companies was flawed. Rather than perform a robust risk analysis customised to the company (i.e. what can go wrong that could have a material impact on the financial statements and related disclosures), standardised control matrices were often utilised. Process maps were prepared to document the existing tax provision processes. Existing processes were matched to the controls matrices and additional controls were added as necessary. These additional controls were often designed by employees that are not familiar either with tax or the risks inherent in the tax figures. This bottom up approach, starting with detailed process flows rather than the risks, was often viewed as a one time pass/fail exercise that was more of an inconvenience that a value-added exercise.

In working with many companies that have experienced internal control issues, we have noted the following challenges:

- Gaps in key controls resulting from the lack of a quality risk assessment.
- A lack of documentation of the control activities that were actually conducted.

- Excel-based provision spreadsheets that are difficult to understand and review.
- Tax provision workpapers that are not organised in an intuitive manner.
- A short closing cycle that left little time for analytical review.

In designing effective controls there are two key elements to consider. The effectiveness of controls within an organisation are measured firstly by their maturity and secondly by the controls complexity.

The maturity of the controls is a measure of how rigorous and robust those controls are for given processes for managing tax risks. The maturity will take into account whether the controls are sufficiently documented, efficiently maintained, assessed and reported on. The more mature the controls are, the more effective they are likely to be.

The complexity of the controls is a measure of the nature and number of control activities within a given business process—and the overall aim is generally to minimise complexity so that controls are simple and straight forward to operate. The complexity of the controls will, to a large extent, be dictated by the complexity of the business. In a tax context, the controls complexity would take into account the structure, size and geographical spread of the business and tax function, the available resources in the tax function to monitor risk and compliance and the standardisation and automation of systems. Increased complexity of the tax control environments leads to increased risk of error.

So how should we design and improve the controls around tax? A suggested approach is as follows:

1. Begin with a true "top-down" approach that starts with a quality risk assessment. Reach agreement on the areas of greatest risk and revise key controls to align with these risks. You should find that you end up with fewer but much more focused key controls.
2. Next review not only the existing controls but perform a walk through to understand how these control activities are actually being performed and documented.
3. Prepare a gap analysis to help guide the implementation process. Make sure that it is very clear, who is responsible for each activity and that they understand the importance of their role.
4. Make sure that mitigating controls are in place, such as clearly defined analytics that will help to spot issues that might have initially gone undetected.
5. Document in workpapers how the control activities were performed rather than simply the sign-offs of the parties involved.
6. Finally, take a hard look at how you compute your provision. Some companies seem to spend a great deal of time on calculations that are not material to the provision, often at the expense of other more critical calculations. Take an inventory of actual time spent and make sure that it aligns with your areas of greatest risk within the financial statements.

§17.03 ESTABLISHING A TAX RISK FRAMEWORK

One of the keys to successful tax risk management is to implement an effective framework for managing the risks. The most widely recognised framework for the management of risk is the Committee of Sponsoring Organisations of the Treadway Commission (COSO) Enterprise Risk Management—Integrated Framework. We have applied the COSO framework and risk management standards to form the basic foundations for a systematic approach to managing tax risk. The core components of this framework comprise:

- Organisational strategy and structure—which covers the tax strategy, risk profile, structures and culture in place to provide for the management of the company's tax affairs.
- The core processes—which address the approach taken to identifying, measuring and dealing with risk, together with the controls and procedures that operate to manage the identified risks.
- The quality and assurance mechanisms—which ensure that the tax risks are monitored on an ongoing basis and are communicated appropriately within the organisation.

The basic building blocks of a tax risk framework are set out diagrammatically below

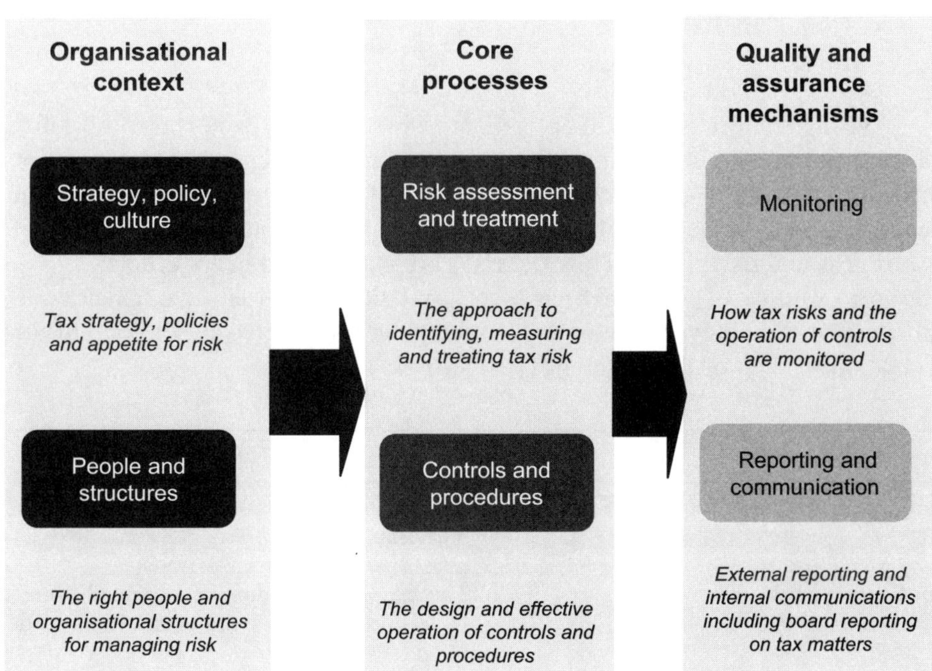

§ 17.04 IMPLEMENTING THE FRAMEWORK

The tax risk framework set out above needs to be tailored to the business and risk profile of each particular organisation. However in our experience, such frameworks should cover each of the following components in one form or another.

[A] Strategy, Policy and Culture

The strategy, policy and culture component addresses the organisation's tax strategy, its risk profile and its appetite for risk. It also includes the engagement of key stakeholders as well as the general culture of the group towards tax risk management. There is a role here for the board and senior management in setting the overall tone for behaviour around managing tax risk. A key deliverable to address this component is a documented tax strategic plan and a tax risk policy.

The tax strategic plan is critical for recognising the role that the tax function plays in maximising value for the organisation, whereas the tax risk policies set guidelines for acceptable tax risk, essentially the appetite for risk. As discussed in chapter 13, the tax strategic plan and risk appetite should ideally be conceived together.

In our experience, the most effective tax risk policies deal separately with the different categories of tax risk. In chapter 11 we set out the specific categories of tax risk as:

- Strategic and transactional risk;
- Operational risk;
- Compliance risk; and
- Financial accounting risk.

The different categories of tax risks arise in relation to each of the key deliverables of the tax function. In addition, non-financial risks such as reputational impacts could arise in conjunction with any one of the above risk types. In practice, we recommend an organisation identifies the full array of potential risks relevant for its business and risk profile. How the risks are categorised is not crucial.

An example of a set of high level tax risk policies is set out below. The policies provide an overview of the agreed position adopted by the organisation in relation to each of the different types of risk.

TAX RISK	*POLICY*
Strategic and transactional	All transactions must have a business purpose. The group will not undertake purely tax driven transactions.
Application of decisions and regulations to specific transactions	The tax function must be involved in: — all business or share acquisitions and disposals — all changes in corporate structure

TAX RISK	*POLICY*
	— all cross-border financing arrangements — all property transactions in excess of $1 million The tax function must be involved in not only the planning of the above transactions but also in the implementation and documentation of each transaction. The group aims for at least 70% certainty for tax positions it adopts but, at a minimum on the balance of probabilities all positions adopted must be more likely than not to be agreed by the appropriate tax authority. Where a tax position is considered to carry greater than 50% but less than 70% certainty, the position adopted is assessed giving consideration to the financial return and potential reputational risk.
Operational *Inherent risks in every day business operations*	Where any new cross border trading arrangements are being set up, the tax function must be involved well in advance of any arrangements being put in place so that appropriate advice can be taken. All cross border transactions must be carried out in line with the group's transfer pricing policy.
Compliance *Statutory risks associated with tax return preparation, completion and submission*	The group will comply with all tax regulations in all countries in which it operates. It will aim to submit all returns by their due dates and in line with local tax law. All positions taken in the tax returns must be supportable and, on the balance of probability, be more likely than not to be agreed by the appropriate tax authority. The tax function will pro-actively manage the relationship with the key tax authorities in order to minimise the risk of penalties arising when tax matters are inadvertently incorrect. The group will aim to have no adjustments to tax returns in excess of the materiality limits for adjustments to the financial accounts, which are set out below.
Financial accounting *Risk associated with tax accounting, financial statements and internal controls*	The group will take a conservative/prudent position in respect of the tax charge in the accounts. A materiality limit of $0.5 million is set for the group tax charge. For the taxes charged

TAX RISK	*POLICY*
	to profit before tax—e.g. employment taxes, indirect taxes, sales and use taxes—the materiality limit is $0.2 million. The financial accounts are expected to be correct within these materiality limits in respect of all taxes, both at the year end and in the quarterly reporting.
Reputational *Risks that impact the Group's image as perceived by the public*	The group does not want its tax affairs to appear in the public domain. The group is only prepared to enter into transactions which could cause this to happen where the transaction type has become common practice. The group will manage its compliance affairs to minimise the risk of any public comment. At the same time, in its dealings with tax authorities, the group will robustly defend any tax position taken in any tax return.
External *Risk associated with factors outside the Group's control, e.g. new taxes, increased rates, new legislation*	The tax function will monitor changes in relevant tax practice and law in order to assess any consequences for the group, with the aim of minimising any adverse impact. The tax function will participate in any tax authority formal consultation process where it is expected that the matter under consultation will have a material impact on the group's tax liability (see Financial Accounting above for materiality levels), or where a significant change in practice is being proposed that will impact the group's management of its tax compliance.

You may wish your tax risk policy to deal separately with the individual taxes borne and collected by your organisation and the above table could be subdivided into the different taxes.

The risk policy in relation to the level of certainty (or likelihood of success) against value may be shown diagrammatically, for example:

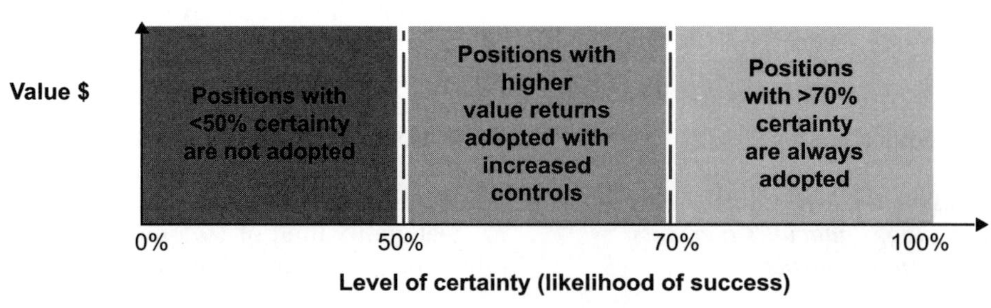

The tax risk policy will generally be supported by specific procedures and controls. Examples of tax procedures and controls are discussed below.

[B] People and Structure

People and structure is about the use of resources (internal and external) to manage risk together with the reporting structure and responsibilities around this. There are risks embodied in each of the key deliverables of tax planning, tax accounting and reporting, tax compliance and audit defence. Accordingly, it is important to have the right balance of resources focussed on each of these and appropriate reporting and escalation structures.

In too many cases, we find staff can not articulate their role in managing risk. It is as if risk management is only the responsibility of tax management rather than a shared role including everyone within the tax function. The risk policy therefore plays an important role in ensuring that people are focussed on the key issues and risks and avoid falling into the trap of trying to 'doing what we've always done' which might result in spending too much time and effort on low risk compliance activities to the detriment of more significant areas of risk (and value), such as cross border transactions or treasury and finance issues.

The emphasis on the people and structure component highlights the critical importance of having access to the right people with appropriate skills to manage tax obligations and inherent risks, supported by external resources in specific areas where they can add value or meet a skills gap. The division of responsibilities between the tax function and functional/business units is particularly important, and this is magnified for an organisation with business units in multiple territories.

The reporting structure and expectations regarding the nature and frequency of communications is also crucial for awareness and escalation of key risks and issues. Frequently, we are told that the tax function is finding out too late about an issue or even that an audit is already being carried out in a particular offshore territory.

In summary we recommend that organisations have a documented tax function structure, responsibilities and reporting lines as well as clear guidance on reporting and communication expectations. For a global organisation, this needs to be done on a global basis showing direct or dotted line reporting to the headquarters team. It could also show where tax risks are being managed by functional/business units as opposed to the tax function.

[C] Risk Assessment and Treatment

Risk assessment concerns the identification, analysis and evaluation of tax risks and will form a core part of the organisation's tax risk management process. The analysis and evaluation of risk involves the consideration of the likelihood and impact of risk; this will form the basis for determining how it should be managed. Part of the analysis of likelihood will consider the risk drivers relevant for your business. The key challenge for a multi-territorial business will typically be to ensure the timely identification of key tax related risks globally and the evaluation of these risks.

Better practices we have seen adopted involve building an ongoing risk assessment and reporting process into periodic reporting and compliance processes. For example, the risk assessment may commence with a one-off global risk review to establish a register of the potential risks and issues in each territory across all taxes (whether or not all taxes are the responsibility of the tax function locally). After several years of experience with risk reviews, there is now a well developed methodology, templates and questionnaires for undertaking such global risk reviews.

How risks are analysed will vary from company to company. Some companies are employing sophisticated techniques to measure tax risk, including the use of statistical measures to estimate likely outcomes of individual or a portfolio of risks. Tools have been developed or adapted from other models to support decision analysis, which essentially involves mathematically assessing the likelihood and impact to evaluate risk associated with different potential decisions or alternative transactions. Our view is that it is important to apply a consistent discipline to assessing risk and the usefulness of tools for risk quantification relies on the accuracy of the input data including judgement applied around the probabilities/likelihoods being applied in the model. The use of such tools for risk assessment is still in its infancy but likely to grow in the future.

The introduction of FIN 48 in the US has also driven some of the latest practices in measuring and evaluating risks. FIN 48 was issued with the stated purpose of harmonising diverse practices with respect to recognising tax benefits and liabilities in the accounts. FIN 48 prescribes rigorous requirements for accounting for uncertain tax positions including a two step approach to the recognition and measurement of the tax benefits attributable to tax positions.

Once the risks have been identified, analysed and evaluated, decisions need to be made as to how these risks are managed. For each risk, you will need to consider what level of residual risk is acceptable and how the risk is to be managed down to this level. The specific response to each identified risk will vary depending on factors such as:

- The ease and cost of mitigating the risk,
- Its potential impact on the business, and
- The availability of alternative mitigating techniques.

The treatment of risk might involve one or a combination of the following three options:

- Tax risk reduction—taking action to reduce the likelihood of the occurrence and/or the impact of the risk.
- Tax risk avoidance—taking an alternative course of action that fully mitigates the risk.

- Tax risk sharing—transferring or sharing the risk in some way through arrangements with third parties.

A key deliverable is a documented tax risk register, setting out both the key tax risks in the organisation together with current tax and accounting treatments adopted and what is being done to manage these risks. We recommend careful consideration be given to how such risks are documented in a register to ensure that the information presented is accurate and supportive of the positions being adopted and does not adversely prejudice the organisation in the event of an audit or review.

An important part of risk assessment is also to consider the total tax risk on a portfolio basis. While individual risks may be acceptable it will also be necessary to consider the totality of the residual risks by category or in the context of the organisation as a whole. For example, organisations in the financial services industry may need to take a view on the inherent and residual tax risk associated with a portfolio of transactions with similar risk profiles such as structured finance transactions entered into with customers where the volume of such transactions is substantial.

[D] Controls and Procedures

The design and operation of controls is a key element in the effectiveness of a tax risk framework. We discussed above some of the factors to consider in establishing effective controls. Some of the better practices that we have noted include:

- Procedures are in place to detect legislative and judicial tax law changes and any business changes (globally) that might impact taxes.
- Use of tax provision technology implementation as a platform to implement improvements in data quality and access, internal controls, eliminate manual processes spreadsheets and workpapers.
- Alignment of responsibilities and open communication between the tax function, finance and the business units.
- Documentation of processes and key controls with a programme of independent testing by the internal audit function.
- A focus on contemporaneous documentation for information retention, particularly in relation to strategic transactions.

A clear trend is the increasing focus on the management of compliance and reporting globally. Many global organisations are putting controls in place that enable ongoing monitoring of compliance globally, whether through internal project management or through a global outsourcing arrangement,

Many of the risks relating to taxes arise from interdependencies between the tax function, different business units and geographies. It is crucial therefore to view the controls around taxes across the whole organisation, not just limited to those controls that are the responsibility of the tax function.

Finally, you will need to ensure that you have clear policies related to the adoption of tax positions. An example of a policy in relation to the adoption of tax positions is set out below.

Description Financial Return	*External Advice Required*	*Internal Sign Off Required*
Positions with greater than 50% but lower than 70% likelihood of success		
<0.5% of PBT	Position will not be adopted	
<2% of PBT	External tax advisor	Head of tax
<5% of PBT	External tax advisor	Head of tax, CFO
>5% of PBT	Tax authority ruling or Counsel's opinion	Head of tax, board audit committee
High reputational risk	External tax advisor Tax authority ruling	Head of tax, board of directors

[E] Monitoring

Monitoring covers both the ongoing review of identified risks as well as the operation of the tax risk controls. This will also include a structured approach to monitoring developments in the law and practice and the impact on identified tax risks in different territories. We have noted that best in class tax functions are planning ahead with rolling reviews across a range of tax areas and activities, often being driven by the group tax risk manager in conjunction with the group's internal audit function.

A potential control and monitoring mechanism is the establishment of a tax risk committee as a focal point for difficult tax decisions and to oversee the organisation's tax risk monitoring programme. The tax risk committee would typically include the head of tax and key internal tax advisors, the CFO and potentially a trusted external tax advisor. A role of monitoring is also to review any change in the overall risk profile of the organisation taking into consideration the portfolio of residual risks. An organisation's risk profile will change over time as new risks are assumed and old risks are resolved.

A deliverable for the tax function will be an annual tax risk review plan which deals with all material taxes. As part of this plan, the role of internal audit or other independent review processes may be noted where relevant.

[F] Reporting and Communication

The reporting component concerns the internal and external reporting and communications practices of the group. Effective risk management requires an organisation to have in place appropriate processes for capturing information about tax risks and issues from business units and offshore territories as well as communicating the risks both internally (to CFO, board, audit and risk committees) and externally. It is also important to have proper communication in place, within the business, with those who are responsible for managing tax risks (e.g. the finance function who might be responsible for dealing with the indirect tax returns).

Critically, internal communications from the tax function need to use a style and language that is understood by the broader business. Over the years, tax functions which are normally resourced by specialist tax people have had a tendency to use technical tax language to explain risks and issues. This has emphasised the perception of tax being a 'black box' and tax risks not adequately transparent to senior management and the board.

Tax functions can ensure that risks are communicated in a business language by including a clear impact statement, including accounting and cash tax impacts. Illustrative reporting such as traffic light reporting to indicate high, medium and low risk areas may also be used if this is consistent with the style of reporting that the organisation is accustomed to. An example of a tax risk map incorporating traffic light style reporting is shown below. For global organisations, this can be supported by a set of traffic lights for each territory, business unit or region. The risk map can also show the likelihood and impact relating to each type of risk as separate components of the inherent risk rating.

Example of a tax risk map

Tax risk assessment (Risk of tax issues greater than $1M arising from activities, or actions or lack of actions, in key business activities)			
KEY BUSINESS ACTIVITIES	Inherent tax risk for group	Assessment of effectiveness of current controls	Current assessment of risk
Strategic and transactional risk			
— Transactions (acquisitions, disposals)	● H	Acceptable	● M
— Restructuring	● H	Acceptable	● M
— Capital management (debt/equity structure)	● H	Strong	● L
Operational risk			
Corporate income taxes	● H	Strong	● L
— Tax depreciation	● M	Needs improvement	● H
— Treasury and foreign exchange	● M	Needs improvement	● M
— Capital gains	● H	Acceptable	● M
— Research and development	● M	Acceptable	● M
— Transfer pricing	● H	Needs improvement	● H
Other business taxes			
— Value added taxes	● H	Needs improvement	● H
— Customs duty	● M	Strong	● L
— Employee benefits taxation	● M	Needs improvement	● M
— Payroll tax	● M	Strong	● L
— Employee withholding taxes	● L	Acceptable	● L
— Other withholding taxes (interest, dividends, royalties)	● L	Acceptable	● L
Compliance and reporting			
— Tax reporting (IFRS, FAS 109, FIN 48)	● H	Needs improvement	● H
— Global tax compliance	● H	Acceptable	● L
— Indirect taxes compliance	● H	Strong	● M
Managing tax authority relationships			
— Audits and reviews	● H	Needs improvement	● M
— Ongoing communication	● L	Acceptable	● L

● H High risk — material potential exposure requiring immediate focus

● M Medium risk — significant potential exposure with reasonable likelihood of review by a tax authority

● L Low to medium risk — other potential risks and issues.

§ 17.05 THE TAX RISK MANAGEMENT PROCESS

In practice, an assessment of an organisation's tax control environment and global tax risk management can be undertaken through a systematic evaluation of the components of the tax risk management framework. Increasingly, we are finding the risk management process being adopted by groups with a global presence as a means to assess global tax risks and controls on a periodic basis.

The risk and control review methodology involves a number of key stages as set out in the following diagram, which is explained in more detail below.

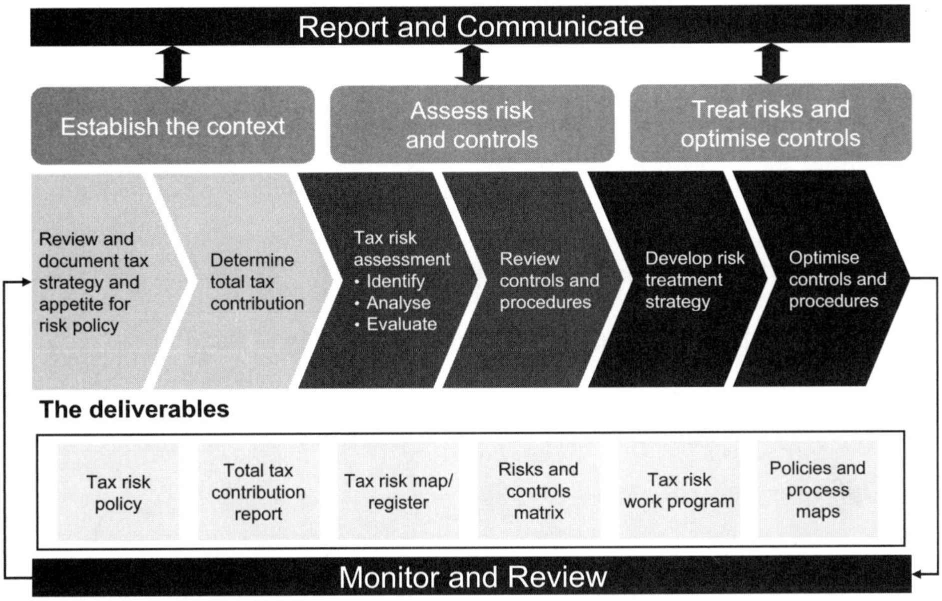

[A] Review and Document the Tax Strategic and Risk Policy

The review of the tax strategic plan and tax risk policy will take into consideration whether there has been group wide engagement and acceptance of the policy and whether it has been endorsed by senior management and the board.

[B] Determine the Total Tax Contribution

A key aspect of assessing an organisation's potential tax risks is to understand the total tax contribution. The total tax contribution comprises the taxes both borne and collected by the organisation and therefore will enable the identification of potential risk areas, whether or not the taxes represent an expense recognised in the profit and loss account.

[C] Assess Tax Risk

The assessment of inherent tax risk areas should involve all key regions, taxes and reporting obligations and will generally involve consideration of the following factors:

- The complexity of the business area giving rise to the risk;
- The volume and potential impact of tax risks; and
- The likelihood of challenge by a revenue authority.

The assessment of inherent risk areas will require significant judgement to be applied in the context of a particular organisation's business activities.

[D] Evaluate the Design and Operation of Tax Controls and Procedures

The evaluation of both the design and operation of tax controls and procedures, in terms of controls maturity and complexity, will enable the assessment of residual (or actual) risk and the identification of areas requiring remediation.

[E] Develop Risk Treatment Strategy

The development of the risk treatment strategy will have the objective of managing residual risk by a range of possible techniques for avoiding, sharing and reducing risk, including remediation of controls and procedures.

[F] Optimise Controls and Procedures

This stage involves enhancing existing or implementing new controls, procedures and systems, dealing with control weaknesses identified at the previous stage. In doing so you will need to bear in mind the maturity and complexity of the control environment as assessed at step 4.

[G] Monitor Tax Risk and Controls

The identified risks and the operation of controls are regularly tested with an appropriate level of communication to senior management, the board and other stakeholders.

§ 17.06 SUMMARY

Proper controls and tax risk management procedures are a key enabler for a tax function. To manage tax risk a robust controls environment needs to be established in the form of a tax risk framework. In this chapter we have set out what such a framework might look like and what practical steps can be taken to implement the framework. The starting point has to be the strategic plan and documenting a tax risk policy which sets out the parameters within which tax risk will be managed. A periodic risk and control review process should be then be implemented to enable the group to focus on where the key tax risks are in the business, to communicate these risks to the various stakeholders and to assess the operation of the controls.

Chapter 18

PROCESS IMPROVEMENT

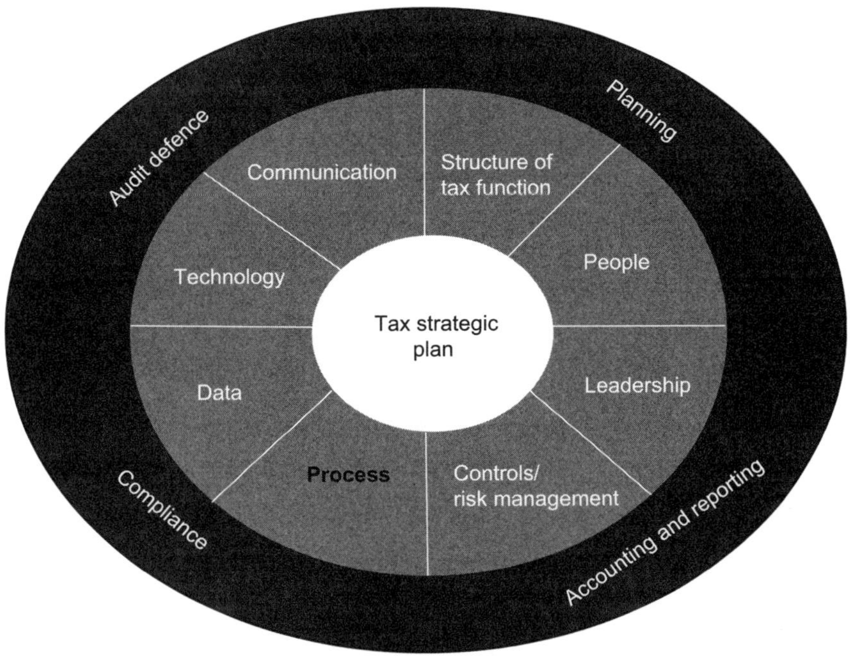

§18.01 INTRODUCTION

As noted earlier in this guide process improvement has not historically been high on the tax function's agenda. Additionally, when an investment has been made to improve the processes of a finance function, little if any of the investment may have found its way to improving the processes around tax. However with a scarcity of qualified tax resources and some significant weakness showing up in tax processes, we believe that the time has come for a much greater focus in driving efficiency into the way that the tax function goes about its day to day activities.

Process improvement is key to reducing both time and cost in tax processes, and at the same time improving quality and reducing risk. For companies that have identified control weaknesses, remediation of controls may provide a good opportunity to review the effectiveness of processes or potentially design new and better tax processes.

In this chapter we look at how the tax function can go about seeking greater efficiencies and improve the quality of its key deliverables through process improvement. We start by discussing what are the key tax processes and then consider some common issues and problems and hence where benefit can be obtained from investment in process improvement.

§18.02 WHAT ARE THE KEY TAX PROCESSES?

Tax processes typically cover a range of the different responsibilities of the tax function from strategic tax advisory processes through to tax accounting for external reporting and tax compliance. Tax processes should play a key role in managing tax risk. This will include the identification of tax risks and issues, the appropriateness of tax technical positions adopted or the operating integrity of tax compliance or tax reporting systems and processes.

A summary of the types of tax processes is set out in the table below:

Deliverables	*Examples of key processes*	*Value to the business*
Tax strategic plan	Developing the strategy Forecasting Capturing information for planning purposes	Shareholder value creation, risk management
Tax planning	Implementing transactions Tax advice to business units Implementing tax changes	Shareholder value creation, alignment with the overall corporate strategy, risk management, cost management
Tax accounting	Tax expense and deferred tax calculations	Improved and more transparent shareholder communications, risk management, cost management

Deliverables	*Examples of key processes*	*Value to the business*
Tax compliance	Data extraction Corporate income tax returns Indirect tax returns Tax payments Managing other compliance—locally and globally	Improved relationships with revenue authorities, risk management, cost management
Audit defence	Collecting and documenting information, negotiation	Risk management, cost management

Unlike many other business processes, tax processes have traditionally been manual in nature with limited automation. Tax controls often rely heavily on the individual skill and experience of the people who own the process with limited monitoring of what they do. A recurring theme is that people with the right skills, experience and application to the job tend to compensate for poor processes and systems. Issues therefore arise where there is a frequent turnover of staff or inappropriate mix of available resources to ensure quality outcomes.

The usual focus for process improvement in the tax area tends to be around tax reporting and compliance. However there are also potential gains from optimising processes in other areas including tax planning, tax risk management and defending audits.

§ 18.03 CHALLENGES TO BE ADDRESSED

Before starting out on how you change and improve processes, you need to reflect on where you are today and define the challenges in terms of one or more of time, cost, risk, quality/accuracy or use of resources. In other words, what are the symptoms of the problems in the current environment? This will help you focus on the priorities for any process improvement initiatives. Some of the challenges you are facing today might include those listed below.

[A] Quality of and Access to Information

Quality tax information is required in a number of different areas. In setting the strategic plan information is needed on the taxes paid and collected by the business. On the tax planning side, quality information is needed for forecasting and in particular for evaluating planning options when transactions are taking place such as disposals. Obtaining quality information for these purposes without a significant effort is a challenge (and is discussed further in the next chapter on the data enabler).

The quality of information issue is exacerbated by the fact that many organisations report for management purposes on a business unit basis, whereas tax is usually reported on a legal entity basis. This can lead to two sets of information which do not always reconcile.

Revenue authorities have always focussed on the quality of information in tax returns. We are also now seeing these authorities reviewing end to end processes and often taking a much more process based approach to tax returns, as opposed to asking specific questions around specific figures. This in itself should be enough reason to improve the quality of those processes used for the preparation of tax returns.

[B] Time to Close Too Short for Proper Analysis

The period between a year end and the finalisation of the tax figures in the accounts seems to get shorter and shorter. There is clearly a limit to how much work can be done in this short period, irrespective of how many people you throw at the problem. However efficient processes coupled with enabling technology can go a long way to alleviating thc problems that the short time scales bring.

[C] Time Spent on Compliance and Reporting versus Other Deliverables

A key challenge for tax functions is getting the balance right between the time spent on tax compliance and reporting and ensuring adequate focus and resources are dedicated to other deliverables, especially developing the strategic plan and tax planning. It is increasingly the case that companies will look to process improvement to reduce the time and cost in both compliance and reporting to refocus the tax function on the more value add activities.

[D] Differing Systems

The primary purpose of business systems, and in particular accounting systems, is to produce financial information, not tax information. However systems need to be in place within an organisation to produce figures for tax planning, tax accounting and tax compliance. Invariably in most organisations there is also no one integrated system that easily produces data for all three purposes; it is more likely that there are numerous feeder systems in addition to the core general ledger. If you then consider that there may be different accounting systems in different geographies or business units, and acquisitions bring with them further differing systems then it can be seen that producing consistent information can be a major challenge for many tax and finance functions.

The use of these multiple and different systems often results in inconsistent data between the systems and often considerable manual work is needed to consolidate and harmonise the data. As a result people are spending too much time collecting, validating and manipulating data and not enough time sitting back and thinking about what the figures actually mean and determining if they make sense.

[E] Cost

Qualified tax staff are an expensive resource and in many organisations we see them spending too much time dealing with mundane data collection, and with manipulation and validation of financial data, as opposed to value adding activities such as tax planning and proactively managing risk. Process improvement is often directed at decreasing the cost of preparing tax information while maintaining the level of reliability in the numbers being used.

[F] Meeting the Needs of the End User

Too often we see situations where the person producing information is not aware as to why the end user is asking for the information and what they do with it once they receive it. For the strategic plan, for example, the head of tax should want to know what taxes have been paid—but at a high level with a materiality limit of, say, $500,000. Does the person in the finance function who has been charged with producing the information know about this materiality limit? For other purposes, that level of materiality in the numbers or categorisations and definitions will not be appropriate. Reworking the same set of numbers for different purposes is a common problem for companies and one that consumes a significant amount of time and effort.

You will undoubtedly have your own list of challenges for your own organisation to add to the above list.

§ 18.04 END GOALS FOR PROCESS IMPROVEMENT

Having decided on the key challenges and hence where the priorities are for process improvement the next step should be to define the end goal. These may include some of the points mentioned below.

[A] Improved Year and Quarter End Processes

Perhaps the biggest opportunity for process improvement is in the tax accounting and compliance processes. In tax accounting the goal may be to improve the underlying accuracy of the tax expense and deferred tax balances without allowing for any increase in the time to prepare the numbers. For compliance the goal may be to improve the management of all tax compliance globally to ensure no surprises.

[B] Integrated Processes

As already mentioned many businesses have different processes for producing information for tax planning, tax accounting and tax compliance. One key goal could be to develop one system (i.e. a data warehouse) which stores information from many different sources, the information then being used for many different purposes. The expression 'gather once, use many' is often heard but, in our experience, it is seldom realised. Where disparate systems do remain, tax functions can of course make more effective use of the group consolidation system, and potentially of XML/XBRL or other 'tagging' technologies.

[C] Optimal Use of Resources

In an earlier chapter we introduced the three groups of people used in managing tax, being the in-house tax function, the shadow tax function and the external service providers. Each of these three groups will have their own particular skills and one of the end goals you should consider is how you use the right people for the right tasks. Outsourcing activities from the tax function either to the shadow tax function (e.g., the finance function) or to external advisors (e.g. tax accounting and/or compliance matters) may allow the in-house tax function to focus on what they are best placed to do.

[D] Automation of Processes

As noted above tax processes have traditionally been manual with significant reliance on the skills and experience of people for efficiency. Increased automation can have a number of benefits. Firstly it takes away a number of the manual processes and allows tax people to review the figures, and spend less time collecting, validating and manipulating the data that goes into their production. Secondly automation can reduce errors since:

- Automation typically permits use of high quality data right from the start;
- Controls can be embedded in the automated processes; and
- Automation leads to less manual intervention

Automation should be viewed as a means not only to improve quality of tax deliverables, but also as one of the primary risk management tools available to tax functions.

However simply automating existing processes is not what we are talking about here. The goal should be defining what the right processes are and then considering what can be done to automate them. Automating poor processes does not stop them from being poor processes. We address the use of technology in more detail in chapter 20.

[E] Improving the Quality of Accounting Source Information

We noted from a recent survey that 40% of all 'sundry expenditure' was coded as such on Friday afternoons. From a tax point of view, how much easier would life be if there was no sundry expenditure and all expenditure was coded to the correct expense code to which it related.

Implementing integrated and automated processes usually relies to an extent on the quality of underlying source information being used for tax purposes. We often find that the source of the problem being experienced by the tax function is actually elsewhere. Process improvement may need to focus on the tax sensitivity, coding and granularity of underlying accounting information.

§ 18.05 MAKING IT HAPPEN

It is all very well spelling out what today's issues are and what an ultimate goal might look like. However the key to success is actually making process improvement happen—a change management objective. We have a separate chapter on change management which looks at getting buy-in for change, how to overcome resistance to change, and managing change in bite sized chunks.

The key objectives of the process improvement project will need to be determined on a case by case basis relative to the desired outcomes but will typically involve establishing business processes that:

- Are efficient from a time and cost perspective in delivering the desired outcome;
- Contain built in controls that are able to be measured and tested;
- Facilitate the organisation's risk management objectives;
- Are documented ('process mapped') and easily communicated; and
- Are monitored for operational effectiveness.

There are various published process improvement methodologies available to guide you through the design and implementation of process change. However in any process improvement exercise we would suggest that, having decided what it is which needs to be improved, you need to go through the steps set out below.

[A] Mapping the 'As Is' Process

This is about understanding and documenting what actually happens today. This is a necessary starting point to address what works and what does not work. Ideally this would be prepared in a diagrammatic form with a mapping of data flows through the process—where does tax data come from, what manipulation is needed, and what reconciliation and rework steps occur on the data. This will also show the different people or functional areas involved and the hand-off points between those people and functions.

[B] Review of 'As Is'

The documentation of the "as is" processes will throw up areas where there is duplication of effort, excessive use of resource, poor data and where there are both gaps and bottlenecks in the process. It should also highlight tax risk areas, opportunities for automation and confusion of ownership. The objective of this step is to identify the precise nature of the problem to be solved through process improvement.

Some of the questions to be considered at this stage are:

- What are the roles of the tax function and required outputs?
- How effective are current key processes?
- What processes work well and which do not?
- Where are the inefficiencies?
- What are our current constraints to process change in terms of people, processes and technology?
- Where are the risks?
- Who are the stakeholders in the outputs of the process and what are their respective business needs?
- What are the symptoms of current problems—level of errors, time/cost inefficiencies?
- Can we determine the real cause of the process problems?

For example, one major multi-national company estimated that over 50% of their time was being spent on tax accounting and compliance and this was consuming significant resources in terms of systems maintenance spend. Despite the time spent on tax accounting and compliance, there was a concern that potentially material issues could arise in the tax accounts and submitted tax returns. After the current processes were broken down to their individual steps, it was identified that significant amounts of time was spent on lower risk areas because the quality of source data was poor, which left less time to analyse complex tax areas like treasury and foreign exchange.

[C] Design of New Processes

Focusing back on the end goals of what you are trying to achieve, and tying in with what you currently do, will allow you to design new processes and to build in automation where that is appropriate. As noted above we are not just trying to automate existing processes; existing processes need to be reviewed and challenged and new processes introduced if that is appropriate. It is these new processes which need to be more automated.

For design, we would normally turn for inspiration to best practices and the collection of our experiences that we have seen work well. Some of the elements of best practice in tax processes we have seen include the following:

- Roles and responsibilities of the people involved are clearly defined.
- There is an appropriate degree of planning and project management overseeing the operation of the processes.

- Interdependencies between different corporate functions and the business units are properly addressed.
- The right controls are in place to ensure data integrity.
- Compliance calendars, processes, roles and accountabilities are well understood and agreed.
- Review and approval controls are in place and operating.
- Risk management processes are integrated into day-to-day tax processes.

In designing the solution you need to have regard to the likely level and mix of internal and external resources and the skills, experience and application to the job.

Coming back to our example, the 'to be' environment for our client trying to improve tax processes was a reconstructed tax accounting and compliance process based on risk management principles with the right mix of internal and external resources. In terms of the internal work on compliance, the client believed that they could reduce the time spent on analysis of data by placing greater reliance on the accounting data, provided there was some increased focus on improving the quality of the data at its source; for example coding of tax sensitive data in the general ledger.

[D] Test Run/Pilot New Processes and Systems

Any new systems should be properly tested before rolling out or going live. It is usual to do a test run on any new systems before their full implementation with a view to working out what works and more importantly what does not work and needs changing. Particularly with high risk areas, such as tax accounting, parallel running of the new and the old systems is critical, particularly where a new system is being rolled out over a year end.

In a complex environment the preferred solution is unlikely to be perfect. Hence all processes require that you adopt an attitude of continuous improvement.

[E] Implementation

Once a new process has been piloted and any faults ironed out it can then be fully implemented. Effective implementation will normally involve good documentation, communication, training and provision of ongoing support.

[F] Monitor and Review

Finally once a new system has been up and running for a period its progress should be monitored and, where appropriate, changes made to the process in order to make it even better than it now is.

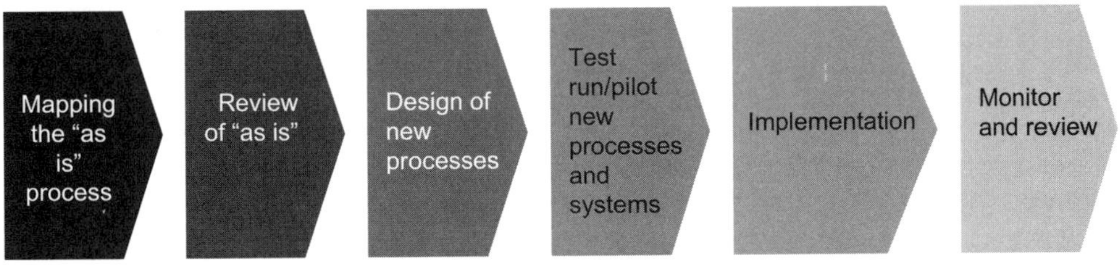

§18.06 SUMMARY

There are a number of key drivers which lead to the conclusion that more emphasis needs to be made on process improvement in the tax function than has been the case to date. This chapter has looked at many of these drivers then moved on to look at how process improvement can be managed.

To the extent that major process improvement is envisaged in an organisation we recommend that process improvement specialists be brought in both to advise and project manage the improvement. As already noted process improvement is not a natural skill of many tax professionals and undoubtedly external support will bring valuable perspectives on the function's problems to help make process improvement a success.

CHAPTER 19
DATA MANAGEMENT

"On two occasions I have been asked,—'Pray, Mr. Babbage, if you put into the machine wrong figures, will the right answers come out?' " Charles Babbage—pioneer computer scientist

§19.01 INTRODUCTION

The lifeblood of the tax function is quality data that supports:

- Tax planning and forecasting,
- Tax accounting,
- Tax compliance, and
- Audit defence.

Tax executives will often indicate their desire to implement tax technology as a way to improve processes and efficiency. However, after gaining a deeper understanding of their current environment, it becomes clear that the potential success of their planned technology and process improvement initiatives are severely limited by their quality and access to data. As a result, it is common to find that the most successful improvement projects begin with a hard look at data. It is this point that causes us to define data management as an enabler for the tax function separate from the use of technology, which we will come onto in the next chapter.

The challenge is that the tax function often sees itself as just a consumer of data from various source systems. Tax is accustomed to taking whatever data in whatever format it can get and then manipulating it so that it works for its needs. The tax function does not always see itself taking an active role in the creation or management of either transaction or master data. Yet, in order for the tax function to improve the quality of the data it receives, it must take an active role in the data management processes at all levels within the organisation.

Before we discuss data management practices and the role of the tax function, we will begin by examining and understanding the data lifecycle.

§19.02 THE DATA LIFECYCLE

[A] Create

Within the context of the tax function, most data is initially created by means of a business transaction. While the transaction may have paper documents that evidence the existence of the transaction, it is eventually recorded within an electronic system. Supporting the transaction is an array of 'master data' that was, at some point, also created and entered into the same electronic system. This master data comprises, for example, the general ledger account numbers, profit centre and/or country codes; these elements provide the context and clarity to the underlying transaction. A key element of the create phase of the data lifecycle is standardised processes to assure consistent capture of similar types of data (e.g. a specific tax disallowable expense).

[B] Sustain

The sustain phase of the data lifecycle focuses on assuring consistency and integrity of the data. Sustaining data implies a controlled environment to prevent unauthorised access to and modification of the data (e.g. merging of two different types of tax sensitive expenditure).

[C] Analysis and Report

The analysis and report phases of the data lifecycle are self-explanatory. Data is grouped based on the defined needs of the user, trends are examined and anomalies are identified. Analysis and to some extent reporting can lead to corrections in the data that arise from errors or omissions. The reporting phase focuses on summarising the data in meaningful output for the consumer. The tax function will be a consumer of data as well as having its own consumers (e.g. the board and treasury). Reports are prepared and delivered to consumers both within and outside the company.

[D] Retire

As in any typical lifecycle, there comes an end. With most tax data this is also true. At some point, there is no longer value and use for the data and it must be destroyed. In tax, however, there is some data that has value so long as the company is in existence. As such, this phase of the data lifecycle for the tax function could actually be further subdivided into retain, resurrect and destroy.

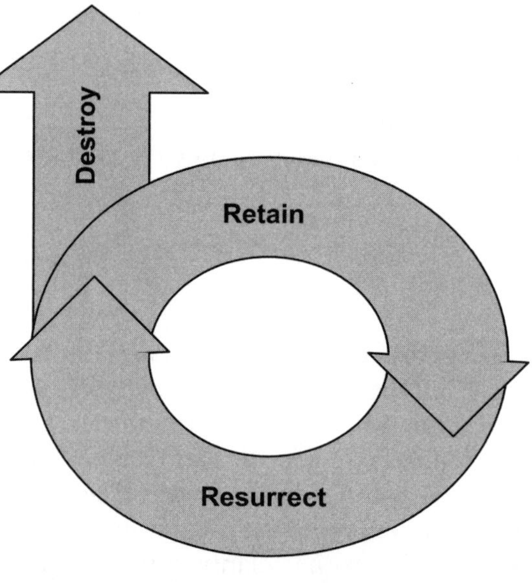

Retain: Many regulatory filings and the laws that underpin them also provide the revenue authority with the opportunity to conduct a review of the filing by requesting additional information as evidence to support the information provided within the filing. Depending on the taxing jurisdiction and the company's practices, the data can be retained either in the original source system, or it can be copied from the original source system in a readable format to an alternative media. For example, data (both transaction and master data with their relationships intact) can be copied from the ERP system into text files. These files can be stored on low cost storage media (magnetic tape). Regardless of the chosen media, if data is extracted from a source system to text files, these retained files should be evaluated periodically during this retention phase to ensure readability in case of a future revenue authority audit.

Resurrect: Having been moved to an alternate media, the data must be able to be resurrected and made available for the defined use. In the case of revenue authority audits, the data must be made available—restored from magnetic tape—in order to respond to the revenue authority's information request.

Destroy: Destroying date is a phase that is often overlooked. Many tax functions that we have encountered would prefer just to retain everything forever. While this does provide a level of comfort of being able to find something 'just in case', the practicality in terms of both cost and risk management dictate that data must periodically be destroyed. Standard records management destructions practices should be applied to data that has truly reached the end of the lifecycle. However the practices may vary from tax to tax and from country to country depending on local regulatory requirements.

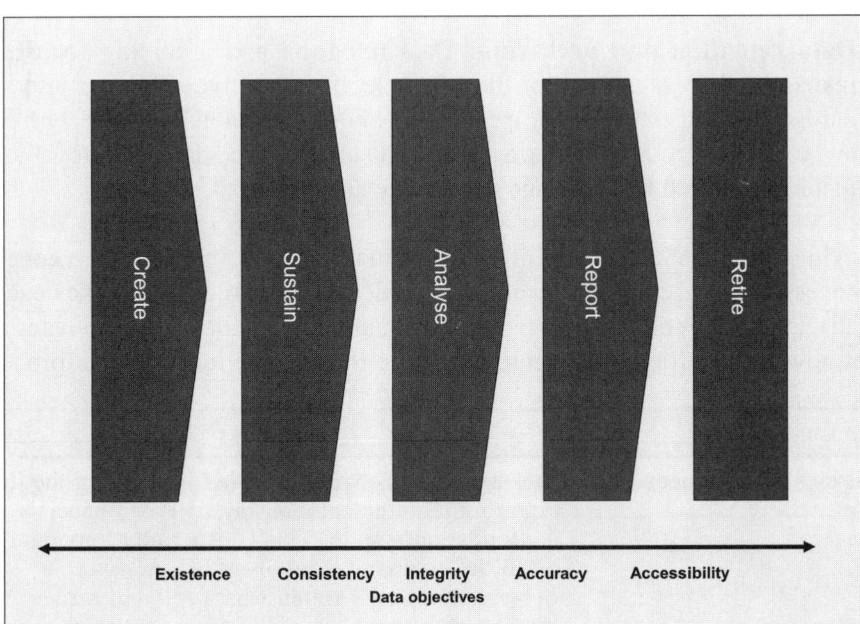

§ 19.03 ENTERPRISE DATA MANAGEMENT

With an understanding of the data lifecycle we must now examine what it means to manage tax relevant data through this lifecycle. Enterprise data management is a process to organise, design and safeguard information throughout the lifecycle. The main objective of data management is to standardise and reuse accurate data, focusing on the set of data that is clearly defined and does not change across departments or countries. Data management cannot focus on just the data but must include the use and distribution of the data and how its distribution can cause error and misinterpretation. The concept of enterprise data management encompasses several other disciplines that are described below.

Master data management: Master data management (MDM) focuses on formalising the processes for creation, maintenance, and retirement of master data. This involves standardising definitions and values for key fields, assigning ownership over master data processes, and monitoring the effectiveness of those processes.

Data governance: Data governance embodies the synchronisation of policies, standards, procedures, organisation and technology for the management of data. Governance is based on identifying ownership, and instilling a level of accountability in data processes.

Data quality: Data quality is about having accurate information, delivered to the appropriate people, in a timely manner. A data quality methodology defines standards for ensuring the accuracy and integrity of data. It is typically highly integrated with MDM and data governance.

Data retention and archiving: Data retention and archiving focuses on managing data at the end of the lifecycle. This involves defining and standardising policies for the proper retirement of data in accordance with legal and regulatory requirements, as well as ensuring retired data is retrievable in a manner required by legal and regulatory entities.

While these are key disciplines for data management, they are often concepts and processes that are unfamiliar to tax functions. The table below takes each of these disciplines of enterprise data management and provides some relevant context of how the tax function might participate in this data management process.

Component	*Examples*
Master data management	• Tax should be actively involved in defining the data/ reporting requirements for any ERP or financial consolidation system. This is especially important when the company is involved in new systems implementations. Tax must be a full and active participant in defining and communicating their

Component	*Examples*
	requirements. A key challenge that we have seen companies face is the conflicting approaches to this requirements definition process between the tax function and other user groups. Typical systems implementations focus on the standard business processes that are directly affected by the systems changes. Tax will define their requirements in terms of their processes e.g. tax provision and tax compliance. The systems integrators will then often struggle to understand how to fit the tax requirements into the system design and often will set those requirements aside in favor of the other business requirements. In order successfully to integrate the data and reporting requirements into new systems implementations, tax needs to participate with the business and define the tax data requirements as an embedded requirement of the overall business process.
	• Much of the data requirements for tax are controlled by master data. Examples would include the charts of accounts, individual location, cost and profit centers that may provide a tie to a local taxing authority, physical material types or groups that may drive whether a product is subject to a transaction tax (e.g. VAT) in a particular jurisdiction. Thus tax should have a role in defining standards and business rules for managing master data. This would include defining key rules around the creation of new master data. For example, if cost centres are used as a relationship to local taxing jurisdictions, then tax needs to specify that one of the rules for creating a new cost centre is that entities that comprise that cost centre may not exist in different taxing jurisdictions.
	• In order for common understanding of data across the organisation, data definitions should be agreed upon and posted to a company intranet site for reference by all stakeholders.
Data governance	• Data governance is the key to ensuring data is accurate and reliable. Tax is heavily impacted by degradations in data quality and should therefore take an active role in the data governance process, including positions in any data centre of excellence or advisory council.
	• Tax should establish data management roles within the tax function, including data owner roles. The individual filling these roles should have a deep understanding of both the data at the data element level as well as the accounting procedures for creating, editing, and retiring key master data.

Component	*Examples*
	• Tax personnel should have the authority to initiate change in MDM processes to ensure tax requirements are met.
Data quality	• The tax function should help define data quality checks in source systems to help identify degradation of data quality in tax data. Goals and objectives for tax data quality should be clearly defined, and be consistent with the requirements of other groups (i.e. finance). As such, the tax function should define positions/roles that are responsible for data quality (data stewards). This does not necessarily mean the addition of headcount to the overall tax function; it likely means the addition of responsibilities to an existing position within tax. • Tax data owners and stewards should be held accountable for the quality of data under their stewardship. The tax data management procedures should include measurement of data quality on an ongoing basis to enforce the accountability. • All tax personnel should have a basic understanding of what constitutes quality data.
Data retention and archiving	• The tax function should have defined retention policies and procedures that are included as part of the enterprise records management programme. The policy should address all forms of records: paper, structured electronic (databases and ERP system data) and unstructured electronic (desktop application files like Word, Excel and e-mail). • As part of the enterprise records management programme the tax department should define a retention schedule for all the records that are identified as part of the retention policy and should work with IT and the corporate records manager to develop necessary procedures to retain and verify retention of necessary business records. • Tax should work with the corporate records manager and IT to define 'legal hold' procedures to assure records are retained for future tax audits, appeals and litigation. • The tax function should work with IT to define the requirements that will allow IT to define the appropriate retention methods and technologies that will support the retrieval requirements imposed by tax audits. Specifically, data should be easily retrieved by tax year and should be able to be produced on demand based on the request of the revenue authorities.

§19.04 THE PEOPLE AND PROCESS SIDE OF DATA

As you examine the different disciplines of data management, it becomes clear that embracing data management in the tax function will require changes with regard to both people and processes. Individuals in tax who are identified as data owners will need to be trained on data management and governance. Yet data owners are not the only individuals in the tax function who will need training. As part of the change management programme for embracing data management, all tax personnel should be educated on MDM concepts.

As part of this change to a data management culture, the tax data owners should have an understanding of data that reaches outside of tax. These individuals must have an understanding of how a change in process impacts tax, finance and operations. One of the ways to effectively build this knowledge is with staff rotations outside of tax for cross-training personnel (e.g. a six month assignment in finance).

§19.05 SUMMARY

Data management is an emerging discipline. Many companies are establishing data management organisations, often including the new role of Chief Data Officer. These organisations have recognised the importance of data to the success of the business. Tax has the opportunity to take advantage of this emerging trend and become an active participant in data management practice. This participation will reap significant benefit by assuring quality tax sensitised data is available for use in tax matters.

CHAPTER 20
USING TECHNOLOGY

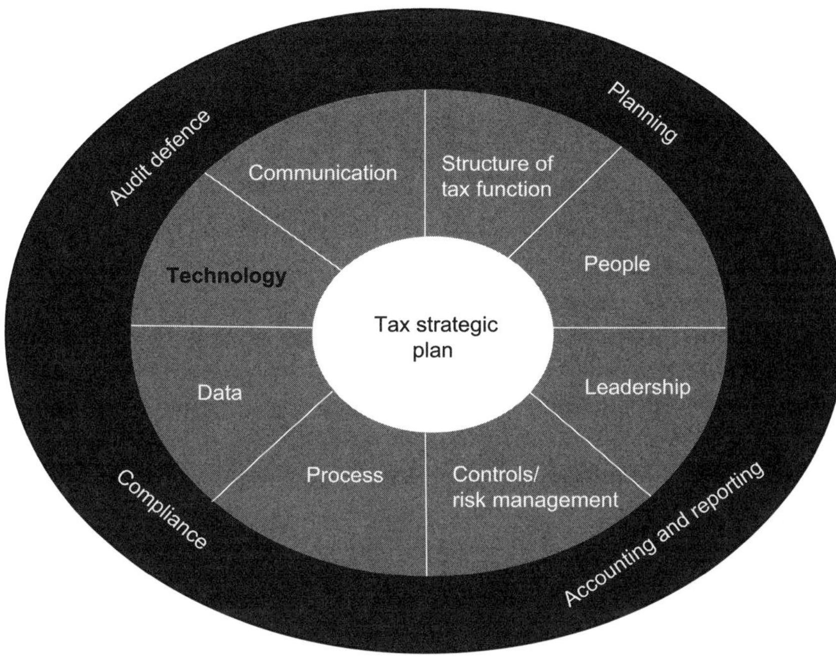

§ 20.01 INTRODUCTION

Having world class people to lead and work within the team is critical to the overall effectiveness of a best in class tax function. However on par with the people is technology. The current, and increasing, sophistication of enabling technologies can make a powerful difference to the ability of the tax function to produce its deliverables within the appropriate timescales and risk parameters.

Let us begin by explaining what we mean by tax technology—what its components are, its functionality and how these various components work together to deliver efficiencies, improve quality and manage risk. Once we have defined tax technology we can then explore the value you should expect to derive from deploying some or all of these components.

§ 20.02 WHAT DO WE MEAN BY TECHNOLOGY?

We have developed an example of a best in class tax technology platform. This is illustrated in the diagram below and developed further in the coming pages.

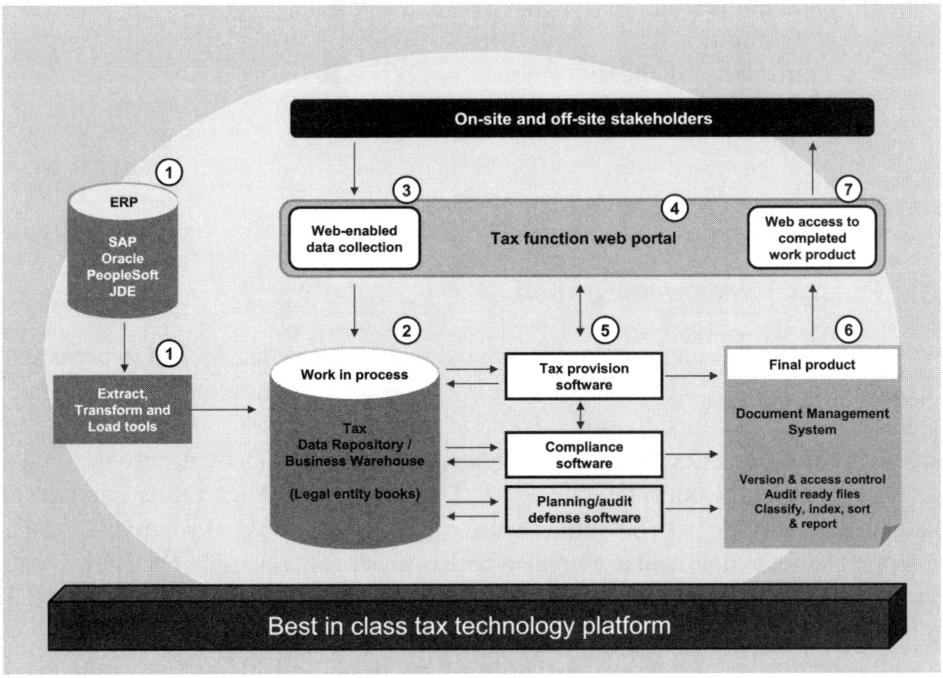

We recognise the term 'best in class' is a vague notion and no single definition of what is 'best' is widely accepted. Moreover, the accepted version of what is best varies considerably from one organisation to the next. With that said, we have based the above model on:

1. Our visits with many of the Global Fortune 1000 companies and observing, first hand, how these leading tax organisations address their technology requirements,
2. Developing our point of view during the course of our many client engagements where we have collaborated with senior tax executives, and their finance and IT leaders, and
3. Our discussions with senior executives from the leading tax technology vendors.

§ 20.03 THE COMPONENT PARTS

You will notice within the diagram the numbers 1 through to 7 which are intended to highlight the distinct components of the technology platform. We will make reference to each of these as follows:

1. Financial system integration;
2. Data warehouse;
3. Data collection;
4. Web portal;
5. Third party applications;
6. Document management system; and
7. Web access.

Let us look at each of these in turn.

[A] Financial System Integration

Acquiring high quality data on demand and in the format needed to prepare tax computations and tax accounting figures is a wide spread and frequently cited impediment to overall tax function effectiveness. Most tax functions spend an inordinate amount of time and effort to collect, validate and manipulate book data so they have a good starting point to begin their tax work. The process to collect, validate and manipulate book data is rife with potential for error and represents a heavy burden on the tax function budget to maintain resources whose primary role is simply to ensure a viable starting point for tax calculations. The key here is better use of technology substantially to minimise the effort required to collect, validate and manipulate data.

To begin, let us recognise that tax data is housed in various company IT systems that may include:

- ERP systems
- Financial consolidation systems

- Payroll systems
- Fixed asset systems
- Inventory systems
- Other industry specific feeder systems (e.g. brokerage systems, R&D systems.)

The traditional approach positions tax as wholly dependent on those who have direct access to the systems or are the system owners such as controllers, accountants and finance personnel. In many instances, data collection requires tax personnel to place periodic requests for reports in what is typically a very inefficient process, resulting in delays while waiting for a reply, and then both validating the report once received and manipulating the data (typically in a spreadsheet) so it is in a useable format to support a tax computation or help produce tax figures for the accounts.

Consider how much better it would be if tax professionals used technology to the fullest extent possible to automate the data collection by reaching directly into the various and numerous source systems, then standardising that data within a 'staging area' and finally, pushing the standardised data set to tax specific systems such as tax accounting software, compliance systems and analytical tools. Much less effort would be necessary to validate data that is sourced directly from finance systems without any intervention. Not only would this free up time for tax people but it would also greatly speed up the financial close process. The benefits can be enormous.

What we are talking about here is not merely linking tax systems to financial systems but rather an integration of these systems. The missing link in the tax technology architecture of old is the tools that have more robust data manipulation capabilities. These tools as a class are defined as Extract, Transform and Load (ETL). What are ETL tools and how can they provide a major boost to the value of tax systems?

> ETL brings together and combines data from multiple source systems into a data warehouse, enabling all users to work off a single, integrated set of data—a single version of the truth. The result is an organisation that no longer spins its wheels collecting data or arguing about whose data is correct, but one that uses information as a key process enabler and competitive weapon.
>
> In these organisations, business intelligence systems (supported by ETL tools) are no longer 'nice to have', but essential to success. These systems are no longer stand-alone and separate from operational processing—they are integrated with overall business processes. As a result, an effective business intelligence environment based on integrated data enables users to make strategic, tactical, and operational decisions that drive the business on a daily basis.

ETL tools have the ability to speak with virtually any other software application to extract and standardise relevant data, and push it to another software application of your choosing. That has the potential to overcome the complexity, inefficiency and risks of collecting the numerous elements of book data from disparate systems required for tax compliance and reporting.

Implementing ETL tools is a complex undertaking and not one the tax function should take on without support from finance and IT. It is highly likely that your company already licenses and uses ETL tools to support the finance or other business operations functions. We therefore suggest you begin your quest to understand how ETL and business intelligence systems can support your tax function by learning how your company is already using these tools in support of other areas within finance. There are also a number of ETL vendors in the market who would be more than delighted to help you in this area.

[B] Data Warehouse (DW)

The second technology component is the data warehouse. The terms data warehouse and data mart are often used interchangeably and while there are certain technical differences between the two, for purposes of this discussion, we will combine the two. We use the term data warehouse to mean:

> An information repository with a consolidated view of enterprise data, optimised for reporting and analysis. Data and information, both transactional and non-transactional, are loaded into the warehouse, often using ETL tools, from data sources as they are generated, or in periodic stages. The transformation of data allows for dynamic queries and analytics, making it simpler and more efficient to run queries over data that originally came from different sources.

The benefits that a data warehouse delivers include the ability to turn data into high-quality information to meet all tax function reporting and compliance requirements for all levels of users. Interactive content can be delivered to anyone in the extended enterprise—customers, partners, employees, managers, and executives—anytime, anywhere.

Simply having a single source for all tax reporting and compliance information is a major leap forward for most tax functions but what else can be achieved within the DW environment that can further enable tax effectiveness?

You should view the tax DW as an information hub that can bring automation to computation of deferred tax items, accept and store information from off-site locations and generally manipulate data so it is in a useable format. It is the storage shed for robust and current tax sensitive data that can be mined or pushed to 3rd party applications to facilitate analysis, audits, planning or forecasting. You should consider developing standard reporting from the DW to serve as your standard set of tax work papers supporting the tax accounting and compliance processes.

Building tax DW functionality can be an expensive proposition. The single most viable alternative is to look within your finance function for either an existing DW or a data warehouse initiative that could be extended to address tax requirements. It is usually simpler, faster and more cost effective to leverage existing IT architecture than proposing to build a new DW. A second alternative is external vendors with existing tax technology solutions who are looking to extend their offerings to provide a standard data model for a tax DW. It is still too early to tell if these vendors can produce a low cost tax DW. And while they may provide a standard data model for the DW, significant investment is still required to identify all the data sources and configure and map the data from the source systems to the DW.

We are often asked about the need and benefits for a DW for a given company. The general answer is that the more disparate the sources of data, the more a DW will provide a significant benefit. For example, it is quite likely that a diversified global company with 20 separate businesses, countless business locations, numerous individual ERP applications and countless subsidiary ledgers will benefit much more from a DW that a single domestic business with one integrated ERP. These benefits will especially arise for acquisition-oriented companies that tend to allow their targets to maintain historical ERP applications rather than quickly integrating their systems.

[C] Data Collection

Tax seeks to collect data from controllers, accountants or tax personnel situated in foreign jurisdictions as well as information from domestic sites that is not readily available from the general ledger (ERP system). Many tax functions continue to rely on spreadsheets and email as the method of data collection from off-site providers. Naturally, this is not a best practice as it is difficult to ensure users do not make changes to the spreadsheet regardless of passwords, protected worksheets, columns and rows, and hash totals built into the model. Many recipients modify the spreadsheet by adding or deleting rows or columns, adding worksheets, hiding cells or hard coding over formulas. These common practices make it very difficult to extract data from spreadsheets efficiently since they lack standardisation when returned. This in turn leads to a significant data validation effort to ensure the information received agrees to the ledger or some other reliable originating source system. The other key weakness of email and spreadsheets is the lack of version control.

Many companies are retiring their data collection spreadsheets in favour of web based tax reporting packages. Essentially they are migrating the functionality and in many instances the same look and feel of the spreadsheet to the internet, typically via a tax web portal. Upon entering data into the web form, it is instantly entered into the tax DW or directly into the tax technology application—in the right place, the right format and immediately available for reporting. This is a highly effective process to ensure standardisation and eliminate the effort required to transfer data from one spreadsheet to another.

[D] Web Portal

Tax function web portals are becoming increasingly commonplace. They serve as the central access point and knowledge sharing nerve centre for tax operations. The illustration below shows how access to tax information can be centralised and easily accessible via the internet.

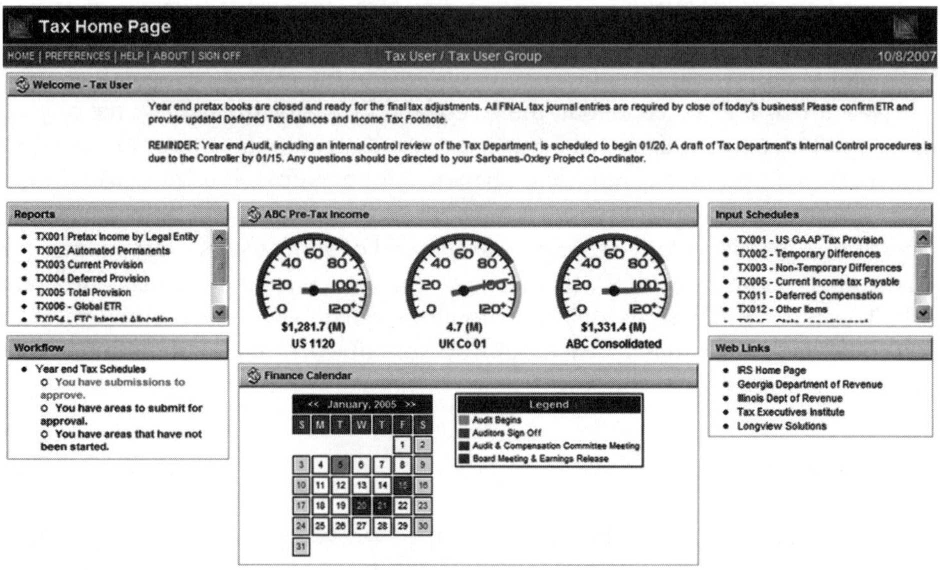

The tax web portal shown above contains links to tax specific reports, web based data collection packages, links to 3rd party research sites and access to workflow tools to manage critical processes. The centre piece of many tax web portal tracks several Key Performance Indicators (KPI's) or tax specific values—in this illustration, pre-tax income in the US, UK and consolidated are represented in a speedometer format.

A critical component of the web portal is the ability to migrate the tax reporting package functionality to web pages that directly update the DW. A close second is the opportunity web portals afford your global tax staff to have visibility into the compliance status on a global basis, into tax document management system and the data warehouse for a first hand view of completed tax returns, workpapers, research memos, financial reports and other company specific work products. The tax document management system is discussed further below.

[E] Third Party Applications

Once book and other tax sensitive data has been collected directly from source systems, standardised through ETL tools and stored in the data warehouse you have a very potent data set available to populate automatically technology applications for virtually any process required, such as planning, tax accounting, compliance and audit defence.

Recent years have seen a growing number of vendors servicing the tax technology market with a number of companies having solutions available to address the following diverse list of needs:

- International planning/foreign tax credits
- State planning, modelling and analytical tools
- Transfer pricing
- R&D credits
- FAS109/IAS12
- FIN 48
- Tax compliance/forms generators
- Transaction tax compliance systems
- Web enabled data collection tools
- Data analysis/mining tools
- Global entity and compliance tracking systems
- Interest and penalty calculators
- Audit tracking tools
- Tax data warehouse
- Document management
- Workflow
- Tax calendar
- Web portal for the tax function

As we write no one company provides a complete package covering all these different needs. There are a number of organisations in the tax technology market focusing on different territories and regions, many with narrowly targeted applications. We would summarise the changes in this area as follows:

- Historically—tax compliance was the core tax technology with complementary modules built around it.
- Currently—tax accounting and FAS109/IAS 12 solutions have gained prominence and currently share the technology mantle as core tax technologies with complementary modules being built around each.
- Future—high end, data warehouse systems with sophisticated financial consolidation, modeling and data collection tools will emerge as the center of the tax technology universe. This will be paired with ETL tools to standardise data sourced from disparate systems. Pushing this collection of high quality, tax sensitive data to FAS109/IAS12 and compliance systems will become routine for the most effective tax organisations.

What is interesting about current provision technology is that the approach taken from vendor to vendor can be quite different. For example, some applications have been built around existing tax compliance tools and stress integration between the two, others are written specifically for the provision, others are integrated with financial consolidation technology and stress the ability for automated extraction. With these differing approaches, the selection process for tax provision technology is critical as no one technology represents the best of the three alternatives discussed above.

As you might expect, true DWs are still rare even among larger global corporations so automated data extraction generally remains a challenge. As a result, many of the newer technology applications are initially being implemented as a means to eliminate spreadsheets and improve processes. Rather than initially focusing on data extraction, many companies are instead focused on efficient data accumulation (via the web input screens discuss previously) as a first step and important change management step toward true automation.

While there are many choices in the technology field, the ability to push data with the highest integrity to one of these third party tools without the requisite validation and manipulation effort is a clear differentiator for those tax functions who claim optimal effectiveness.

[F] Document Management Systems

The shared network drive remains the popular choice as the primary repository for completed tax returns, research memoranda, tax opinions, correspondence and supporting workpapers. Unfortunately, the shared network drive is woefully inadequate, offers very little control and virtually none of the features of a formal, dedicated document management system. We have provided below a brief list of the main features and benefits one can expect from a document management system.

- Secure and organised electronic workplace for all returns, receipts, work papers, tax planning and audit projects.
- Consolidate worldwide unstructured data from all sources including any electronic documents, fax, email, images and electronic forms with access from any company location in the world via the Internet.
- Audit ready files.
- Secure access control and logging.
- Classify, categorise, sort and report all documents.
- Mine previously filed work papers, revenue audit responses and tax research papers using detailed context relationships and advanced search.
- Version control around all documents—especially key spreadsheets, including the ability to restore prior versions and a complete audit trail of who made changes and when they were made.
- Eliminate dual file systems and the effort to ensure both are consistent, current and readily available between manual files and workpapers, and electronic versions on the shared network drive.
- Reduce delays, floor space needs and fees for tax records retrieval and storage—onsite and offsite.
- Enhance workflow within the tax function by assigning responsibilities for specific events in the work process with documentation being routed automatically to the next defined individual in the process.

[G] Web Access

The development of the Internet has facilitated instant access to information from virtually anywhere in the world at any time. This information accessibility should be no different for the tax function. In addition to serving as the tax function nerve centre and key access point for data collection the web portal can be leveraged to be the means by which tax personnel (and others in finance if desired) can gain remote access to completed work products—such as tax returns, supporting workpapers, and legal opinions. Unencumbered access to data and finished work product enables speed and accuracy in completion of specific tasks regardless of location or time zone.

§20.04 LEVERAGING EXISTING FINANCE FUNCTION IT SYSTEMS

Historically the tax function has tended to operate as a silo separate from the finance function. The impact of this is that finance and IT leaders have become accustomed either to ignoring tax when looking at IT projects or bringing tax in so late in the systems development or deployment lifecycle that it is no more than a token step in the project plan. This tendency has been a major contributor to today's inefficient tax processes and control issues and is no longer acceptable. Similarly in most companies there is an expansive IT infrastructure that is not appropriately leveraged by the tax function.

First and foremost, tax must invest in training in the self-service tools available to access, query and report critical information for tax reporting and planning. This includes the key tools around the ERP systems that would allow tax to access directly the information rather than submitting a request to a third party and waiting for results. Furthermore, it is likely that the IT and/or finance functions will have deployed sophisticated ETL tools, consolidation programs, business warehouses and/or data mart applications that enable the finance function to carry out their role. One of the first steps in a tax technology improvement project will be to look inside the organisation at these tools and applications to see how they can be further refined to deliver on many tax function requirements in a very cost effective manner.

§20.05 TAX IT PERSONNEL

It's now a well established best practice to have one or more tax IT people that are aligned with the tax function. Particularly in those tax functions having deployed some or all of the best in class tax technology platform, a tax dedicated IT person will be critical to the successful implementation, training and maintenance of an effective tax IT architecture.

While some may initially balk at adding headcount within tax for an IT role (or within IT for a tax role) it is our experience that headcount within the tax function is positively impacted by adding dedicated IT specialists. Their work contributes to an environment that relies heavily on automation which allows for greater flexibility in managing overall tax headcount.

§ 20.06 BENEFITS OF TECHNOLOGY

Traditionally senior tax executives have not had the need to propose significant investments in technology short of the subscription to an on-line research service or for corporate income tax compliance software. Until very recently, it has been a rare occurrence where tax has required and requested a six figure investment for technology projects that may include data warehousing, web enabled data collection tools, automating deferred tax computations, data acquisition projects, spreadsheet remediation or tax web portals.

The current emphasis on lower risk tolerance, shortages of tax talent, shorter financial close cycles, increased transparency and the increasing regulatory burden has led many tax functions to examine how technology may aid them in their effort to maintain or improve their overall effectiveness. As we look back at our recent client experiences in the tax technology space, and our ongoing dialogue with leading global companies, we have distilled the ten most commonly achieved benefits which have been realised through the greater use of technology.

Benefits of Technology	*Explanation*
Free up staff	Efficiency gains are attainable via technology that can result in reducing the hours required to complete tasks by 10%–20% or more. Most tax functions are redeploying that newly created capacity to high value tasks such as risk management, planning, financial reporting and controls.
Higher staff retention	Requiring less effort to collect, validate and manipulate data leads to greater opportunities to focus on meaningful tax analysis, reporting and planning. These tasks tend to be more rewarding and encourage the growth of your staff which in turn leads to improved retention.
Improve quality of information	Using technology to gain faster access to book data directly from source systems encompassing both domestic and foreign jurisdictions can help to overcome use of estimates or even out of date prior year data as the starting point for tax computations.
Increase analytics	Having more time available to perform analytics is achievable particularly around data collection processes. The market for tax analytical technology is growing rapidly. Applications for foreign tax credit planning,

Benefits of technology	*Explanation*
	dividend repatriation strategies and ETR forecasting are widely available and perform well.
Retain institutional knowledge	What value can be placed on the knowledge carried by your staff in their heads? While difficult to quantify, most agree the value is material and important. Technology platforms such as document management systems permit the permanent retention and ongoing development of a bank of company specific tax issues, their resolution and the related documentation to support conclusions.
Enhance knowledge sharing	Tapping the value from internal collaboration is a best practice receiving much attention from leading tax functions. Using technology as a platform to collaborate via tax intranets or sharing research via the document management system represents an opportunity to increase effectiveness and manage risk.
Connect tax personnel globally	Many material weaknesses linked to the tax function relate to matters emanating from outside the home country. Accessing data and fully understanding tax positions and accounting methods adopted in all territories is a requirement in today's environment. Using technology to close the gap via tax web portals, workflow tools and document sharing are becoming increasingly important.
Simplify response to audits	Fast, accurate and complete responses to tax audit requests is one of the best ways to ensure development of a strong collaborative working relationship with the revenue authorities. Best practices suggest that this type of relationship best positions your organisation during a tax audit. Having rapid access to a complete set of 'audit ready' documents that support your originally filed tax positions is increasingly being addressed via tax web portals and document management systems.
Strengthen internal controls	When done correctly, the implementation of new technology will include the design and implementation of new processes.

Benefits of technology	*Explanation*
	The result can be a much improved control environment evidenced by new processes supported by enabling technology.
Improve forecasting capability	Accurate forecasts of the effective tax rate and cash taxes are critical to the effective management of tax. Many companies struggle with forecasting methodologies, use old data and lack insight as to how major transactions may impact ETR in key jurisdictions. The emergence of FAS109/ IAS12 software with the ability to model the ETR is a major technology enabler. In addition, linking the tax accounting system and the ERP to collect the most current data is another critical technology element enabling better tax forecasting.

However technology improvements alone will not deliver the benefits you should be looking for. You should not make the error, as we have seen some do, of focusing too narrowly on technology as the solution. For example a common mistake is handing the existing tax provision excel-based tax provision workpapers to a technology vendor or outside consultant with the instructions to make the newly chose technology work in the same way. Generally this approach is not effective as evidenced by the number of spreadsheets that remain after the implementation and the complaints from staff indicating that they would rather revert back to their old spreadsheet approach. It is critical that you think about the people, process and data—as noted in previous chapters.

§ 20.07 TAX TECHNOLOGY AS A JOURNEY

The benefits of improved technology are clear. However we have observed many companies who have been very excited by the promise of what tax technology can do for them only quickly to experience implementation failures and budgetary resistance. We recommend taking a long term view of your tax technology strategy and look at it over a 1–3–5 year period; take things at a pace you can absorb. This longer term approach has been tested successfully many times and compares very favourably to the big bang approach that attempts to transform the tax function beyond its capability to digest the change.

Developing incrementally not only spreads the budget, but more importantly lets the change take root. Human nature does not lend itself naturally to significant changes in our work processes or easy adaptation to new tools to accomplish our tasks. It is important to recognise what we already know and design your technology transformation plans to align with this instead of trying to overcome it.

§ 20.08 SUMMARY

The opportunities for greater use of technology and to generate the benefits that these bring have never been greater than they are today. A best practice tax function should be reviewing its IT plans and working through what needs to be introduced. Not only will the greater use of technology be beneficial to those people who are doing too much manual manipulation of data, but it will also greatly improve the quality of information through better businesses controls and risk management.

CHAPTER 21

COMMUNICATION

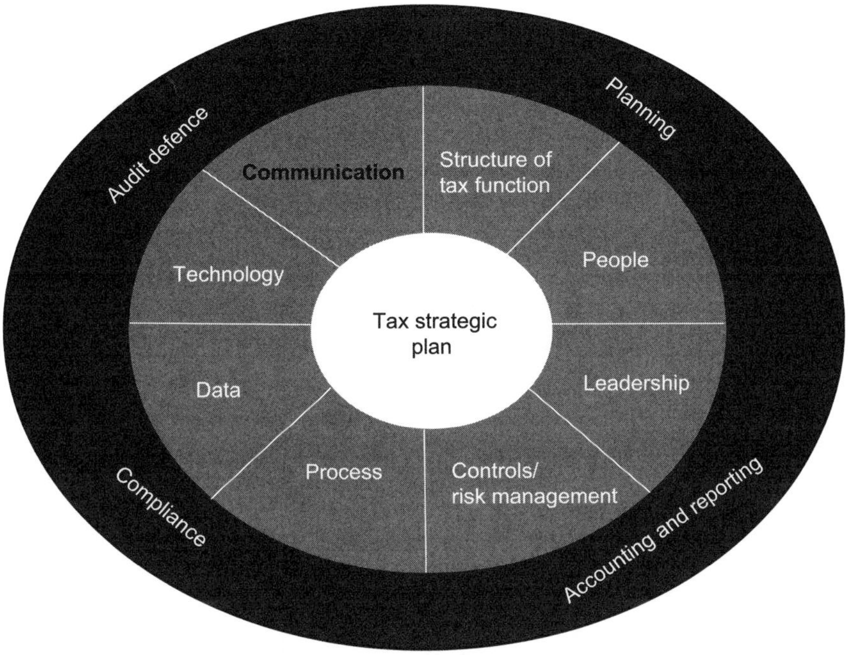

"There is no such thing as a misunderstanding—there is only a failure to communicate"

§21.01 INTRODUCTION

One of the themes running through this guide has been the need for proper communication with the numerous different stakeholders in the tax affairs of an organisation. Each of these different stakeholders will require different things from the tax function; indeed the tax function will require different things from each of the stakeholders. Additionally, different forms of communication will work better with different stakeholders.

The purpose of this chapter is to encourage people to think through systemically what their different stakeholders need from the tax function, what is needed from the stakeholders and how this two way communication should take place. When life gets busy (and when is it not busy?) quality communication often slips. In our opinion communication is too important to ignore and we conclude this chapter by recommending that a communication plan is put in place with a view to ensuring that, at the very least, all the key stakeholders are in regular communication on the tax matters of their organisation.

However before talking about individual stakeholders it is worth making some comments about some general principles of communication which need to be taken into account when the tax communication plan is put in place.

§21.02 PRINCIPLES OF COMMUNICATION

[A] Structured Approach

A best practice approach to communication with the stakeholders in tax might look like this:

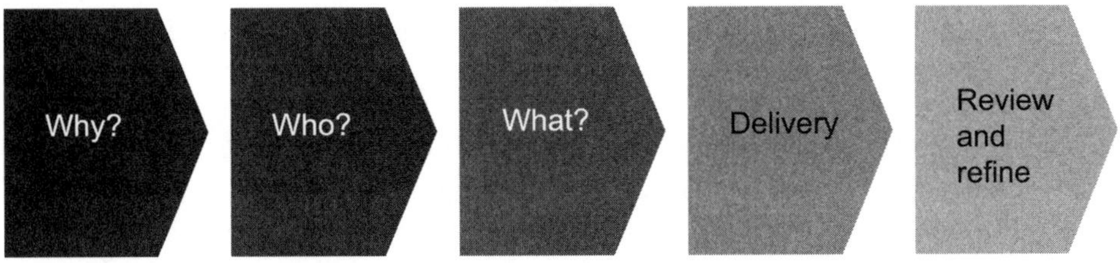

- Why—this is around the overall objectives of the communication. What are you aiming to achieve through the communication? What do you want the stakeholders in tax to do once you have communicated with them?
- Who—this is focusing on which stakeholders in tax (both internal and external to the organisation) need to be communicated with and where the different stakeholders sit in the order of priorities.
- What—which picks up the messages which need to be delivered around tax; for example there will probably be messages which need to be delivered

internally around risk management, equally there will be some messages to be delivered around tax accounting. When we look at the external stakeholders there will be messages around corporate responsibility.

- Delivery—having sorted out what tax messages need to be communicated and who needs to receive the messages (the tax stakeholders), there is then the question as to what is the best method of delivery; and
- Review and refine—once a delivery mechanism has been in position for a period of time, then the success of the communication needs to be assessed and if necessary refined.

This approach may feel overly proscriptive. However the overall perception from many non-tax people is that tax is a complex subject, being something which is outside their comfort zone. It is often a subject they have avoided. We therefore see communication as being one of the key enablers for the tax function and if it is that important, it needs to be done properly.

[B] Stakeholders

In looking at the various stakeholders in tax you will need to think through what response you want from them in respect of the communication. The responses will fall into the four categories set out below, together with examples of where they apply to tax.

1. Knowing—this is just imparting of knowledge to them (e.g. the investor community).
2. Thinking—where they start giving some thought to the knowledge which has been imparted and how it might impact on them (e.g. customers, suppliers).
3. Feeling—where they start to buy-in, or not, to what they are seeing and hearing (e.g. the board), and finally
4. Doing—where they actually take some actions in relation to the communication with them (e.g. finance people who are providing information for tax returns).

To get people to phase four, they normally have to go through the first three phases to get there (and sometimes more than once). One of the major failings in any communication programme is the expectation that the recipients of knowledge would automatically move into the doing phase without having had a chance to think things through and feel comfortable with what they are being asked to do.

[C] Quantity

We live in what is called a 'communication age' where there is a vast amount of information being thrown at each and every one of us both as part of our jobs and as part of everyday life. Often we have great difficulty sorting out what is important from what is irrelevant. Equally we have a tendency to ask for everything we might possibly need, without really understanding the impact on those we are seeking this information from.

For each stakeholder in tax, we therefore break information down into three categories, namely that which:

1. We must have to do our jobs;
2. Is important to have—but it is not crucial; and
3. Is nice to have.

As a recipient of information we need to stop and think about the cost/benefit of that which fits into the 'nice to have' category and whether this is something which we could really do without. As a deliverer of information we need to put ourselves in the shoes of the recipient and ask whether we are giving them enough information or whether we are overloading them with too much (which often results in them taking none of it on board).

[D] Quality

As we all know different methods of communication are more effective than others. There is almost an inverse correlation between the effort needed to communicate and the ease with which the messages are received by those we communicate with. For example consider the relative effort and impact of:

- Face to face meetings;
- Telephone calls;
- E-mails; and
- Databases.

§ 21.03 INTERNAL STAKEHOLDERS

In other parts of this guide we have highlighted where the tax function needs to communicate with various different internal stakeholders and the subjects where good communication is needed. In this chapter we will summarise briefly the comments we have made elsewhere and refer you to those sections for more detailed comments.

[A] The Board and Senior Management

In the chapter on developing the strategic plan we talked about communication with the board and getting their buy-in to the overall strategy for managing tax. We talked about the tax function having regular (i.e. at least once a year) access to the board. The board needs to have a high level understanding of the group's tax issues, be involved in approving the overall strategy and be comfortable that the controls in place to deliver the strategy; the tax function needs the board's approval that the tax strategy is acceptable and consistent with where the rest of the business is going.

More regular communication will be needed with the CFO (and probably the CEO as well). In many organisations the head of tax and the CFO meet on a monthly basis to ensure the CFO is aware and is consulted on all major tax issues and the tax function is aware of what is happening more widely in the business.

[B] Business Unit/Functional Departments

Interaction with those within the business was covered in a number of chapters including those on other stakeholders in tax, and on tax risk management, and will be further covered in the chapters on tax accounting and reporting and on tax compliance. The message here is that tax needs to be embedded in many parts of the business and it is crucial for proper management of the tax affairs of a group that the tax function have good working relationships with those in the business. This is often achieved by tax people 'marking' their counterparts in the business so that mutual understanding and trust builds up between the two. As shown in the diagram below a trusting and open relationship between tax and the business is much more conducive to a joint solving of issues.

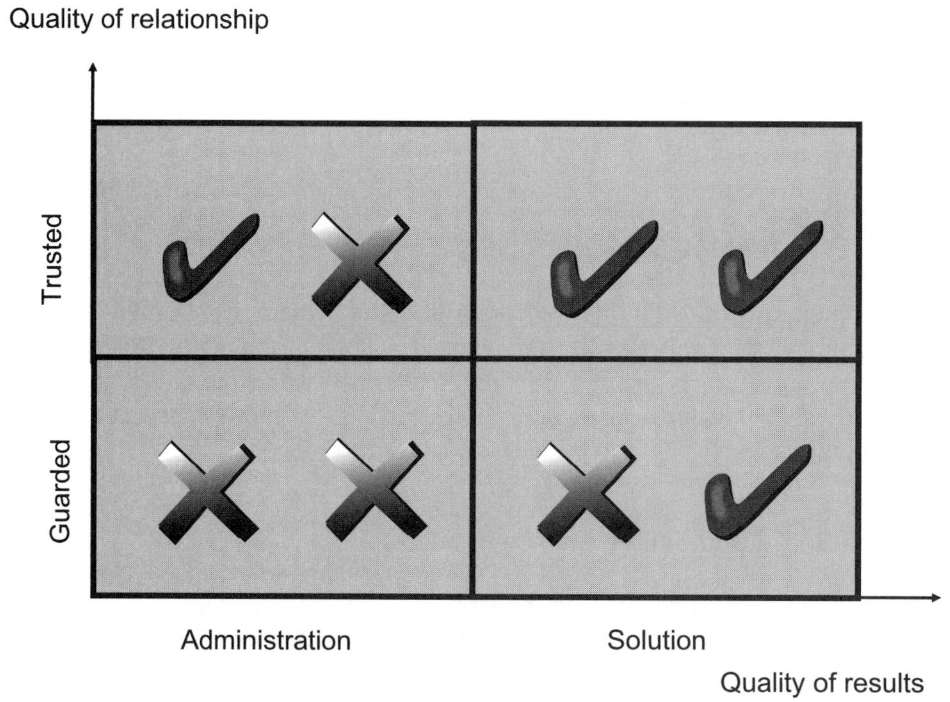

Where a business is measured on a PBT (profit before tax) basis, achieving a close relationship between tax people and the business can be quite a challenge.

[C] Within the Tax Function

One of the key areas of communication is within the tax function itself. Where there are only a small number of people this can probably be fairly informal. However for larger tax functions and particularly where there are people based in different business units or countries more formal processes are essential. This may be no more than a monthly call for those who have not been contacted for a few weeks; it could be a monthly report to the head of tax from their direct reports.

We do recommend the tax team, as a group, getting together at least once a year to focus on the bigger picture as opposed to their day to day activities. In the same way as we recommend the head of tax taking the tax strategic plan to the board once a year, so should the tax team consider where they are going and what they are going to focus on going forward. This is also an important opportunity for the head of tax to articulate their expectations for communications from the wider team especially where it is decentralised. Whether this meeting is part of agreeing what is taken to the board, or is feedback from the board meeting will depend on individual situations. However having this meeting around the same time as any board presentation makes a lot of sense.

§ 21.04 SERVICE LEVEL AGREEMENTS

For those who want to put some formality around the communication process, we have set out below a simple service level agreement (SLA) which we have used with some of our clients. This allows the tax function and the different parts of the business firstly to think through what they need from each other, secondly how they are going to communicate and finally put some measurement around how well the communication is working. SLAs are not for everyone; however where there have been issues and a proper structure is needed they may be helpful.

Between:	**[Stakeholder] and Tax function**
[Stakeholder] needs from Tax function	
Must have: Should have: Nice to have:	
Tax function needs from [Stakeholder]	
Must have: Should have: Nice to have:	
Communication protocols	
The Tax function will: The [Stakeholder] will:	
Measurement of success (Key Performance Indicators)	
(Probably no more than 4—to include key improvements)	
1 2 3 4	
Signed by: [Stakeholder] .... Tax function .... Date	
Date of next review:	

§21.05 EXTERNAL STAKEHOLDERS

Communication with revenue authorities was covered in the chapter on regulatory compliance. However, there is more to be said about communication with both the investment community and government authorities and these are dealt with below.

[A] Tax Transparency Framework

In the chapters on investor expectations and the one on corporate responsibility we flagged up the need for companies to be more transparent about the taxes they pay. In PwC we have taken this concept a stage further and introduced the tax transparency framework. We would encourage groups to think about what they want to communicate in their financial statements, their corporate responsibility reporting and in other external communication.

In an increasingly transparent world the tax affairs of a group might be reported under the three headings set out below:

- Tax strategy and risk management, where the communication should include:
  - a clear discussion of the company's tax strategy and objectives;
  - full details of how the company's tax strategy and function is managed and who in the organisation has responsibility for governance and oversight;
  - clear disclosure of the material tax risks faced by the company.
- Tax numbers and performance, which should include:
  - a clear explanation as to why the current tax charge is not equivalent to the accounting profit at the statutory rate of tax;
  - a transparent reconciliation of the company's cash tax payments to the tax charge included in the income statement;
  - disclosure of forward looking measures for tax, including forecast accounting and cash tax rate.
- The group's total tax contribution and the wider impact of taxes. This should include:
  - detail as to how tax impacts the wider business strategy and results of the company;
  - disclosure of the impact of tax on shareholder value;
  - clear communication of the economic contribution of all taxes paid by the company.

By way of example, consider the following extracts from recent reports of two large multinationals.

Taxes paid directly to governments by country*		
	Borne	Collected
South Africa	1,034	551
Chile	1,032	10
United Kingdom	235	325
Australia	234	57
Austria	48	90
Brazil	85	48
Russia	83	20
France	44	39
Venezuela	77	1
Canada	5	56
Poland	46	14
Others	196	125
Total	3,119	1,336

* Unaudited amounts of taxes payable directly to governments operations (borne) and amounts collected and remitted to gove employee taxes and net value-added tax (collected).

Tax compliance and planning
The Group has a tax strategy which has been reviewed and endorsed by the Board of Directors of Anglo American. Central to this strategy is that the Group's "Good Citizenship" business principles are followed in pursuing our tax planning and in dealing with tax authorities globally, and that the tax strategy is aligned with the Group's long-term business strategy.

Source: Anglo American report to Society 2006

Tax

Vodafone paid £2.5 billion in taxes across the countries in which it operates in the 2007 financial year. We believe it is important to state clearly and precisely our views on tax in the context of corporate responsibility.

We operate within a clearly defined Group Tax Code of Conduct. This sets out the principles, responsibilities, conduct and approach to working relationships of all tax professionals working in (and with) Vodafone.

We believe our obligation is to pay the amount of tax legally due and to observe all applicable rules and regulations in all of the territories in which we operate. At the same time, we have an obligation to maximise shareholder value and to manage financial and reputational risk. This includes minimising and controlling our tax costs. We accept that some may not share this view and believe that transparency regarding our position is the best policy.

Source: Vodafone corporate responsibility report 2007

Both of these are examples of the increasing trend for greater transparency in what is reported around both taxes paid and collected. Both have gone a long way beyond what is needed under local regulatory requirements.

The point to focus on here is what message you want to give to the external community and how do you best do so. This is clearly a question which should involve more than just the tax function. The investor relations and perhaps also the company's external public relations advisors should probably be involved. Use of diagrams and pictures will certainly help get the message across.

In considering what message you want to give the external community it is also necessary to think through who you want to get the message across to. One of the key external stakeholders is the different government authorities in the countries in which your group does business. Setting out the table above showing how much you are contributing to their treasury is a powerful way to demonstrate both your importance to them and the fact that the headline rate of tax in the accounts is but a small part of your overall tax contribution.

[B] Influencing Governments

Your total tax contribution in a particular country is also a good starting point for a dialogue with the government. However in many countries the discussions between companies and government authorities goes much further than how much tax you should or do pay to them. Indeed in some countries, such as the US, lobbying of governments has become a business in itself. It is our opinion that it is the duty of a responsible tax function to engage with government authorities both in respect of tax policy and the creation of tax law. This is not just a question of arguing for a favourable tax break; it involves helping get a better tax system that is less burdensome to all concerned.

How you deal with governments in this respect will vary considerably from country to country. Local custom and culture will clearly need to be taken into account. However there are some generic comments which we believe apply across a number of different jurisdictions.

- What do you want to influence?

The issue on which you wish to influence government could range from a high level tax policy issue, through a change in tax law to just how existing tax law is operated in practice. It may be something on which the government has asked for consultation; it may be one where you, as a business, feel strongly something should be changed.

- Who to speak to?

In trying to influence change to tax law or practice, there are a vast number of different entry points. The issue may be of such magnitude that you start at the President/Prime Minister level. It may be that you start at the tax policy makers; or alternatively it may be the local revenue authorities who can help you achieve your objectives.

Many heads of tax are members of their industry bodies and working through an industry body is an excellent way of getting some weight behind a particular issue. It is also noticeable that those who are regular contributors (perhaps through an industry body) are those who are listened to more often. There is a question here about being credible in this space.

If there is a local angle then involving a local member of parliament/ congressman could be a way forward. In some countries—notably the US—using paid lobbyists to advise on how to argue for change, and then having them take forward the arguments, is a well-worn route.

What is clear is that you need to think through very carefully as to what is the right point of entry. It may be that your local chairman or CEO has very good contacts and you can tap into their network.

Finally, do not discount the power of the press. Using the press to help lobby for a change in legislation is often a long-term strategy; a regular drip feed of articles to the press can have significant impact. At the same time, it needs to be borne in mind that trying to conduct a tax dispute with the authorities through the press can be counter-productive.

- How to influence government

Again different methods will work better in different countries. Probably the single biggest issue for governments is to look at the cost/benefit analysis of any changes they are being asked to make, and in particular the impact on their revenues. (They are usually being asked for a tax cut, not a tax rise.) Therefore a well presented argument which includes this analysis is going to have more impact than something which is not so thorough.

In summary influencing government is something that can and should be undertaken by tax functions. There are numerous different ways of doing this and best practice dictates that you evaluate your own position, the contacts you have and then put a plan of campaign into operation. This should involve others within the organisation; indeed the largest businesses often have a government relations advisor to help on exactly this type of work.

§ 21.06 THE COMMUNICATION PLAN

This chapter has discussed a number of different stakeholders, what they need from the tax function, what the tax function needs from them as well as a number of different methods of communication. The best practice tax function should pull these various strands together into a communication plan. This would set out:

- Who you will communicate with;
- What both sides need from each other;
- How the communication will take place, and
- How often it will happen.

The content may be similar to the SLA above; but this is an internal tax function plan which will drive the communication between the tax function and both internal and external stakeholders.

§ 21.07 SUMMARY

We would challenge whether tax functions have given as much attention to communication in the past as the subject warrants. If we go back a number of years the tax function was often seen as a black hole and not really connected with the rest of the business. Clearly things have moved on a long way since then but we believe there is more still to be done. We recommend that you consider bringing together a communication plan so that you are clear what messages you want to give and to which stakeholders, and what you need from them. You also need to be clear where the priorities lie. The challenge then is to make sure that the plan is implemented.

Chapter 22

TAX PLANNING

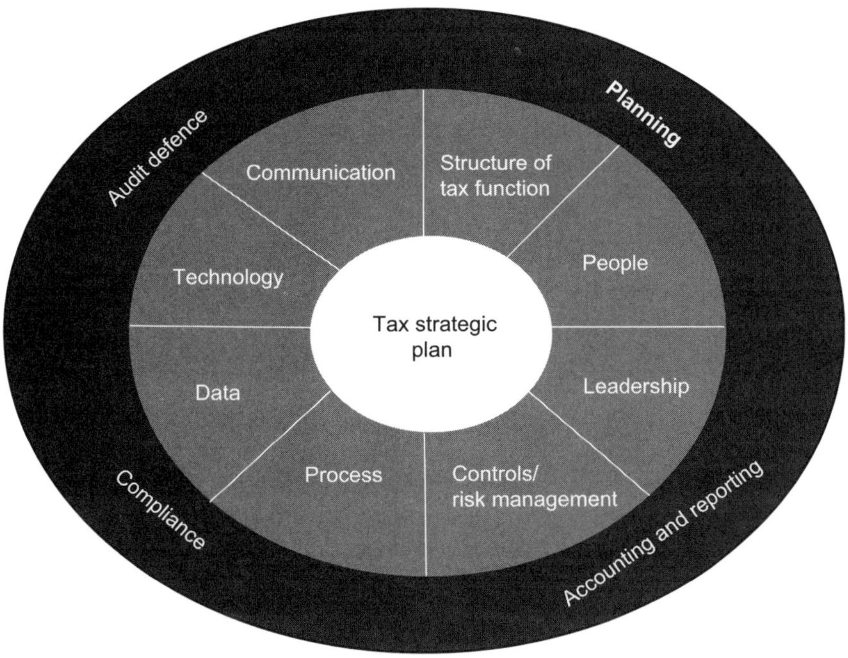

§22.01 INTRODUCTION

The previous eight chapters have focused on the tax function enablers, those things which need to be in place if the tax strategy is to be properly and efficiently implemented. We now come to look at the end product—the four deliverables for the tax function, the first of which is tax planning.

A core objective of the tax function should be to optimise value within the business. Tax planning which is focussed on optimising tax outcomes in relation to strategic transactions and day to day operations is the main vehicle through which the tax function contributes value to the business. In many cases, tax could be key to the achievement of corporate goals and critical to competitiveness. Tax planning therefore is one of the key deliverables for a tax function.

So how do you decide what tax planning you should or should not do? What factors do you need to take into account when a tax planning strategy or idea is under consideration in respect of your organisation? The purpose of this chapter is to set out some of the areas which need to be considered in answering these two questions, and to provide a template which can be used to evaluate which ideas should be taken forward and which are not appropriate for your organisation.

§22.02 THE OVERALL STRATEGY

In the chapter on documenting the strategic plan (chapter 13) we introduced the tax planning template, and asked the question as to how actively you want to manage your tax charge, what appetite for risk you were prepared to accept and what resources you were prepared to spend on tax planning. Any tax planning you undertake needs to be consistent with how you scored your business on the template.

In the chapter on corporate responsibility (chapter 6) we raised the need to consider your organisation's position on corporate responsibility in relation to tax planning. Certain types of tax planning will not be considered acceptable to your organisation from a corporate responsibility perspective, let alone within your acceptable risk profile. The important point here is that any tax planning you carry out also needs to be consistent with your corporate responsibility agenda.

§22.03 BENEFITS OF TAX PLANNING

The value that can derive from a particular tax planning strategy could relate to cash savings, cash flow benefits and benefits to the P&L account or effective tax rate. Alternatively, the value of some tax planning could relate to protecting against unintended or adverse tax consequences, such as double taxation or uncreditable foreign taxes. Additionally there is a role in supporting business units achieve their business strategy objectives in a tax efficient manor. Indeed the overall benefit might include a combination of these different items. In any tax planning exercise it is worth focusing on which of these benefits are arising and how these particular benefits fit in with the overall tax strategy. If you have not already done so, it may be worth developing modelling tools which can look at both the cash benefits and the accounting implications under a number of 'what if' scenarios.

§ 22.04 RISK MANAGEMENT

As noted above in the chapter on documenting the tax strategic plan we set out a template for looking at both the aggressiveness of tax planning which was appropriate to an organisation, together with the level of risks which you might be prepared to accept. However not only is it the level of risk inherent in the tax planning idea which is important, but you also need to consider the risks of the tax planning not being properly implemented. Revenue authorities are typically asking for all the underlying documentation relating to tax planning and if the paperwork does not support what you believe has been done then there is a high risk that the tax planning will not deliver the benefits expected.

Additionally, revenue authorities are 'scoring' companies on their risk profile. Companies which are being seen to be more aggressive in the tax planning arena are coming under more scrutiny, not only on their tax planning but also in other areas. This emphasises the need for any tax planning to be consistent with the organisation's risk profile and be managed within the parameters of the risk management framework.

§ 22.05 IMPACT ON THE BUSINESS

There is an interesting debate to be had around the impact of tax planning on the day-to-day operations in a business. Some will argue that if a tax planning idea impacts the business on a more than marginal basis, then that tax planning should not be carried out. The argument here is the tax tail should not be wagging the commercial dog. However when considering all business planning and indeed most day-to-day commercial decisions, tax should be considered and the appropriate tax planning included in the process.

However, some tax planning strategies will involve a fundamental change to a company's business model. The introduction, for example, of commissionaire arrangements, the moving of intellectual property and the introduction of cost plus manufacturing activities could all fall into this category. We are increasingly seeing a very positive shift towards planning which is integrated with the fundamental operations of the business where the value created from planning justifies real business change.

§ 22.06 RECOGNITION OF TAX BENEFIT

Many companies, particularly public companies, have placed a much greater emphasis on achieving effective tax rate savings rather than cash savings.

We have seen a number of cases where companies have decided not to try and obtain significant cash tax benefits, on the grounds that these benefits can not be recognised in the accounts. This lack of recognition might be due to accounting interpretations not allowing the benefits to be recognised until they are reasonably certain; they might be because a tax credit in the P&L account is compensated by a deferred tax debit.

Equally there is often nervousness that if a benefit is recognised before the tax treatment has been agreed by the revenue authorities, there is a risk of a restatement of the figures in later years' accounts.

While making earnings a priority is a very reasonable approach, achieving cash tax savings can be of significant value as a means of supporting the company's business financing needs. Tax executives should collaborate with the treasurer and CFO to make sure that initiatives that will significantly increase tax cash flow are analysed on a cost of funds basis consistent with how the company analyses its internal cost of funds.

§ 22.07 PROJECT MANAGEMENT

In any tax planning exercise there are a number of steps which need to be taken. These include:

1. Evaluation;
2. Implementation, and
3. Ongoing care and maintenance.

Many tax planning strategies fail to deliver the expected benefits either because of poor implementation or because, after the planning, someone does something which causes the planning to unravel. Poor implementation, rather than the tax planning itself, is in our experience one of the most common sources of tax risk. We would suggest procedures are put in place to ensure that the implementation is carried out as intended. For example, ensuring the tax function oversees the implementation where a business unit or the finance function is responsible for carrying it out. We also recommend a post implementation review (possibly from someone who has previously worked for a revenue authority) for any significant tax planning.

Our view is that most tax planning should not be done in isolation by the tax function and should involve the relevant business units and other corporate functions, such as the finance function, treasury and legal. The planning may also require the auditors to be involved to opine on the accounting treatment. The project management therefore needs to incorporate these stakeholders in the planning.

§ 22.08 COMPLIANCE AND DISCLOSURE

We have stated elsewhere in this guide that we do not see non-disclosure of information to tax authorities as a viable option. Therefore in any planning it has to be assumed that the full facts will be available to the revenue authorities. Indeed in the US certain types of tax planning have to be disclosed as 'reportable transactions'. It therefore follows that in any tax planning consideration should be given at an early stage to how the planning will be reflected in the appropriate tax returns. Not only is disclosure important, but it also impacts the future ability to negotiate the tax treatment with the revenue authorities.

The more aggressive a tax planning strategy is the more likely it is to be challenged and indeed the more likely it is to end up in the tax courts. Before entering into any form of tax planning, companies should ensure that the inherent risk in the planning is in accordance with the company's desired risk profile and consider whether senior management would be prepared to support the issue being pursued through the tax courts if challenged by a tax authority.

§ 22.09 EVALUATING TAX PLANNING IDEAS

The starting point for tax planning for any business should be an understanding of the corporate objectives and tax profile of the company. However there are still a number of tax planning ideas being brought to tax functions where the planning is not driven by the operational side of the business. We have been often asked by clients as to how they should evaluate these ideas.

While there is no one right answer, we do set out below a template which you might find useful. The approach involves the company evaluating what is important to them in tax planning and then to take a particular strategy or idea and score it against those particular criteria. By weighting the criteria you can then come up with a 'weighted result' which you can compare with a pre-set benchmark as to what is acceptable and what is not.

The criteria will undoubtedly differ from business to business. Those where cash is the overriding factor will have different criteria to where the accounting profit outcome is more important. Companies which have a low risk threshold will have different criteria to those who are more aggressive. What is important is that the criteria are set before looking at any particular tax planning ideas. Each idea can then be evaluated against the overall criteria for the organisation.

EVALUATION OF TAX PLANNING

Summary of tax planning strategy or idea:

	Key criteria	*Relative importance (out of 10)*	*Score (out of 10)*	*Weighted result*	*Maximum score*
1	**Strategic**				
	• Fit with tax strategic plan	X	Y	(X × Y)	(X × 10)
	• Risk appetite				
	• Corporate responsibility				
	• Simplicity (v complexity)				
	•				
	•				
2	**Benefit**				
	• Cash saving				
	• Cash flow saving				
	• P&L recognition				
	• Timing of accounts recognition				
	• Shareholder value				
	•				
	•				
3	**Risk**				
	• Likelihood of success				
	• Success of others				
	• Impact on business				
	• Reputational impact				
	• Revenue authority challenge				
	• Legislative change				
	•				
	•				
4	**Cost/downside**				
	• Payback period				
	• Return on investment				
	• Implementation cost				
	• Defence cost				
	• Of failure				
	•				
	•				
	Total			Score: %:	Max score: Target %:

The 'score' (4th column) ranks how well an item meets the requirements of that criteria. A score of 10 represents the best possible fit (i.e. high cash benefit, high chance of success, low risk, low cost). A score of zero represents no fit.

§ 22.10 SUMMARY

Carrying out tax planning as part of a company's strategic business planning and day-to-day commercial transactions is a key deliverable of the tax function. Minimising both cash taxes and accounts charges for tax are areas where the tax function can contribute significant value and therefore they warrant an appropriate amount of time and effort. However the ground rules around tax planning have changed in most countries over the last few years and companies need to ensure that whatever tax planning is carried out is in line with their overall tax strategy.

CHAPTER 23
TAX ACCOUNTING AND REPORTING

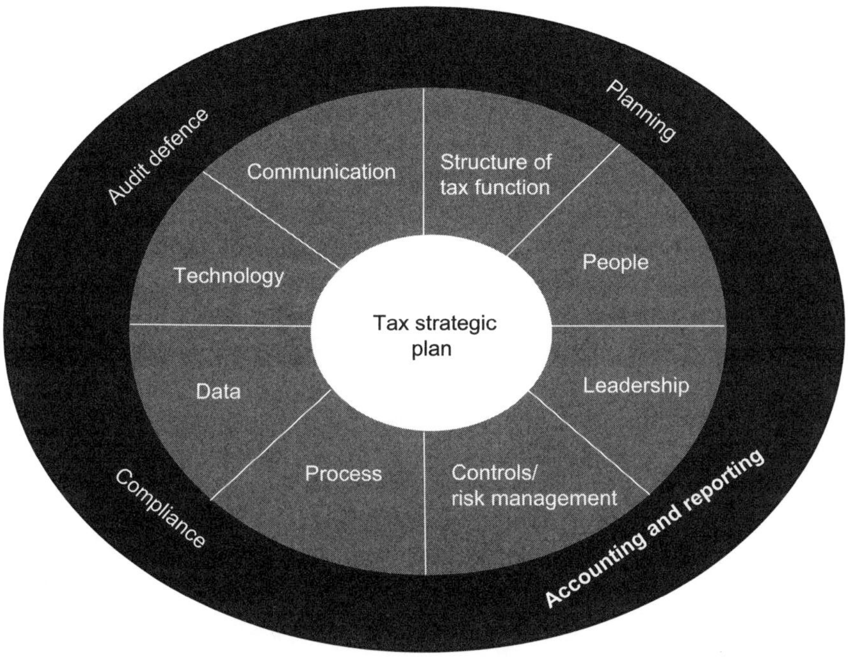

§23.01 INTRODUCTION

Over the past few years we have seen tax accounting and reporting become increasingly important such that it is now one of the key deliverables in relation to tax. The high number of material weaknesses reported in this area under the US section 404 rules has highlighted the fact that many tax accounting processes are not as effective as they should be. As a result the focus from management and hence the time and resources spent on tax accounting and reporting has increased considerably around the world.

The purpose of this chapter is to flag up some of the key issues around the approach, the people, the processes and the technology in delivering a best practice tax accounting and reporting system. Let us start however with reminding ourselves of the deliverables and the main risks in this area.

§23.02 DELIVERABLES

The key deliverables in this area are the figures for the corporate tax charge in the financial statements (in the P&L account, on the balance sheet, the figures appearing in the various notes to the accounts together with any notes on tax policies). However tax figures are also needed for forecasting and increasingly, as noted in the chapter on communication, we are seeing groups reporting, in their accounts, their total tax contribution—all the taxes they both suffer and collect.

Tax accounting is therefore not just about getting the figures right. It also involves understanding who the stakeholders in tax are and how the accounts can be used as part of the communication strategy. The tax function may also be responsible for the tax accounting for other taxes, such as indirect taxes and employment taxes.

§23.03 RISK ISSUES

'No surprises' is often the underlying agenda here. Groups look for the effective tax rate either to be consistent throughout the year, from the quarterly and half year reporting through to the year end accounts or, at the very least, to be in line with projections. The accounts need to be consistent with the forecasts. However there are a number of issues which are giving rise to risks (and surprises) in the tax accounting and reporting area.

The first of these is the underlying uncertainty in the figures themselves. However good both the people and the processes are in preparing the figures, they are based on interpretation of tax law where the company's view and that of the local revenue authorities may be different. This will include not only where revenue authorities are challenging figures in tax returns which have already been submitted, but will also include uncertainties over interpretation in respect of the current year figures which have yet to be submitted.

Both tax rules and accounting rules have becoming increasing complex. For multinational groups people are often dealing with a number of different tax systems and more than one set of accounting standards, sometimes for the same entity (e.g. the US FAS 109 and also IAS 12, though this may change if global accounting standards finally converge). The second key risk we are therefore seeing is that there is a lack of suitably qualified people to do the work to the required standard. What is needed are individuals with both tax technical as well as accounting knowledge. Not only is there a shortage of such people, but as we write this guide there is limited training available in the global market to ensure that people do have the requisite tax accounting skills to do this work.

Thirdly the processes for delivering tax figures have historically not been well documented and controls in this area, which are predominantly manual controls, have often been less than adequate as compared to today's best practice. There is certainly considerable opportunity for process improvement as we explained in an earlier chapter.

As already noted, CFOs do not want surprises from the tax figures in the accounts. The implications of getting them wrong will range from personal embarrassment, through prior year adjustments to restatement of the accounts and possible disclosure of material weaknesses in the controls. Between them, these possible implications are a strong driver to ensure that the tax figures in the accounts are correct within established materiality limits.

§ 23.04 PEOPLE

One of the first questions to address is who has ownership within an organisation over tax accounting and reporting. In the majority of cases we see it is the tax function who has the overall ownership; however we still also see a number of cases where the tax accounting and reporting is very much driven by the finance function with tax having very limited input (perhaps only on tax technical matters and discussions around status of tax returns with revenue authorities).

This ownership question needs to be addressed at both local level and at head office/consolidation level. In one model, local finance people input basic financial information into the standard collection pack used for the consolidation. The tax function then extracts these figures and uses these as the basis of the tax provision calculated on behalf of the local entities. In another model, the local entities complete calculations of local tax and then input the accounting entries required for year end reporting. These numbers are then consolidated by group tax or the finance function.

Certainly where tax people come from a legal training/background then there are arguments that they are not necessarily best placed to sort out tax figures for the accounts. Equally it could be argued that accounting people may not properly understand the tax issues, and hence the uncertainties in the tax figures, and that they are also not best placed to take ownership.

In our experience the collaborative model whereby people who understand the tax issues work very closely with people who understand the accounting is the best way forward. Probably the initial preparation of the figures has to be with tax people, as it is usually based on figures which are in or are going into tax returns which have been/are to be sent to revenue authorities. We would stress that clarity of ownership around both the figures and the process is vital.

Due to the shortage of people with the appropriate skills we are also seeing an increasing use of external third party providers to help in this area, either on a co-sourcing or an outsourcing basis. In some cases this can result in the full outsourcing of the preparation of the figures; in others it could just be a review, for example, in certain countries to ensure that the relevant accounting principles have been properly applied.

§23.05 OVERALL APPROACH

To a large extent the accounting standards (e.g. FAS 109 and IAS 12 together with FIN 48) dictate what work needs to be done in relation to the tax figures in the accounts. However the published numbers need only be materially correct and this has led, in many organisations, to the development of streamlined approaches to tax accounting that rely on the use of assumptions to reduce the amount of work required to produce the final figures.

Some of the different approaches we have seen are noted below:

[A] Risk Based Approach

Best practice dictates that the work performed on the accounting figures should focus on the areas of greatest risk. The starting point should therefore be a risk assessment exercise and a decision as to where the time and resources should best be spent. For example some groups have decided to use assumptions around the tax rate in smaller (and hence less material) companies/countries. The focus of such groups is just on the material subsidiaries. This approach should link in with the risk and controls framework discussed in chapter 17.

[B] Period 11+

Preparing figures at the year end is a time consuming exercise. For a group of any size or complexity the consolidation process is also time consuming and logistically difficult. There is therefore often very limited time to stand back and consider what the figures actually mean. This has led a number of groups to do their detailed work based on period 11 figures with an adjustment post year end for period 12, with possibly less detailed work on the period 12 figures. This allows more time at the year end to analyse and comment on the figures. The same methodology could also apply at the half year and possibly also at the quarter end.

[C] Manual v Automated

To deliver tax figures of the required quality and to the reporting deadlines, companies have traditionally thrown people at the issues with limited use of technology around data collection. More recently a number of companies have brought in some degree of automation of their process either by making use of global finance systems, developing tools specific to the tax function or licensing 3rd party technology designed to support the tax accounting process.

[D] Tax Compliance and Accounting as a Single or Split Process

There is an ongoing argument in many countries as to how the tax accounting process should feed into the tax compliance process. Some groups take the view that it makes little sense to compile the tax computation numbers for the year end and then do basically the same work again for payment and submission of tax. Other groups take the view that the work is done to very different levels of accuracy (based on materiality), at different times of the year and often by different people and so should be kept distinct. As tax compliance and tax accounting systems become more integrated it will become much more efficient and effective to integrate the two processes.

§ 23.06 PROCESS

The tax figures in the accounts are made up of two distinct parts. The first are the figures relating to prior years, the second the current year tax charge. Separate processes may be needed for these two parts.

For prior years there will already be some figures in the accounts. They will be based on estimates made at the last year end (or perhaps even earlier). However since those figures were included in the accounts, tax returns will have been submitted, revenue authority correspondence, audits and investigations will have started (and may be concluded) and tax payments will have been made. The first part of the tax accounting and reporting process is therefore a 'true up' of the prior year figures. Decisions need to be made as to what tax provisions are needed in the accounts in respect of these earlier years. The introduction of FIN 48 in the US has tightened up the rules for some companies in respect of what can and can not be included here. Certainty over prior year tax positions is obviously a major bonus and the increasing concern over tax accounting is clearly a driver towards settling outstanding tax issues with revenue authorities.

In looking at the prior year position it is not only the corporate income tax figures which need reviewing. The prior year deferred tax position also needs to be considered. We are aware of a number of groups where deferred tax balances have been built up which, with hindsight, are extremely difficult to reconcile with the tax position as per agreed and submitted tax returns. The true up exercise therefore needs to consider both current and deferred taxes. This is certainly something which can be done prior to the year end.

The current year corporate tax charge is, by its very nature, one of the last figures in the accounts which can be finalised. It is dependent on a number of other figures being sorted before it can be agreed. This together with the increasingly shortened timeframe between the end of an accounting period and the announcement of the results has led to a number of different processes for arriving at the figures as noted above.

§23.07 TECHNOLOGY

The risks in the area of tax accounting and the time pressures at period ends logically dictate that for the larger groups some form of automated tax accounting and reporting system should be considered. Building in-house tax technology is usually cost prohibitive and requires resources be dedicated to maintaining and updating the system. However, as noted in chapter 20, there are an increasing number of technology solutions being developed in the market to help companies to deliver their tax accounting and reporting. Some of these (and currently the majority) are stand alone tax accounting systems. However in the future we may well also see ERP systems which fully incorporate tax accounting.

The technology on the market typically has two functions:

- The control of the tax accounting process, providing process control and workflow to ensure that all the work required concluding the tax accounting process happens on schedule and that delays are anticipated and dealt with.
- Tax accounting calculation software, allowing for collection of source data from systems, manipulation of this data for GAAP requirements and then reporting the data provided for multiple GAAPs. It is this element of the tax accounting software that is most attractive in the current environment where a single set of results can be reported for different GAAPs at the touch of a button.

Today there is probably no one market leader in this technology space and, for those organisations moving towards the automation route, one of their challenges is to choose the most appropriate package for their needs. The ultimate goal is an integrated accounting, tax reporting and tax compliance solution although at the moment there is a lack of products on the market offering a viable comprehensive solution.

However whatever tax provision technologies you decide to use you need to be aware that they will not necessarily solve all your control issues. Failure to properly implement provision technology has been cited as a contributing factor leading to a material weakness in tax. The value proposition around provision technology does not revolve around its unique ability to solve control deficiencies of itself. It is more an important enabler that allows experienced tax personnel to spend more of their time on analytics and less time collecting and validating data; it is about how processes can change in a technology enabled environment and not about how the solution is the software in isolation.

§ 23.08 CONTROLS

Having formal and documented controls around what they do is not something which tax people are generally used to—and this may explain the number of material weaknesses arising, under section 404, from tax accounting. However it is not just section 404 which demands proper controls; they are also part of general best practice. In preparing the tax figures you will know where the material items are and you will also probably know where the key risks lie. These are clearly the areas where proper controls need to be built into the process. The point to note here is that the controls are not just a review at the end of the process; they are part and parcel of the process itself. (For more details on controls see chapter 17.)

One of the key controls is around the people. We have already discussed the shortage of properly qualified people for tax accounting work. Best practice controls will include clear divisions of responsibility and proper training for both tax people and those in the finance function. Both types of people need to have enough knowledge of each other's specialism for the collaboration between the two to be seamless. The people need to have enough experience to know what can go wrong, to spot when this is happening and react accordingly when it does.

§ 23.09 NEWLY FORMED TAX FUNCTIONS

Whether formed via spin offs from a larger public company, merger of equals or an IPO, newly formed tax functions face a substantial hurdle to ensure they have proper processes in place, and, where applicable, they are compliant with section 404. The effort necessary to ensure compliance in the first year is considerable and comes at a time when other issues seem to be a priority, such as staffing and technical issues in connection with the transaction.

§ 23.10 ABOVE THE LINES TAXES

The comments set out above predominately relate to the tax charge in the accounts which represents current corporate income taxes and deferred taxes. However, there are also a number of taxes, such as indirect taxes and employment taxes, where the figures appear as part of the profit before tax, rather than in the tax line itself. Some of the points above will apply equally to these taxes as they do to the tax charge itself. They may not be quite so visible in the accounts, but if there are not proper processes in place to review the provisions which may be required, then there are risks of some nasty surprises appearing at some later date.

§23.11 SUMMARY

Tax accounting and reporting is an area where the risk of getting things wrong can be very high profile with resulting reputational damage. Errors can even have an effect on the pricing of publicly offered stock. It is an area where we expect to see significant changes and developments over the next few years. This is an area ripe for process improvement and for more technology driven solutions.

CHAPTER 24
REGULATORY COMPLIANCE AND AUDIT DEFENCE

"Compliance is where the rubber meets the road"

§24.01 INTRODUCTION

For tax functions, compliance has always been viewed as a key deliverable and for many organisations remains *the* key deliverable. Whether that enables the tax function to achieve the right balance between compliance and the other key deliverables is an issue that has been discussed in other chapters. But the fact remains that ensuring compliance is both timely and accurate continues to be the most common KPI for a tax function. It is the window through which the wider world views the organisation and is therefore a critical element of its overall risk profile. With that in mind, this chapter discusses how better performing tax functions manage compliance, locally and globally.

Audit defence is inextricably linked with regulatory compliance. In theory the higher the quality of the compliance process, the better the returns and the less for revenue authorities to audit or investigate. Therefore in this same chapter we also discuss audit defence, another of the tax function deliverables.

§24.02 WHAT WE MEAN BY COMPLIANCE

Firstly, we will explain what we mean by compliance. In keeping with the approach we have taken in relation to defining an organisation's tax strategy or determining its total tax contribution, compliance means any filing and reporting obligation required by regulation in a particular territory concerning a tax, whether or not the responsibility of the tax function.

§24.03 THE KEY COMPLIANCE CHALLENGES

In managing compliance, there are some common challenges that organisations, especially global organisations, experience. We would categorise some of the challenges as follows:

[A] Managing to Deadlines

Compliance deadlines are hard deadlines that typically carry significant penalty ramifications for the organisation if missed. Keeping up with constantly looming deadlines, especially for growing organisations with limited resources is clearly one of the key challenges in relation to compliance. Lack of resources (often in conjunction with a lack of focus on compliance) is the key reason why organisations miss deadlines, in some cases year after year and finding themselves multiple years behind.

[B] Managing People Resources

Managing people is often cited as the main issue for a tax function in relation to compliance, particularly hiring and retaining people with appropriate skills for compliance work. Those tax functions that have been grown as a compliance team may have developed significant teams of compliance people of all levels. Providing challenging and rewarding work and career progression options for compliance people is a real dilemma for tax functions.

[C] Global Compliance Management

Historically many companies have given the primary responsibility for tax compliance outside of the headquarters country to the local or regional finance function. In fact, many tax functions only had a very limited role with respect to global tax compliance. Over the past few years we have seen a very positive trend toward the tax function assuming primary responsibility for global corporate income tax compliance. Proactively managing compliance so the tax function knows the status of all group tax returns, payments, and current and pending audits is a major undertaking but critical to the company's overall risk management and control environment.

[D] Technology

Accessing data either directly or through a myriad of accounting or tax personnel from the many disparate accounting and tax systems relied on by tax functions is an ongoing challenge in managing compliance.

[E] Data

The input of quality data has a direct impact on the efficiency and quality of the resulting regulatory filing. With many tax functions, data is accepted on a 'take what you can get' basis. The result then is significant manipulation of data in order to get it into the form that is needed to begin the compliance process. The result is a disproportionate amount of time spent in the compliance process on data manipulation rather than data analysis. This lack of quality, tax sensitized data also has a direct impact on audit defence, often requiring a significant amount of time to produce the supporting detailed transactions that reconcile to the tax filing.

[F] Managing the Cost of Compliance

Compliance is typically not viewed by organisations as a value-add deliverable for the tax function, so there is often a strong focus on cost and efficiency. In our view, the approach to compliance is a critical component of an organisation's overall risk profile and excessive focus on cost can compromise the tax function's risk management objective. Accordingly, there is a trade off between cost and risk management when it comes to compliance.

§24.04 HOW DO BEST PRACTICE TAX FUNCTIONS MANAGE THE COMPLIANCE CHALLENGES?

We have been asked many times what better performing tax functions do to manage the compliance challenges. While the approaches are many and what works for one organisation will not necessarily work for others, there are some common themes.

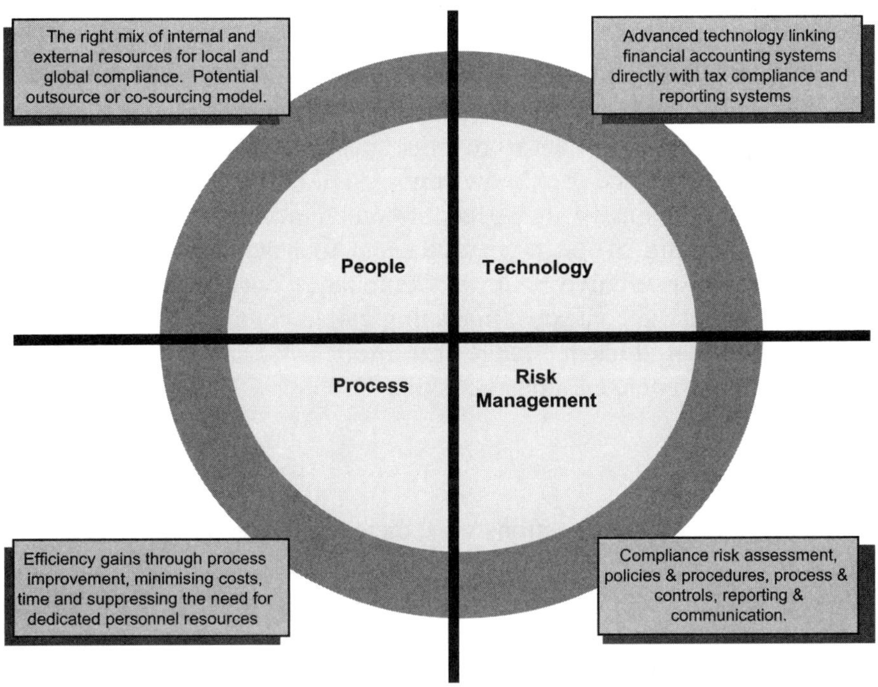

§24.05 PEOPLE AND STRUCTURE

Some key features of those organisations that are adapting well to the people challenges in relation to compliance include:

- Acknowledgement that efficient tax compliance requires a specialised skill set. An individual well qualified to undertake a complex analysis of an international tax agreement and the supporting case law with gusto, may not be very good at process design, project management, ongoing communication monitoring and planning. If these skills are not sufficiently available within the core tax function or it is not the desire of the organisation to hire and maintain the level of resources required to manage compliance on a timely basis, then the team needs to be supplemented from elsewhere inside or outside of the organisation.

- Acknowledgement that compliance is a business imperative being a critical part of the risk profile of the organisation. This means that people who specialise in compliance are given the right recognition, rewards and opportunity for development. Where possible there are dedicated resources for significant compliance periods to avoid the inefficient 'pick up and put down' approach to compliance.
- Properly defining compliance roles internally or externally through compliance outsourcing arrangements. For many organisations, there will be a mix of resources who have an involvement with compliance including business units, finance function, tax function and external service providers. Achieving the right mix of resources is critical from an efficiency perspective as well as balancing various other demands. Segregation of preparation and review roles is important from a risk management perspective.
- Overall confidence in acknowledging skill deficiencies through utilising third parties to assist in aspects of compliance. This may take the form of outsourcing of the preparation and management of compliance or high level qualitative reviews. Compliance outsourcing is particularly prevalent in the context of managing global compliance where the organisation's activities in a range of territories will not warrant a substantial finance presence, let alone tax skill.

§ 24.06 PROCESS

Better performing tax functions view the compliance process as key to both gaining efficiencies and therefore cost management as well as risk management. The single biggest impact on compliance process improvement is often achieved in relation to data collection. We have found that some organisations can spend up to 80% of their total compliance time on collecting the right data and in many cases, reworking that data.

Some of the other elements of process improvements we have seen include:

- Getting the timing of compliance right, better integrating the annual tax calculation and income tax return process and reducing the time lag between these parts of the process to avoid rework and duplication of effort.
- Improving the quality of source data. This can often involve a programme of awareness training for those responsible for coding data to the accounting system and, in particular, training accounting/finance function staff on tax problem areas in accounts. This can also establish accountability for accuracy.
- Project managing the compliance process using project management tools (or at a minimum a spreadsheet) to maintain responsibilities, task

status and timings Larger groups benefit from appointing a designated compliance co-ordinator. For a global organisation, a global compliance co-ordinator is an essential element of overall risk management.

- Connecting tax planning and advisory with compliance. Better performing tax functions formalise the connection between planning and compliance by ensuring the preparation of detailed and timely transaction summaries that clearly set out accounting and compliance treatments and scheduling time for briefing of the compliance team (whether internal or external).

§24.07 MANAGING THE COST OF COMPLIANCE THROUGH OFFSHORING

In addition to improving internal compliance processes, companies are looking at other ways to reduce the total cost of compliance while not adversely impacting on compliance risk. For some time, companies have looked to outsourcing as a means to reduce the cost of compliance particularly where, as discussed above, there is a skilled resource gap or it is not a company's preference to build an internal team with permanent employees dedicated to tax compliance.

A trend for companies that manage significant compliance burdens is to consider offshoring their compliance obligations to lower cost territories, often extending the scope of services provided by a shared service centre. An outsourcing arrangement with an external service provider may also involve some form of offshoring as means to minimise the cost of delivery. As you might expect, offshoring arrangements are most successful when high volume repetitive services are involved. While we have certainly found to date that the quality of the compliance service that certain offshore territories are capable of delivering is high, it may be difficult to offshore certain aspects of global compliance due to differing laws and tax compliance technologies. However, we see offshoring models for tax compliance continuing to develop in the future. (For further comments on shared service centres see chapter 29.)

§24.08 TECHNOLOGY

Increasing pressures for process efficiency, transparency and risk management has increased the use and sophistication of dedicated tax calculation software. Historically, many tax functions have used spreadsheets to support compliance (and tax accounting). The increasing use of software is not restricted to tax specific software, extending to enterprise resource planning systems, as well as other communication and project management tools. Typical features of this growing sophistication include:

- Process efficiency through automation of data from accounting systems, including general ledger systems.
- Building 'tax intelligence' into accounting and tax systems to automate various tax related calculations.

- Enhanced utilisation of work flow tools and web based tracking systems.
- Systems based capture of workings, notes and documents to provide an audit trail supporting the figures in tax returns.

There is a clear trend towards global organisations looking for technology solutions for global reporting on tax risks, compliance and tax accounting and to assist them with collecting and storing tax data. (For further comments on technology see chapter 20.)

§ 24.09 DATA

Technology and data are tightly coupled when it comes to reducing the pressures on the tax function for process efficiency, transparency and risk management. While sophisticated technology is helping with these pressures, the degree of manual intervention and data manipulation required often restricts the effectiveness of these new technologies,

Best practice tax functions are looking to:

- Have greater focus on data quality and the 'tax sensitivity' of accounting source data; i.e. how useful the information is for tax purposes without significant rework. This includes active participation in enterprise data governance processes to assure that tax data requirements are incorporated into the creation and maintenance of enterprise data.
- Increase the level of detail of data available to the tax function for transaction analysis and audit support.

(For more details on data management see chapter 19.)

§ 24.10 CONTROLS AND RISK MANAGEMENT

Tax functions are increasingly seeing the link between risk management and compliance and ensuring that their compliance policies and procedures align with their risk management objectives. As discussed in chapter 13, we recommend an organisation should define its compliance risk profile as part of its overall tax strategy.

Accordingly, we best practice in respect of compliance risk management might include:

- A defined compliance tax risk profile and compliance error thresholds that align with the risk profile of the organisation.
- Regular assessment of the key risk areas in compliance being undertaken and used as the basis to plan the scope and detail of work required across all taxes (e.g. what aspects of an income tax return are subject to detailed review).

- Effective project management of all compliance obligations to ensure they are met on a timely basis (e.g. payment of tax and filing of all VAT returns, across all territories).
- A structure put in place for reporting on the status of worldwide compliance obligations that integrates with external service providers. Many organisations have already moved to centralise the management of global compliance, using predominantly one external compliance service provider under a global contract.

§24.11 MANAGING AUDITS AND REVIEWS

Compliance is obviously the key link with revenue authorities in terms of the presentation of the tax positions adopted. It is a common feature of tax administration in all territories that tax filings can be the subject of review by a tax authority. This review might be superficial, based on the information in the filing and publicly available information, or it might be comprehensive, including examination of internal company information and interviews of personnel.

Therefore, better performing tax functions commonly adopt regulatory compliance strategies that properly consider how the positions taken in tax filings can be defended against review and adjustment by tax authorities. Such adjustments may arise either when the tax authority processes the tax filing on lodgement or at a later date when the filing is subject to review by the authority. The time that a filing remains 'open' for review will vary from territory to territory, and in some cases will remain open indefinitely.

Tax functions should ensure that their approach to defending filing positions will take into account a number of territory specific matters, including:

- The review processes adopted by the local taxing authority;
- The nature of the relationship the local taxing authority is seeking to have;
- The reason that the tax authority has chosen to conduct the review, including any hypothesis on the risk perceived to be present;
- The time available for the taxing authority to review the tax filing;
- The scope of authority the taxing authority have to review the filing;
- The coercive powers available to the taxing authority to require disclosure of documents or information;
- The sanctions that can be imposed on a company for non-compliance with requests from the taxing authority; and
- The financial penalties that can be imposed on a company for adopting positions in their filings that the taxing authority does not agree with, and the impact of defence strategies to decrease such penalties.

Taking into account these factors will often lead to better outcomes in a review. For example, in a number of cases we see that taxpayers can avoid extensive use of coercive powers by volunteering selected key documents at an early stage of an information gathering process, or by providing a presentation on the overall business model or transaction in focus.

Another area that is often overlooked relates to identifying opportunities to manage the scope of a taxing authority audit. Many tax functions allow the taxing authority to set the audit plan without taking advantage of special programs designed to streamline the audit process or accelerate the closing of the audit cycle. Given today's resource challenges and the importance of managing tax reserves, it is more important than ever to reduce audit cycle times and internal resource requirements.

Some other matters will have more general application, regardless of jurisdiction. We see that better performing tax functions develop a good relationship with their taxing authority—which can lead to better treatment from that authority in a number of areas, for example:

- The taxing authority will generally have more regard for the company's arguments in support of its filing positions;
- The chances of coercive powers being used to access documents will be lowered;
- There will be a greater likelihood of reduced penalties imposed on any incorrect filing positions; and
- If the territory has a system whereby the taxing authority can issue administrative rulings, then favourable rulings may be more forthcoming in a more timely fashion.

A tax function can look to outside sources for good relationships with a tax authority that can influence the overall outcome. For example, we have seen instances where external advisors with excellent tax authority relationships have been used to achieve outcomes in audits and reviews that were not considered likely to be achieved by the company itself.

Additionally, it is generally accepted that well documented tax positions will have greater likelihood of being upheld on review. What is meant by this is that companies should ensure that, in relation to transactions that have substantial tax outcomes, the following types of documents should be identified and retained in a discrete location so that they can be accessed with ease in response to any enquiries from a taxing authority:

- Core transaction contracts;
- Contemporaneous accounts;
- Other relevant transaction documents;
- Valuation materials;
- Contemporaneous commercial advice; and
- Final tax technical advice.

In one transaction, a well organised tax function had undertaken an extensive process of pulling together all relevant documentation at the time of a major restructuring, so that when the transaction was reviewed by the taxing authority a number of years later all the company had to do was pull out the pre-prepared document set and send it in. No further information requests were issued by the taxing authority and an enormous amount of time and resources were saved by being able to close off the information gathering process by the taxing authority in one hit.

If documents are subject to legal professional privilege, or documents are otherwise protected from disclosure to a taxing authority under local territory laws, then those documents should be marked clearly as being protected from disclosure.

The strategy for engagement with a taxing authority during the course of a review or audit will, as noted above, depend in part of territory specific matters. However, generally the most successful strategies will include a number of key elements:

1. Identify relevant evidence to support the filing position;
2. Make or obtain an objective and honest assessment of the prospects of defending a filing position, in light of current law;
3. Consider carefully what the desired outcomes are and how they might be achieved;
4. Establish 'rules of engagement' with the taxing authority, including a clear understanding of contact people on both sides and a jointly-developed plan for conducting and completing the review; and
5. Understand escalation processes, if any are available, including to who issues should be escalated.

In respect of these matters, independent external advisors will generally be able to provide objectivity on filing positions, based on the relevant rules of evidence in a particular territory. Such advisors, if they commonly deal with matters of controversy, will also be able to provide strategic advice or direct assistance in dealing with revenue authorities and Courts.

Prudent companies should also be mindful of the potential effect adjustments to filing positions may have on corporate accounting and financial reporting. With this in mind, when devising a strategy to manage a taxing authority review of filing positions, in circumstances where a such a review has commenced or is seen as likely to commence, companies should have regard to the corporate governance, reporting and disclosure issues that may arise from any potential adjustments and proactively manage those issues in advance.

§24.12 SUMMARY

Compliance and audit defence have always been key deliverables for the tax function. However they are not areas where best practice has been consistently applied across that many tax functions. Data collection, in particular, is often time consuming and frustrating hard work. Compliance in particular is an area where a focus on process improvement could well be an investment well spent.

CHAPTER 25
MANAGING CHANGE

"If you're not riding the wave of change, you'll soon find yourself beneath it"

§25.01 INTRODUCTION

In the Why section of this guide, we highlighted that tax functions are operating in a fast moving business environment and that they face changing regulatory considerations, changing tax regimes and changing reporting standards and control environments. Change is a constant in the tax world. The ability to respond to these changing conditions and to lead the tax function (and others) through these changes will be key to the effective performance of the tax function. In short, change management skills are vital skills for any head of tax.

This chapter is about how a tax function might go about managing change, which will include anything from minor day-to-day changes in how you work through to major transformational projects and even the significant changes that accompany mergers and acquisitions.

> *"Managing change is only going to get harder, because change is going to keep getting faster".*
>
> MNC head of tax

The way in which change needs to be managed must of course vary to suit the circumstances. However while much of what is written about change management focuses on big ticket transformation, we believe that many of the principles of managing change effectively apply right across the change spectrum for a tax function.

§25.02 EXAMPLES OF CHANGE

To anchor this chapter in reality for tax functions let us start by giving some examples of where we have worked with tax functions on a change agenda. These examples include:

- Where two groups have merged, bringing together two tax functions that are organised and work in very different ways.
- Where a new head of tax has been appointed (or where a new CFO has been appointed).
- Where an organisation has historically had tax losses and will shortly become a tax paying entity again.
- Where there has been an acquisition or divestiture that significantly changes the tax footprint in a major tax jurisdiction.
- Where there has been a business reorganisation, including where a business has introduced a shared service centre.

- Where, following the production of a tax strategic plan, it is recognised that the current organisational structure for the tax function is not 'fit for purpose'.
- Where there have been material weaknesses or significant deficiencies (under section 404) in the tax accounting controls.

We could give many more examples, some reflecting large changes and some small. However the examples above do highlight the fact that managing change is something which all tax functions should have on their agenda.

§ 25.03 CHANGE IS ABOUT PEOPLE

We know from recent research (Source: CSC Index/AMA Survey) that 41% of change projects fail and that of the 59% that 'succeed' only half meet the expectations of senior management. A survey that PricewaterhouseCoopers ran in conjunction with MORI in the late 1990's found that 9 out of the 10 top barriers to change are people related, with limited change management skills, poor communications and employee opposition all being cited.

In other words, management of change is not just about effective project management (as important as that is). Whether change is about organisation, process, technology or location, it is clear that all these changes impact on people. Organisations are first and foremost social systems. Focus on the human impact of change is therefore critical.

§ 25.04 WHO NEEDS TO CHANGE?

Over the last few years we have witnessed, and we continue to witness, major change in the nature of tax functions. More MNC tax functions are now typically recognised as being key to the business. Some have an increasing profile in the organisation and are engaging more regularly and effectively with other departments. This of course has meant change in the nature of the tax function itself and of the approach and skills of those within it. These changes will continue for the people within the tax function.

However part of the tax function's engagement with others in the business will involve changing the behaviours of those who have not had, or do not recognise having had, a tax agenda of their own. As the actions of many different groups of people may have tax implications (e.g. on tax risk), the tax function can find itself trying to change the behaviours of widely disparate groups of people outside even indirect 'dotted line' control, and these are often people with very different priorities. This presents a particularly tough challenge, which is perhaps evidenced by the difficulties tax functions typically experience in getting tax issues to the top of others' agendas and to-do lists.

The same comments might apply to those people in the shadow tax function (though these people should recognise that tax is on their agenda). The starting point here is to recognise who the different stakeholders are; who is it who needs to change their behaviours in order for tax to be better managed?

§ 25.05 RESISTANCE TO CHANGE

Resistance to change takes many forms, from outright obstruction, through lip service acquiescence (masking subtle opposition), to reluctant half-hearted compliance. However it is a misconception that it is basic human nature to resist change. People only resist change when it makes them feel anxious or out-of-control or it has clearly negative consequences for them personally. Effective change management therefore involves anticipating stakeholders' reactions to ideas of change and working to ensure they will understand and support the changes planned, rather than resist it.

It is also important to recognise that those personality types who do welcome change may not be those with the strongest reliability/dependability/process-following characters. This contrasts with those with more disciplined tendencies, which are often key to successful implementation, but who may generally be more unsettled by change.

§ 25.06 OVERCOMING RESISTANCE

The tax function will often have a powerful rationale for the need for change, including legal or regulatory requirements, material risk issues to address and of course the impact of tax on shareholder value. However compelling as some of these arguments will be, it will not normally be logic alone which leads stakeholders to change their individual behaviours or to acclimatise to different circumstances.

What motivates people is an individual matter and therefore different stakeholders may need to have their issues addressed in different ways. This means that there will normally be a number of strands in an effective change management programme. These would typically include some of the following:

- Involving the stakeholders. People generally react better when they feel included in decision making and planning. Perhaps you should share plans with the team even before they are fully formed and have the team help refine them. (By way of example we have facilitated a number of tax strategy workshops where all/the majority of tax function have been present).
- Ensuring the reasons for the change are properly understood and that plans are backed by well reasoned analysis (addressing the 'why?' questions as well as the 'what?' and the 'how?').
- Good up-front communication, avoiding stakeholders being left in the dark and thus ensuring their concerns are identified and addressed. We find putting the reasons on paper, and encouraging comments, are a good way of avoiding future misunderstandings.

- Ongoing communication, reinforcing the key messages about the need for change, the benefits it brings and the actions and behaviours needed to support it.
- Ensuring team and individual objectives and performance measures align with/support the change programme. Ensuring appropriate training, coaching and support is available.
- Recognising that change normally takes time, generally longer than one would expect. Leadership, energy and support may need to be sustained over quite a period.

§ 25.07 PROJECT MANAGEMENT

Change management and project management are not the same thing. Change management involves a particular focus on people issues and the psychology of change. Project management involves the organisation of resources, activities and timetables. Many change programmes (especially those of larger scale) will of course need to be supported by effective project management. Space does not permit detailed consideration of project management issues here, but some features we have observed as being present in many better managed projects include:

- Setting out a proper project plan.
- Ensuring the plan is focussed on achieving goals, not just the execution of tasks.
- Setting out measurable milestones (managing the project in 'bite sized chunks', demonstrating successes along the way and so showing stakeholders benefits in return for investment/disruption).
- Focussing on getting the basics right first, rather than making the project wholly reliant on completion of more complex activities.
- Identifying project risks and plans for managing them.
- Holding regular project meetings where progress is tracked, plans revised and issues addressed.

One trend we do note is the increasing use of specialist project managers on larger tax function transformation projects. They will often bring change skills and experience with them. However we suggest it will still be key for the head of tax to ensure that the overall transformation plan does embrace broader change issues, rather than focus only on completion of tasks, and that the project manager's plans support these change goals.

§ 25.08 MODELS AND METHODOLOGIES

There are a large number of change management models, methodologies and tools available. We find it hard to land on a single 'one size fits all' methodology.

However the following model from our performance improvement consulting colleagues[1] is we believe a very good starting point. Asking questions, probing at each of the three areas it highlights is a great way to test and develop the thinking behind a change programme.

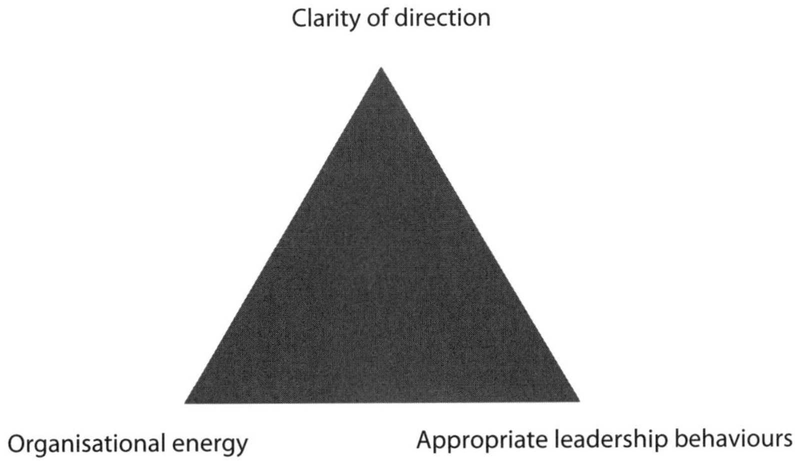

For example:

Clarity of direction: How would various colleagues/stakeholders describe the direction of what is being asked of them? What questions and concerns will they have? What's in it for them?

Organisational energy: How are stakeholders bought in to the plans? How effectively will objectives and reward support change? What is being done to reinforce change messages?

Leadership behaviours: How do ones own style and actions reflect what is being asked for? How does other stakeholder behaviour evidence one's leadership style is appropriate and helpful?

This is of course only a starting point and we have only scratched the surface of the thinking behind the model here, and there are of course many other models. However one thing that strikes us from having reviewed a number of models is the inclusive language which recurs in each of them. Commentary on change management almost always refers to the need to "involve", "consult with", "consider the views of" stakeholders, to "share" and "communicate" with the team and to "train" and "support" others involved in the change process. As a leading organisational learning guru put it: "People don't resist change. They resist being changed!" or as an ancient Chinese proverb put it "Tell me and I'll forget, show me and I may remember, involve me and I'll understand."

---

§ 25.08 [1] Why has my change programme stalled? David Wardrop-White, Carolyn Rose. Pricewaterhouse Coopers LLP, June 2007.

§ 25.09 SUMMARY

Change management, like process improvement, is not always a natural skill of people running tax functions. However not changing is not an option—the tax world is moving too fast to stand still. The question for a best practice tax function is therefore whether they muddle by, adapting to circumstances as they arise, or manage change in a more organised manner.

> *"Everyone thinks of changing the world, but no one thinks of changing themselves".*
>
> *Leo Tolstoy*

CHAPTER 26

MANAGING THE COSTS OF THE TAX FUNCTION

§26.01 INTRODUCTION

In-house tax functions typically consist of highly skilled, specialist (and thus expensive) individuals, who in turn contract the services of expensive advisors. The costs of a tax function will therefore always be under scrutiny. However the costs of managing tax go considerably wider than just these two types of cost. Additionally the value provided by best practice tax management is often very difficult to measure. While it might be possible to put a figure on tax saved by good tax planning, how do you put a figure on the benefit of effective risk management activities?

This chapter is about the costs of managing tax, how it is calculated together with some thoughts as to how the costs might best be managed. We start however with why it is important to understand the full costs of managing tax, not just those costs which fall within the tax function's budget.

§26.02 WHY MEASURE COSTS?

We believe tax functions have an interest in making sure the true cost of tax management is better understood. There are a number of reasons for this.

- A significant element of the costs of managing tax does not lie within the tax function or the tax function's budget.
- It is easy for cost-cutters to point the finger at the direct costs of the tax function and push for them to be reduced. However once the true, wider costs of tax management are properly understood, it can be recognised that 'cutting off the brain' of the tax function may not be a cost-effective move. Indeed there may be a stronger case for investment in better processes and in better provision of information to the tax function.
- Understanding hidden tax management costs may help identify process efficiency. Indeed if understanding the costs is a part of a bigger exercise involving mapping end-to-end tax processes and data flows, it can be a key part of understanding risk, controls, resource allocation and performance improvement potential.
- When business, and particularly big business, is engaging with government or with the tax authorities, it is important that the full cost of compliance is recognised as part of the burden on business.

§26.03 WHAT DOES MANAGING TAX ACTUALLY COST?

Our experience is that few companies have an accurate picture of the costs of their various tax management activities. The tax function budget may be a good starting point for assessing costs, but it is unlikely to provide the full picture. Costs to take into account will include:

[A] Direct Tax Function Costs

These include salaries, benefits, social security costs, pensions, profit share and employment taxes. It may also be necessary to factor in recruitment, severance and training not forgetting the cost of temporary staff. Overheads and other central costs will also be part of the picture. As a rule of thumb, our discussions with businesses suggest that the full cost of an employee is often over 200% of their base salary.

[B] Shadow Tax Function Costs

Staff outside the tax function will also carry out tax work. Typically a major part of this will consist of recording, analysing and supplying tax information to the tax function and answering queries from the tax function, but it will also include dealing with tax returns on VAT, sales taxes, duties and payroll taxes. The accounting, finance, legal, treasury and management information/IT departments are areas where significant shadow tax function costs often lie. However business units will also have a role to play, for example in managing tax risk, and their costs for doing this need to be included in the overall costs of managing tax.

Our experience is that the shadow tax function costs often exceed the tax function's own internal costs, and are almost always much higher than the tax function believes them to be. However very few businesses have attempted to quantify the costs of the shadow tax function. We think they should. Some of our process review work has uncovered huge hidden tax analysis 'cottage industries' within finance functions. Understanding the full costs (and risks) attaching to this type of work will often make a much more persuasive case for investment in process improvement.

[C] Advisors' Fees

External advisors' fees are probably relatively easier to ascertain than the costs of the shadow tax function. However where individual business units/ subsidiaries (and in particularly those overseas) are permitted to instruct their own advisors, it becomes increasingly difficult for either the tax function or the CFO to keep a good picture of what is being spent and where. Things can get even more complicated where different advisors are used in different territories.

[D] Senior Management Time

Finally there is the time spent by senior management, typically the CFO but increasingly the board as a whole, in discussing the tax strategy and keeping an overview of how the tax position is being managed. Our experience is that this is often rather a modest cost, and one that companies would sometimes do well to increase.

§26.04 COST BENCHMARKING

We believe it is good practice to understand how tax function costs arise, not least as a first step to delivering greater efficiency. However while some of the benchmarking exercises we have seen where tax functions are compared can be the basis for interesting discussion, the comparisons can become dangerous if used as performance measures. This is due to:

- The different roles, approaches and strategies different tax functions follow.
- The difficulty in measuring value added by the tax function.
- The difficulty in establishing true comparable costs, notably due to differences in shadow tax function costs, but also due the varying quality of inputs tax functions receive and the different geographical spread of their activities.
- Differences in how companies are structured (i.e. global footprint, complexity of global structure, number of legal entities, number and nature of business units, acquisition strategy, quality of accounting systems).
- Most importantly, the importance of the trade-off between tax function cost and risk.

§26.05 COST VERSUS RISK

Tax risk is covered elsewhere in this guide. Therefore aside from pointing out the somewhat obvious correlation between tax management costs, degree of inputs and oversight and the level of control over tax risk, we shall restrict comment to suggesting that when tax functions do set out their costs, they would do well to link them to the work done managing the tax charge, fluctuations in it and in preventing unpleasant surprises for the group.

§26.06 INTERNATIONAL ISSUES

Costing gets particularly difficult when it spans multiple territories. Tax is typically managed in different ways in different jurisdictions, and of course the tax compliance burden varies hugely from country-to-country. Nevertheless we believe that it is in most tax functions' interest to look at costs on a global basis, not just at the domestic level.

This is partly because it will normally be in the tax function's (and the business') interest to ensure the importance of managing the global charge and risk is properly understood. However it is also because, as tax data flows will increasingly run across borders (not least with the rise of single ERP systems and finance and accounting SSCs) there will increasingly be pools of cost which relate to several jurisdictions. There will also increasingly be the opportunity to effect process improvement and cost reduction which impacts across multiple territories.

> Tax compliance costs vary hugely from country to country. Research shows that in order to meet their tax compliance obligations a standard, modest sized company can expect to spend:
>
> Singapore. 49 hours
> UK. 105 hours
> USA. 325 hours
> China. 872 hours
> Brazil. 2600 hours
>
>

§ 26.07 MANAGING COSTS

From time-to-time, most businesses go through cost reduction exercises, often with a particular focus on cutting the cost of back office operations, with an increasing focus on core activities. Managing costs is therefore clearly an important issue for most tax functions.

However businesses must bear in mind that the manageable elements of the tax charge and tax risk may be far more significant than the costs of running the tax function. The biggest achievable cost savings may well be in respect of reductions both in the tax charge and in managing the downsides of risk, not in the tax function's budget. The purpose of having a straight line result on the strategy templates (see chapter 13) was to show the correlation between the costs of managing tax and the ability to manage both the tax charge and the tax risks.

Some years ago, the UK Government launched a 'Spend to Save' initiative where they increased resources available to the UK tax authorities in order to increase tax revenues. Companies looking for bottom line cost cutting may need to consider mirroring this approach. However one of the big issues for tax functions is that the benefit they add is often below the line, while their costs are charged above the line in arriving at the profit before tax. We are aware of significant tax planning initiatives being rejected solely on these grounds.

Tax function costs are a function of three basic variables:

- The volume of service delivered to the business.
- The price of inputs (principally staff salaries and advisors' fees).
- The efficiency with which services are delivered.

If costs are to be cut, tax functions either need to:

1. Do less (usually by cutting headcount), and probably therefore have to gain consent from the businesses that they will henceforth receive a lower level of service, or
2. Reduce fees paid to external advisors, or
3. Look for opportunities to improve efficiencies.

There is perhaps a fourth option of moving costs/activities that do not logically belong in the tax function to other functions/business units within the company. While this may be a political rather than a real cost saving, it does come back to the role of the tax function, what they should be doing and what should more correctly be carried out elsewhere in the organisation.

In terms of reducing levels of activity, it may be that there will be some potential to jettison some non-essential activities without having a major impact on the value added to the business. The tax strategy should clarify those areas of activity the tax function will focus on and those it will not. Indeed putting a tax strategy in place and agreeing on the areas of focus may well highlight which current activities are adding least value to the business—with the resultant changes leading to cost savings.

It may be possible to cut the total salary bill without a reduction in service levels, primarily through ensuring the staff mix is more appropriate and avoiding the use of overqualified staff for junior level work. It may also be possible to cut advisors' fees through more careful scoping of their work, requiring improved efficiency or through 'bulk buying'.

Significant savings will often also be achieved through improved efficiency, which can be brought about through:

	Ease of achievement
Process streamlining	Normally requires significant time investment to build, implement and maintain new processes
Process standardisation	Can involve significant cultural change as well as process design, implementation and maintenance
Outsourcing	Easy to achieve by leveraging off the investment made by the service provider

As noted in earlier chapters we believe that there are some real opportunities through both process improvement and the use of technology to improve efficiencies in many organisations and hence take costs out of some of the existing tax processes.

§26.08 MAXIMISING SHAREHOLDER VALUE

When seeking to control the cost of managing the group's tax affairs, it is important to distinguish between measures to improve efficiency and measures which reduce the level of service the tax function delivers. Nobody is going to argue against improved efficiency, but if cutting the cost of the tax function results in a higher tax charge or greater tax risk, the net result may be a reduction in shareholder value. Having a proper tax strategy in place will help ensure that the tax function receives the appropriate level of resource and that the business gets value for money from the tax function.

Where tax functions are gathering or reporting details of their costs, we would suggest that any such exercise should:

- Identify shadow tax function costs and, where necessary, give others guidance as to how to do so.
- Seek to identify areas where costs could be reduced (across the in-house, shadow and external parts of the tax function), but also address the risks attendant in doing so for each.
- Also seek to identify areas where additional value could be delivered, outlining the likely additional investment necessary to deliver this.

§ 26.09 SUMMARY

The cost of managing tax in an organisation is not a straightforward subject. Costs lie in many different parts of the organisation. Some relate to compliance and regulatory processes, some to added value and risk management. To the extent that processes can be improved there is scope for cost reductions. However not providing adequate resources towards value added and risk management activities can be counter productive.

CHAPTER 27
MEASURING PERFORMANCE

"WYMIWYG—What You Measure Is What You Get"

§ 27.01 INTRODUCTION

It has been long established that measures and targets influence performance. Our experience with tax functions is that, while the position is beginning to change, relatively few have formal targets or metrics—and where they do, they often revolve around those things which are both easily measurable and are relatively easy to achieve; for example they usually include submitting all the returns by the statutory filing date.

The challenge, we believe, is to have performance metrics for the tax function which tie in with the overall tax strategic plan. The KPIs (key performance indicators) need to reflect the key strategic goals. Only when this is happening will the tax function genuinely be able to show the value they are adding to the business—and be in a position to justify better the extra resources many functions say they need.

This chapter looks at both what should be measured and how that measurement might be carried out. As this is a difficult area, some tax functions have argued that time spent measuring performance is time that could otherwise be spent managing performance. We do not agree. Provided the right measures can be found, movements in the measures will reflect the impact the tax function is having on performance, and measuring is therefore a key management discipline. The key question is therefore "what are the right measures for a tax function?"

§ 27.02 WHAT ARE GROUPS TYPICALLY MEASURING?

Our experience is that the most common measures are still those which focus on the basics which include 'no surprises', filing the returns on time, and keeping to budget. Indeed a recent tax function survey published by the Tax Executives Institute in the US reported similar measures as three of the top six measures used to evaluate tax functions. The same survey reported that only 20% of groups assess the economic value added by the tax function. In short, most (but not all) groups are still relatively unsophisticated in their approach to tax performance measurement. There is a disconnect between what should be measured and what is being measured.

§ 27.03 WHAT SHOULD A TAX FUNCTION BE MEASURING?

In documenting the tax strategic plan (see chapter 13), we recommend that for each key area of focus there should be SMART objectives. These are the important matters where the tax function should be ensuring they deliver during the year. The starting point for setting the KPIs for the tax function as a whole should therefore be these strategic objectives.

If we go back to the enablers and deliverables there may also be specific objectives around each one where a KPI can be set. Some of these, particularly around the enablers (e.g. people or processes), may be more difficult to measure than others (e.g. compliance). This does not make them any less important. However it is important that these additional objectives/KPIs do not override those included in the tax function's strategic plan.

Strategic objectives and KPIs may be at a fairly high level. It is also necessary to take these down to specific measurable objectives and actions at the individual level in order to measure individual performance. These will include not only the KPIs of the head office tax function, but also of those people who are responsible for tax in some way and are located in business units and other countries. High level strategic tax objectives can be linked to individual objectives in this way:

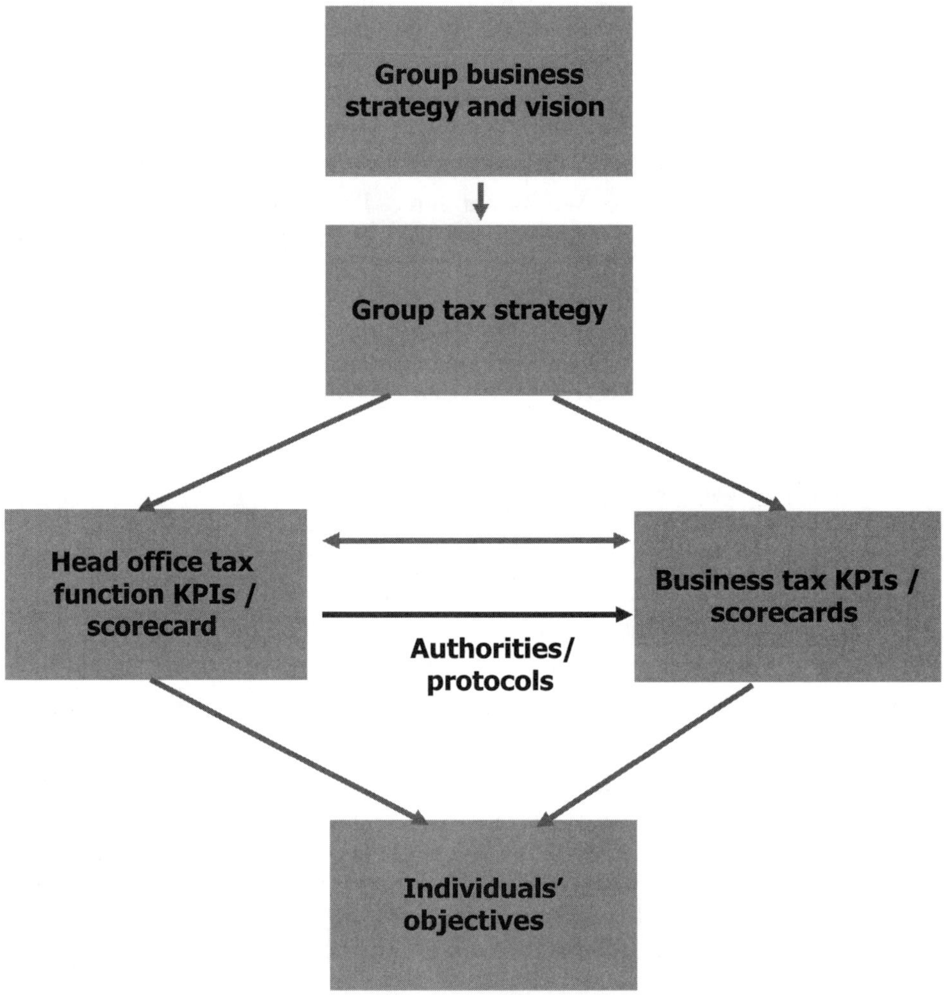

§27.04 WHAT ELSE CAN BE MEASURED?

There are a number of other measures we do see in use by tax functions or hear CFOs and boards suggesting should be used. These include:

- Value added—while this is a key metric for a tax function it is not an easy one to measure, particularly where part of the value is the avoidance of risk. However we do see some tax functions which operate value management systems where tax projects and planning activity are logged and tracked over time.
- Competitor comparison—looking at the tax rate of direct competitors. As noted in the chapter on benchmarking, there are usually very good reasons why your nearest competitors have a different tax rate. This may be their geographic spread, their business model or even the impact of tax losses.
- Reduction in effective tax rate—there are many different drivers of the effective tax rate, not all of which fall within the remit of the tax function. This is therefore a difficult one for a tax function to deliver without considerable support from others in the business. Often the most effective way to reduce the tax rate is, for example, some form of business reorganisation such as a move to a commissionaire arrangement. A better measure may be the structural/natural rate (essentially the long-term tax rate which would be expected to apply, eliminating short-term fluctuations).
- Reduction in cash taxes—cash taxes are an important driver of shareholder value, though from what we see it remains of secondary importance in most organisations to the effective tax rate as a tax function metric. The cash tax rate may also be slightly easier for a tax function to manage, but a number of the issues noted above under reducing the effective tax rate are equally applicable here.
- Customer satisfaction—this is one which we believe is underused. The tax function has a number of customers or stakeholders. Obtaining independent feedback from them is an important measurement, particularly as communication is one of the key enablers for the tax function. We have even been asked in some cases to obtain independent feedback on behalf of a client from revenue authorities.
- Tax return production or compliance deadlines—we often see these as the first measurement for a tax function (and they can sometimes include turnaround times in response to tax audits). While meeting compliance deadlines is important, having these as the key measurement gives a message about a very compliance focused tax function, at the expense of adding value. This also drives people to focus on deadlines rather than quality.
- Tax return adjustments—it is debatable as to whether having material adjustments, arising out of tax audits, is something which should be

encouraged or not. No adjustments suggest that the filing positions taken are very conservative; significant adjustments suggest your filing positions may have been too aggressive. Too many adjustments does suggest a weakness in the processes, particularly if the final agreed figures show material variances from the estimated figures used for tax accounting.

- Independent reviews—we are increasingly seeing the results of section 404 examinations performed on tax controls by the independent auditor, or even by your internal audit function, used as a measurement of the tax function.
- Risk based measures—this is an area which has grown in importance and we see more-and-more groups pursuing targets linked to the group risk management frameworks.

§ 27.05 A MORE BALANCED APPROACH

More sophisticated groups are also using balanced scorecard metrics for the tax function. Two key themes we would briefly highlight here are:

- That a balanced scorecard needs to balance financial measures with non-financial measures. As well as the more traditional measures relating to financial performance and internal processes, there needs to be a focus on both 'customers' and 'learning and growth', in effect taking into account likely impact on future financial performance. Some illustrations of how this may be reflected in tax function measures are set out below.
- That as well as including 'lagging' outcome measures that reflect past performance, scorecards should focus on 'leading' performance drivers which will influence future results.

Balanced scorecarding best practices for tax

For the customer perspective

- Consult tax function customers (as a part of strategy setting)
- Establish service level agreements, and monitor performance
- Conduct customer satisfaction surveys
- Measure tax resource allocation against customer requirements

For "learning and growth"

- Attach importance to communication, collaboration and knowledge sharing (especially outside normal contacts)
- Measure staff "feelgood factor"
- Look at staff retention/turnover
- Address information system capabilities
- Ensure staff development objectives are on the scorecard

The table below may help you document both what you intend to achieve during the year (the KPI column) and what you have achieved:

	KPI	*Achievement During Year*
Area of focus 1		
Area of focus 2		
Area of focus 3		
Area of focus 4		
Tax strategic plan		
Structure of tax function		
People development		
Leadership		
Controls and risk management		
Process improvement		
Data management		
Use of technology		
Communication		
Tax planning		
Tax reporting and accounting		
Compliance		
Audit defence		

§27.06 SUMMARY

When PwC published the predecessor to this guide, "The Best Practice Tax Function" in 2002, we commented that the 'jury is still out' in the case for numerical performance measures and that "we know of relatively few tax functions that currently operate formal measurement processes for the function as a whole".

We no longer believe that the jury is out. Most tax functions now have formal performance measures. However many of these measures still focus on the basics rather than on the real value that a tax function adds. Nevertheless we do see a trend towards more sophisticated performance measure and targets. We predict that metrics and related objective setting will be an area of particular focus for tax functions in the next few years.

"However beautiful the strategy, you should occasionally look at the results."—Winston Churchill

CHAPTER 28
BENCHMARKING

§28.01 INTRODUCTION

Having been involved for a number of years in advising tax functions on what is best practice, we have being asked many times about benchmarking for individual in-house tax functions. We have therefore set out in this chapter firstly some of the reasons people have asked us to benchmark their tax functions and have then gone on to look at some of the issues involved with such an exercise. We have focussed on what can sensibly be benchmarked, how best this can be done and finally the value to be obtained from benchmarking exercises. Various alternative approaches to benchmarking are also considered.

§28.02 WHY BENCHMARK?

The benchmarking exercises we are asked about fall into three main categories. The first category is where the tax function has decided it wants to be best in class/top quartile and it needs some objective evidence to show either that it has achieved this objective or what still needs to be done to get there.

The second category is where benchmarking of the tax function is part of a bigger exercise, for example the benchmarking of the whole finance function. In these cases the finance function is often being looked at on its effectiveness in processing financial data (e.g. time to close), and it is often the case that those carrying out such reviews attempt to look at the tax department against similar parameters. However, new approaches to evaluating finance function effectiveness are starting to look at a range of other more subjective measures which attempt to benchmark the value added by the finance function against best practice standards. We have yet to see these new approaches being extended to the tax function.

The third category we see is rather less specific to one particular company and involves benchmarking against trends in the tax market place. Benchmarking in this latter category is driven by global or local surveys which capture data on tax function attitudes and priorities, asking questions such as "compared with two years ago, are you . . . ?" or "in two years time do you expect. . . . ?" These surveys are useful in providing a steer as to where others have gone/are going and hence how you might organise yourself going forward.

§28.03 WHAT TO BENCHMARK?

One of the biggest debates we have with people wanting to benchmark their in-house tax function is what measures they want to benchmark. For example, if you are aiming to be best in class what is it you would measure to show you fit into this category? Some examples of what you might like to benchmark yourself against are set out below.

[A] Taxes

One of the easiest things to benchmark is your group's effective tax rate. Information for other groups is readily available in published accounts. To look at your rate and compare it with others over, say, a five year period may give you a useful guide as to how well you are managing your own tax rate. The PwC survey entitled the 'Global Retail & Consumer Tax Benchmarking Survey' produced some excellent material around effective tax rates (ETR) in that industry.

There are also some more recent surveys undertaken of a group's total tax contribution, which goes wider than just the effective tax rate in the accounts. Surveys of total tax contribution capture data on a group's actual taxes borne (paid) and taxes collected and remitted to government. This data enables a range of other measures to be benchmarked, either against other groups in an industry or a group of similarly sized companies by, say, market capitalisation. Some of these measures can include:

- Individual taxes borne and collected against industry;
- Total taxes borne and collected compared to turnover; and
- The company's total tax rate, which measures the percentage of company profits paid in all taxes and provides a useful indicator of a business' total cost of taxes.

Like other measures, the benchmarking of total tax contribution provides a series of indicators that highlight possible issues and inconsistencies that then need to be analysed. In the same way as comparing ETRs, the value of the benchmarking is analysing the reasons for differences from the benchmark.

With the increasing focus on tax reporting, work has also been done on the extent and quality of tax reporting and disclosures in public accounts. In the UK for example, PwC conducted a review of the tax reporting of the FTSE 350 with the purpose of establishing some subjective benchmarks for best practice in reporting.

[B] Size of Tax Function

We are frequently asked to comment on the size of the tax function compared to other companies—do we have the 'right' size tax function? While questions around trends can be helpful in this area, other objective evidence gets a bit trickier as different groups are structured in different ways. As already discussed in an earlier chapter those who provide tax services to a group will include not only the tax function but also the shadow tax function and the external advisors. The results of any benchmarking exercise will clearly be affected both by how much of the tax work is dealt with by shadow tax people, outside the tax function, and how much use is made of external advisors. For these reasons we have not found the size of a tax function to be a particularly good measure to benchmark. While there is clearly some correlation between size of group and size of tax function, there are many groups that do not fit into a standard pattern—as we discovered when we did such a survey a few years back.

Cost is another area we have been asked to benchmark. However if you look at the tax function's budget as a whole, some groups will include the shadow tax function, others will exclude it. Some will have some tax related costs within operations (particularly those groups with overseas subsidiaries), others all the costs going through the tax function. We have seen a number of surveys in this area and they do provide some guidance to groups. However benchmarking is about comparing like with like—and the variety of different ways tax is structured and run within organisations means that there is limited like for like information that can be benchmarked. If we narrow the costs down to those relating purely to tax accounting and compliance, it is possible to get a better picture and the cost per return or the cost per entity does give you some qualitative information.

Another area we are often asked to comment on is the split of work between the in-house team, the shadow tax team and the external advisors. As we have discussed earlier, there are such a variety of different ways tax functions are structured it makes it very difficult to interpret any information in this area.

[C] Value Add

What we would like to find is some way of measuring the value added by a tax function—and possibly extend this into some form of cost/benefit analysis. This surely is the real measure of a tax function. The nearest we have got to measuring the value added is by looking at the ETR; it is interesting to note from our retail and consumer benchmarking exercise that there is a correlation between the ETR and where people rate themselves on a scale of 1 to 10 in relation to both their active management of tax and their attitude to taking tax risk.

However the ETR ignores taxes that appear 'above the line' which is the focus of total tax contribution and both the ETR and benchmarking based on total tax contribution do not properly cover the value being added by effective tax risk management and business support.

§28.04 OBTAINING QUALITY INFORMATION

As noted above the only publicly available tax information is that which appears in published accounts. In tax benchmarking it is therefore often difficult to obtain quality information (other than the ETR) and information that has hard evidence to support it. In the various surveys which we have seen we suspect that the responses to a number of the questions being posed are often at best subjective judgements and are probably, in a number of areas, estimates based on gut feel rather than anything more scientific. One of the issues to be addressed therefore when considering benchmarking an individual tax function is the cost of obtaining scientifically based, and hence quality, information.

§ 28.05 USING THE RESULTS

Those surveys that look at trends can be helpful in focussing the minds of heads of tax; for example we are all seeing that tax risk management is increasingly on the agenda of both tax functions and boards. It would be a brave head of tax who, in the light of benchmarking evidence to support the above comment, decided that tax risk management should be pushed down, rather than up, the agenda in their organisation.

However in our experience, and hence one of our concerns, is that the majority of heads of tax with whom we have shared benchmarking data have found good reasons, and often very valid reasons, for differentiating themselves from whatever norm is shown by the benchmarking data.

We have even found that heads of tax can usually find reasons why their ETR is different from the norm/top quartile; a high ETR should perhaps be the measure that most causes behaviour to change. It is publicly available information and it has been independently reviewed (by the auditors)—if your tax rate is in the highest quartile for your industry does that not tell you that others may be managing their tax affairs more effectively than you are?

You should consider what else your ETR is telling the wider market. We have seen commentary from equities analysts suggesting ETRs that vary from the statutory rate can also be indicative of the quality of underlying earnings. In other words, value is being placed on real cash operating earnings upon which tax is levied. While this is a simplistic analysis, it does highlight the point that proper analysis of a company's results against the benchmark is the crucial step.

§ 28.06 AN ALTERNATIVE APPROACH

There are ways other than benchmarking against other businesses for achieving a best in class/top quartile tax function—and that is what this guide has been all about. By reviewing what you are doing against the content of earlier chapters you can benchmark yourself against a best practice standard and conclude whether you are meeting the criteria you set out to achieve.

Another way of measuring how well you are doing is by discussion with your peer group in other businesses. There are a number of "benchmarking clubs" in which such discussions take place and attendees, we are sure, come away from such meetings with a better feel as to how well their organisation is doing, as compared with their peer group, in whatever area was under discussion.

As noted above discussions around variances with comparable benchmarking data often lead to the conclusion that one company's metrics should rightly be different from another's, because the different tax functions have different roles and strategy, and the different businesses have a different geographical footprint. Benchmarking data can be helpful in informing the debate and illustrating conclusions, but we do not believe it will be the only or even the most cost effective way to drive an exercise to measure a tax function's value or performance.

None of these three alternatives set out above really address the issue of benchmarking the tax function when the exercise is part of a larger benchmarking, for example, of the finance function as a whole. The difficulty we see with such reviews is that they focus very much on the costs of the tax function at the expense of the value that the tax function brings to the business. With cost being very measurable, and, as noted above, value being much more difficult to measure this is clearly a tricky area.

Overall, our view is that benchmarking the performance of the tax function requires the analysis of a combination of objective measures, such as the ETR and total tax contribution as well as subjective benchmarking against a set of best practice standards discussed in the earlier chapters in this section of the guide, in particular how effectively a company uses the eight enablers and manages its key deliverables of the strategic tax plan, tax planning, tax accounting, tax compliance and audit defence.

§28.07 SUMMARY

Benchmarking studies have proved very useful in getting both tax functions and boards to focus on tax as a manageable component of shareholder value and to encourage a more active tax management approach in their businesses. However if the objective of benchmarking is to change behaviors then, with the exception of reviews of the ETR and possibly surveys into trends over a period of time, we have not seen a great deal of evidence that benchmarking has achieved its objectives. In practice, we consider benchmarking against a set of best practice standards (which we acknowledge do change over time) such as reviews of tax strategy and tax function roles as set out in this guide, are likely to be more beneficial in driving change.

The holy grail that we are searching for is an objective measure of how much value a tax function is adding to the business—now that would be worth benchmarking!

CHAPTER 29

WORKING WITH SHARED SERVICE CENTRES

§29.01 INTRODUCTION

We are seeing an increasing number of businesses operating through shared service centres (SSCs). The purpose of setting up an SSC is usually to bring the accounting and financial processing for a number of different countries/companies together into one central location. The rationale is to create greater efficiencies and greater consistency across the group and often little or no accounting or financial expertise is left behind in individual countries.

The use of an SSC brings with it both opportunities and risks from a tax point of view. We consider that these opportunities and risks are of sufficient importance (and the use of SSCs sufficiently widespread) to warrant a separate chapter on SSCs. The purpose of this chapter therefore is to highlight the impact of an SSC on the tax management of a group and consider what is best practice in such circumstances.

§29.02 TAX DELIVERABLES

The key question to be addressed is which of the tax deliverables, and for which taxes, can be dealt with in the SSC and which, by their very nature, need local expertise and therefore have to be done in-country, usually by an outsourced third party due to the fact that, as noted above, there may be few if any in-house finance people in individual countries.

[A] Tax Accounting

As we noted in an earlier chapter tax accounting is best managed through a combination of people who have tax expertise and understand the tax position of the company in-country, and people from the finance department of the group. It is unlikely that the people at an SSC will have the requisite tax expertise to be able to sign off with confidence the tax figures of all the in-country subsidiaries for which they are responsible. It may be that they can do this for countries where the business is either not material or there is a very simple tax system. However for countries where the business is material and/or the tax rules are complex, then we would suggest that in-country expert tax expertise will be required as part of the team preparing and signing off the tax figures in the accounts. Where the group is SEC listed and FIN 48 applies, then knowledge of local tax systems and practices will be crucial in making the appropriate judgements.

[B] Tax Compliance

In any business there are many and varied different taxes where tax returns will be required. Some of these are relatively straightforward (such as withholding taxes) and the processes within an SSC are well suited to dealing with these. However other tax returns, for example corporate income tax returns, are considerably more complex and it would be unusual for an SSC to retain people with the appropriate expertise to deal with all the corporate income tax returns for all the different countries which the SSC is responsible for.

In-between these two extremes there will be some taxes which, while they may be specific to individual countries, maybe relatively straightforward to administer. There will also be other taxes, such as indirect taxes, where the processes are relatively similar across a number of countries but where there are differences that are significant enough to make dealing with the compliance for these taxes far from straightforward.

The data required for most (all?) of these tax returns will lie within the SSC. The question which then has to be addressed is where the skills lie for doing the tax returns and how you manage the risks from these returns being done in an SSC, often by people who are not tax specialists, and usually not tax specialists in all the particular countries for which tax returns are required.

[C] What Should an SSC Be Responsible for?

Picking up the themes from the headings above, where all that is required is a process then a SSC is ideally suited to deal with the tax matter. However where local in-country tax knowledge is required, and in particular where in depth knowledge is required, then, in order to manage the risks, it is vitally important that local expertise is brought to bear.

We have summarised the position in the diagram below. The higher a return is on the scale the more local knowledge is needed to manage the risks; this is usually provided by an in country third party advisor.

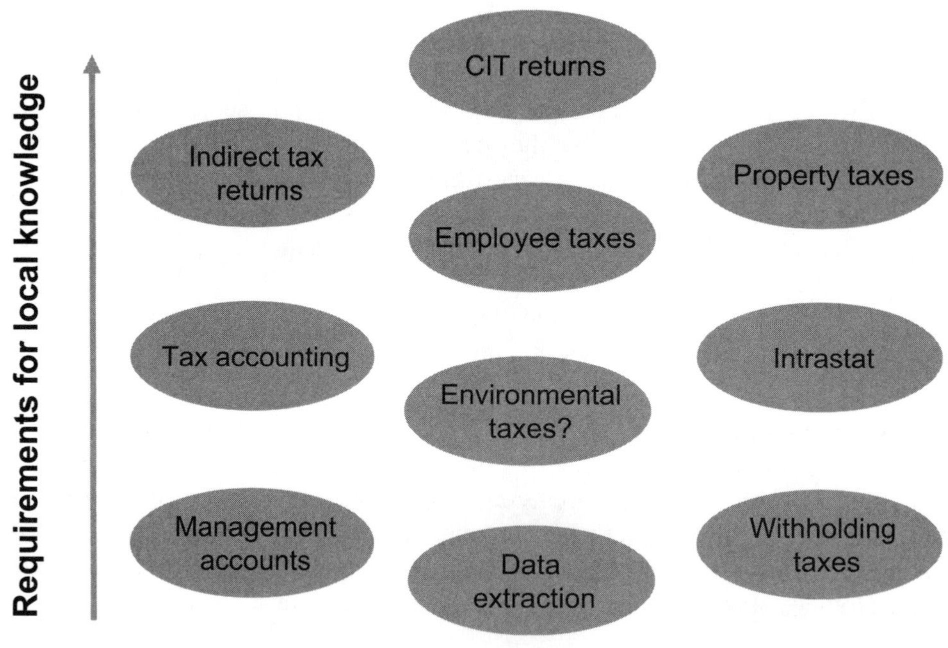

As you will note we have put a question mark against the environmental taxes. This is a developing area and it is difficult at this point to see where they might end up on the scale.

§29.03 TAX ENABLERS

The use of an SSC also raises opportunities and challenges around the various tax enablers.

[A] Controls and Risk Management

The migration of processes to an SSC, or the implementation of new processes, all create risk of tax process failure. Our experience is that during an SSC implementation tax issues are often given lower priority than other matters.

The key to managing ongoing tax risks where an SSC is involved is to separate out processes (where an SSC is usually very effective) and knowledge of local tax systems (where whatever training you put in place there will always be gaps in both technical knowledge and understanding of local practices). By way of an example we are aware of one group who had excellent processes in place for dealing with its VAT returns; however, when the Spanish authorities introduced a new and different return, they had no way of knowing that this new return existed and was stung with a very significant penalty of failing to submit a return which they did not even know about.

Where the decision is made that an SSC will deal with a particular tax return, a system needs to be put in place whereby changes to tax law and practice are picked up and the SSCs processes adapted to cope with these changes. The people who know about legal and practical changes will usually be in country.

[B] People

There will be many people within an SSC whose actions will have a direct impact on the tax position on the group. These people will be involved in tax figures going into the accounts and tax returns, and also providing information to the tax function for tax planning purposes. It is also likely that they will be looking at a number of different taxes, and quite possibly, for a number of different countries.

Even where their activities are purely part of a process they will need to have some understanding of why they are carrying out their activities and the implications for the group of any errors they may make. As well as ensuring the appropriate quality of the people dealing with tax, there is clearly a training issue here which needs to be addressed. Additionally the turnover of staff in SSCs is often higher than in other parts of the business, which again reinforces the need for the training to be repeated at regular intervals.

[C] Process and Technology

We have talked in earlier chapters about process improvement and, on the back of the number of material control weaknesses within tax, how important process improvement is. We see the use, and in particular the introduction, of an SSC as an ideal opportunity to drive improvements into the tax processes and, where possible, introduce consistencies across how tax returns are dealt with for different companies and countries.

On the technology side the move to the SSC can provide the economies of scale which allow an investment in technology tools, an investment which would not satisfy a cost/benefit analysis on a country by country basis. We would encourage tax functions to use the move to an SSC as a catalyst for making process improvement happen.

At this point it is worth flagging up one of the key risk issues involved with moving to an SSC, which is the loss of knowledge of the current 'as is' processes. Once the move to an SSC has been announced (or even suggested) people in country will be starting to think about their next job and an understanding of how local tax returns are dealt with can very rapidly walk out the door. Documenting how returns are put together today is a key first step in the move to an SSC.

[D] Communication

The use of an SSC does raise some big questions around communication. It is high risk for people in SSCs who are dealing with both the tax figures for the accounts and tax returns not to understand what is happening in the business—and this is especially difficult if that business is based in another country. Equally it is important for them to be kept abreast of tax legislation, practice and interpretation in the countries whose returns they are responsible for.

There is no one easy answer here, other than to say that communication processes need to be put in place and they need to happen. The starting point is perhaps an analysis of where the larger risks are and how they will best be managed.

Additionally those SSCs who are looking to add value to the business have a role in providing quality information to support tax planning. Understanding what the tax planners need and why they need it will be key to delivering this.

[E] Leadership

The metrics of those heading up SSCs are often around efficiencies and how well processes are working. At times this agenda can be in conflict with putting proper risk management procedures in place. Additionally those heading up SSCs are not usually people with a tax background and they may not always have a complete understanding of the risks involved in managing tax.

In our opinion it is the responsibility of the group head of tax to take a leadership role here and ensure that the SSCs processes and procedures do not give rise to unforeseen tax risks, penalties and liabilities.

§ 29.04 SUMMARY

The setting up of an SSC provides an ideal opportunity for improving some of the processes around both tax accounting and tax compliance. However at the same time an undue focus on centralised SSC processes can result in changes to the way tax is operated in-country being overlooked. A key to successfully management of tax within an SSC is therefore finding the right balance between process/ process improvement and risk management. Leadership from the tax function and proper communication between those in the SSC and those based elsewhere is vital.

CHAPTER 30
CONCLUSION

It is very clear that the world of tax is changing—and is changing very rapidly. Revenue authorities are increasingly focussed on their 'tax gap'. The corporate agenda has moved towards compliance and regulatory reporting. The number of stakeholders in tax has increased and the corporate responsibility agenda has entered the tax arena.

The *Why* section of this guide explains why it is so important that the tax affairs of an organisation are properly managed. In the *What* section we have sought to put some structure around what needs managing. The starting point is a properly documented tax strategic plan. We believe there are then eight enablers which underpin the efficient implementation of the strategy. These enablers are the structure of the tax function, the development of the people, leadership, controls and risk management, process improvement, data management, the use of technology and last, but by no means least, communication. The results of the strategy and the enablers are the four deliverables for a tax function which are tax planning, tax accounting and reporting, tax compliance and audit defence.

In the *How* section of this guide we have explained what we consider to be the best practice methodologies around both the eight enablers and the four deliverables. We have set out to share our current thinking in each of these areas while at the same time fully recognising that there is no one right answer which will fit all organisations.

In summary we believe the most effective tax functions of the future will need to:

- Lead on all matters relating to tax;
- Pursue a clear strategy;
- Be flexible to cope with change; and
- Be actively engaged with the stakeholders.

If in the course of reading this guide we have given you some food for thought as to how you run your own in-house tax function, then we have achieved our objective. The debate will continue as to what an effective tax function actually looks like. We look forward to being part of this debate with you going forward and wish you every success in whatever role you have in managing tax in your organisation.

In conclusion:

Give us the courage to change those things we can change,
The serenity to accept those we can't,
And the wisdom to know the difference.

Index

References are to section numbers.

C

D

E

F

G

H

P

Q

R

S

T

U

V

W

X

Appendix A

BEST PRACTICE CHECKLIST

Tax Function Effectiveness Best practice checklist

To review whether you are operating a best practice tax function in your organisation you should score each statement below based on 5 – strongly agree; 4 – agree; 3 – neither agree nor disagree; 2 – disagree; 1 – strongly disagree

Enablers	Statement	Score
Tax strategy	We know what taxes we pay/collect (our total tax contribution).	
	We have agreed our approach to corporate responsibility in relation to tax.	
	We understand our overall attitude to tax planning.	
	We have a documented tax strategy.	
	The tax strategy is discussed/agreed at board level at least once a year.	
	We know our key areas of focus for managing tax.	
	We have SMART objectives for each area of focus.	
Structure of the tax function	The structure of the tax function supports the implementation of the tax strategy.	
	The structure of the tax function is aligned with the business.	
	It is clear what the tax function is responsible for – which taxes and which enablers/deliverables.	
	It is clear what the 'shadow' tax function is responsible for.	
	It is clear when we use external advisors.	
	The structure is flexible enough to cope with ongoing change.	
People	We have sufficient tax resources to deliver the tax strategy.	
	Tax function staff have the appropriate skills to deliver the tax strategy.	
	Tax staff are continuing to develop their skills.	

PRICEWATERHOUSECOOPERS

Enablers	Statement	Score
Leadership	The head of tax has access to the board.	
	The head of tax is an effective ambassador for tax within the business.	
	The head of tax is good at managing change.	
	The head of tax is an effective manager of the tax function.	
Control/risk management	Those involved in managing tax risk understand our attitude to tax risk.	
	We have a documented tax risk policy.	
	We understand where the major tax risks are in the business.	
	We have evaluated the tax controls around the major risks.	
	We have put in place appropriate controls to manage these risks.	
	We monitor the operation of the key controls.	
	The tax function knows the position on corporate income tax compliance around the whole group.	
Process	We have a process for evaluating tax planning ideas.	
	We have mapped the key processes for managing tax (including tax accounting and compliance processes).	
	We have reviewed the processes for inefficiencies.	
	We have implemented new processes where there were inefficiencies.	
	We have people with the right skills to operate the processes.	
	We monitor and review our processes on a regular basis.	
Data	We have good data for tax forecasting.	
	We can easily obtain the data we need for tax accounting.	
	We can easily obtain the information we need for tax compliance.	
	We receive data in a standardised format.	
	There is a proper audit trail from the accounts to the tax returns.	
Technology	We use tax technology systems to prepare our tax figures.	
	Our tax technology systems are integrated with the financial systems.	
	Our tax technology systems are integrated with each other.	
	We do not use spreadsheets/email as a way of collecting tax data.	
	We do not spend a lot of time re-keying information.	
	We store information in an electronic data management system.	
	We have someone specifically responsible for tax IT matters.	
Communication	We know who the key internal and external stakeholders in tax are.	
	We have a formal plan for communication with the stakeholders.	
	The stakeholders understand the tax strategy as it effects them	
	We understand what they need from the tax function and what the tax function needs from them.	
	We are in regular contact with our stakeholders (including revenue authorities).	
	Total score	

Score (maximum 250):
200 – 250: You are operating best practice in many areas
150 – 200: You are operating best practice in some areas
100 – 150: There is more you could be doing
Below 100: There is more you should be doing

For further information, please refer to the Tax Function Effectiveness book
www.pwc.com/taxfunctioneffectivenessbook

pwc.com

The member firms of the PricewaterhouseCoopers network provide industry-focused assurance, tax and advisory services to build public trust and enhance value for its clients and their stakeholders. More than 146,000 people in 150 countries across our network share their thinking, experience and solutions to develop fresh perspectives and practical advice.

Ref 2008BHM22820.